PIG/PORK

Also available in the Bloomsbury Sigma series:

Sex on Earth by Jules Howard
p53: The Gene that Cracked the Cancer Code by Sue Armstrong
Atoms Under the Floorboards by Chris Woodford
Spirals in Time by Helen Scales
Chilled by Tom Jackson
A is for Arsenic by Kathryn Harkup
Breaking the Chains of Gravity by Amy Shira Teitel
Suspicious Minds by Rob Brotherton
Herding Hemingway's Cats by Kat Arney
Electronic Dreams by Tom Lean
Sorting the Beef from the Bull by Richard Evershed and Nicola Temple
Death on Earth by Jules Howard
The Tyrannosaur Chronicles by David Hone
Soccermatics by David Sumpter
Big Data by Timandra Harkness
Goldilocks and the Water Bears by Louisa Preston
Science and the City by Laurie Winkless
Bring Back the King by Helen Pilcher
Furry Logic by Matin Durrani and Liz Kalaugher
Built on Bones by Brenna Hassett
My European Family by Karin Bojs
4th Rock from the Sun by Nicky Jenner
Patient H69 by Vanessa Potter
Catching Breath by Kathryn Lougheed

PIG/PORK

ARCHAEOLOGY, ZOOLOGY AND EDIBILITY

Pía Spry-Marqués

Bloomsbury Sigma
[illegible]t of Bloomsbury Publishing Plc

50 Bedford Square
London
WC1B 3DP
UK

1385 Broadway
New York
NY 10018
USA

www.bloomsbury.com

BLOOMSBURY and the Diana logo are trademarks of Bloomsbury Publishing Plc

First published 2017

British Library Cataloguing-in-Publication Data
A catalogue record for this book is available from the British Library.

Photo credits (t = top, b = bottom, l = left, r = right, c = centre)
Colour section: P. 1: Vladimir Wrangel / Shutterstock (tl, tr, cl); Wayne Hutchinson / Alamy (cr); Arco / G. Lacz / Alamy (b). P. 2: Pía Spry-Marqués (t); Dr Siniša Radović / Archive of the Institute for Quaternary Paleontology and Geology, Croatian Academy of Sciences and Arts (b). P. 3: Lebrecht Music and Arts Photo Library / Alamy (t); D. Nixon / Creative Commons Attribution 3.0 Unported (b). P. 4: Rafa Sanchez Ruiz / Shutterstock (t); rtem / Shutterstock (b). P. 5: Reuters / Alamy (t); Donald Broom / University of Cambridge (cl); Science Photo Library / Alamy (b). P. 6: Viethavvh / Creative Commons Attribution 3.0 Unported (t); Tamorlan / Creative Commons Attribution 3.0 Unported (b). P. 7: Elisa Frost (t); Classic Image / Alamy (b). P. 8: Mauro / Creative Commons Attribution 3.0 Unported (t); Keystone / Stringer / Getty (b).

Library of Congress Cataloguing-in-Publication data has been applied for.

ISBN (hardback): 978-1-4729-1139-1
ISBN (trade paperback): 978-1-4729-4539-6
ISBN (ebook): 978-1-4729-1140-7

2 4 6 8 10 9 7 5 3 1

Illustrations by Samantha Goodlet

Typeset by Deanta Global Publishing Services, Chennai, India
Printed and bound in Great Britain by CPI Group (UK) Ltd, Croydon CR0 4YY

Bloomsbury Sigma, Book Twenty-five

To Daniel

For teaching me so much about life
and for making me realise it's probably best not to
write a book and raise a small child at the same time!
Te quiero.

Contents

INTRODUCTION

Chu-Lin and Espinete

I suppose I should start by recounting a sweet childhood story about a school trip to a farm where my friends and I got to feed and stroke a few nice piglets with our small hands, and how this experience made me fall in love with pigs. But it wasn't like that at all. The truth of the matter is that the only thing I recall from that trip is being bitten by a lamb to which I had a given a finger to suck on. Yes, I must admit, that probably was not the cleverest of ideas, but I obviously didn't know any better at the time. I also vividly remember how much my finger bled as a result of the lamb's innocent bite, but little else of the day is stored in my memory of what must have been a magical day.

I must also confess that of all the animals I encountered growing up as a child in Spain, pigs didn't feature very prominently. I have many animal memories, but all of them are pig free. For instance, I remember going to the Madrid Zoo to take part in one of the birthday celebrations of Chu-Lin, the first panda to be born in Europe, where we got a piece of his birthday cake that tasted very creamy and sickly. I also remember keeping silkworms in a shoebox and picking mulberry leaves in the nearby Retiro Park to feed them. Then there was the snail I kept in another shoebox, whose shell I accidentally crushed when trying to give it a 'hug'. I also remember when my dear goldfish died, and instead of having him buried far away from me – we lived in a fourteenth-floor apartment and didn't have a garden – I decided to keep him nearer to home and put him in our freezer despite my mother's objections. But there are definitely no pig memories. I don't even remember pigs featuring on the TV or in films.* I do remember *The Lion King*, *Sesame Street*, which, in its Spanish version, had Espinete the pink hedgehog and Don Pimpón, who was meant to be a finch (though knowing today what a finch actually looks like I can't quite see the resemblance), and the crazy *Maya the Bee*. There were also *Hello Kitty*,† and Snoopy of *Peanuts* fame.‡ But still no childhood memories involving pigs.

I have now realised that this lack of pigs in my awareness was due to the fact that the pigs I grew up with were not on farms, in zoos or on TV screens. They were on my plate instead: the chorizo in the sandwich I ate after school; the

---

* Upon further reflection, there was the film *Babe* (1995), which I didn't particularly like, and judging by the reviews on imbd.com, it seems I'm not alone in my thinking.

† My best friend María had quite the obsession and owned all sorts of official merchandise.

‡ I had a really cool toothbrush and cup holder.

lard in all those delicious pastries from the shop across the road; the gelatine in the sweet-sour strawberry strips that I was only allowed to eat at weekends; and the tasty pork loin with chips we got for lunch once a week in the school canteen.* I have always loved pork in all its shapes and forms,† and I was never really shocked by the sight of dead piglets inside the butcher's glass counter, or by the numerous legs of ham hanging from the walls of many food shops, bars and restaurants in Spain.

I guess, like most children, I developed an interest in animals early on, but unlike many of my peers I never dreamed of one day becoming a veterinarian or biologist. I wanted to be a paediatrician or the Queen of England.‡ So when the time came to decide on what further studies to pursue, many of my friends and family were rather puzzled by what appeared to be my random choice of a subject: I wanted to read archaeology and anthropology at university. However, my interest in the variety of peoples and societies across the world, and their origins, perhaps wasn't *that* random. I was born in Geneva (Switzerland), raised by a Spanish mother and a British father, and have two older Swedish half-siblings, with whom I have spent time in their native Stockholm. Growing up, I spent many summer holidays in Nice studying French, and in southern Italy living with the family of my Italian godparents.

* The deliciousness of this meal wasn't the norm, though; when it came to school lunches they were all pretty disgusting, especially the fish we got served on Fridays.

† I was not a fan of trotters or other 'suspicious-looking' body parts.

‡ There are probably thousands like me. From a young age I had what back then felt like a very great crush on Prince William and dreamed of marrying him one day; I understand from the press he is now taken – and so am I – so I guess it just wasn't meant to be?

Over the years my varied national and cultural experiences made me realise how different yet similar human groups are. It made me want to learn more about what it is that makes us human and how our cultural differences came about – hence the choice of archaeology and anthropology. My undergraduate studies not only took me on a journey of human behavioural discovery, but also taught me about our diets in the very distant past. I became fascinated by the past (and present) hunting-and-gathering economies of humans, and before I knew it I was doing a PhD on what people were eating in southern Croatia about 18,000 years ago. Though humans ate all sorts during the Palaeolithic, my doctoral research focused on the animal side of their diets, so my three and a half years were spent studying zoology and analysing red deer tibiae, European wild ass phalanges and wild boar teeth (more on that later).

Animals were, once again, in my life. It was around this time that I also began wondering more and more about different cuisines, and why pork features so prominently in the Spanish diet that I savoured growing up as a child in Madrid. The cuisine from my other side of the family, the British one, also had pork products (such as bacon and black pudding), but with its beef and other meat dishes seemed to me to be slightly more 'balanced'; but perhaps that was just me. I started thinking about Spain's multifaith background and history, and it soon became apparent that this pork obsession of ours might have something to do with the Catholic-driven Spanish Inquisition and its non-pork-eating Jewish and Muslim targets. That led me to wonder about why Judaism and Islam prohibit the consumption of pork, and I began reading more around the subject. One thing led to the next and, again before I knew it, I was putting together a proposal for the *Pig/Pork* book you are now holding. Just as many friends and relatives were surprised by my choice of undergraduate studies, many colleagues were also surprised to hear that I was writing a book about pigs. 'I didn't know you liked pigs, Pía,' said one with a rather puzzled look on her face after I told her I was writing this book. Neither did I, I guess, but I felt I wanted to find out more about the animals that had featured so frequently on my plate as a child, but with which I had had little contact (seeing dead piglets on the butcher's counter doesn't count).

Perhaps this choice of writing subject wouldn't be as much of a surprise if this were happening twenty years in the future and we had all grown up watching Peppa Pig, the anthropomorphic character, sister to George and daughter to the unimaginatively named Mummy and Daddy Pig. My son, who is now two, is obsessed with the fictitious little piglet's family, and I sometimes wonder when he will make the connection; when he will figure out that the *lomo* (cured loin of pork) he so much loves, and which his mum and dad also grew up with, is in fact the flesh of one of Peppa Pig's real-life relatives. A Spanish friend of mine recently told me how her niece, on finding out that chorizo is made from pork, decided she no longer wanted to eat it because she didn't want to hurt Peppa or anyone from her family. While this anecdote is funny, it also highlights how many of us have become so disengaged from our food that not only do we not know where it comes from, but we also know very little about the animals behind it.

Animals, however, are more than just food; pigs, as this book shows you, are here, there and absolutely everywhere. Each and every part of a pig is used, and that's why you find pig traces in such a disparate range of things as the glue holding this book together, probably derived from the bones of pigs and other animals; pig hairs in paintbrushes; and even pig haemoglobin in certain cigarette filters. Pigs have been a part of our human past since prehistory: they were, for example, the source of inspiration for prehistoric art from Spain all the way to the Indonesian island of Sulawesi. They have been a source of human conflict, and several wars were named after them. Experiments on their bodies have helped advance many fields of study, such as dermatology and tattoo artistry, though I get the feeling that the indispensable role these (guinea) pigs play for these and other disciplines – and for human life and survival in general – is something only a 'select' few are fully aware of. Perhaps this has to do with how, deep down, we feel uncomfortable with the fact that other species are being experimented on to improve *our* chances of survival; perhaps, also, it has something to do with the paywalled nature of much of the scientific literature. What I do know, though, is that a part of learning more about ourselves as a species requires us to gain an understanding of other species, including pigs, and vice versa. We are as much a part of pigs' lives as they are of ours. Dogs might be 'man's best friend', but pigs are our most resourceful and, dare I say it, closest friends. I hope this book does that relationship justice.

A note on pig evolution

The wild boar species (*Sus scrofa*) and domestic pig subspecies (*Sus scrofa domesticus*) this book mostly focuses on are, in terms of piggy evolution, just the tip of the iceberg. I have, however, chosen to begin this book in the Palaeolithic period, the Old Stone Age, because it is during this time that our full-on obsession with (wild boar) pork appears to have first emerged. Before discussing this subject, I thought it would be helpful to take a quick look at the millions of years' worth of evolution that gave rise to the wild boar and the domestic pig we know and love today (note that there are many weird and wonderful domestic pig breeds across the world today – see Appendix, page 241).

Taxonomically speaking, wild boar and domestic pigs belong to the Suidae family, the earliest unproblematic evidence for which has been found in African, European and Asian early Miocene epoch deposits about twenty million years old. By around fifteen million years ago, during the middle Miocene, the Suidae had spread widely across these three continents, and studies have confirmed the emergence of several Suidae subfamilies: the Listriodontinae, Cainochoerinae, Hyotheriinae and Tetraconodonotinae. Each had its own peculiar physical characteristics, which are believed to have emerged from the different and new environments the subfamilies colonised throughout Africa and Eurasia following their emergence.

At some point in the Miocene, around thirteen or so million years ago, a further subfamily emerged: the Babyrousinae, or 'pig-deer'. Very little is known about these creatures, which were so anatomically different from the rest of the Suidae. They are the black sheep of the family, the odd piece in an otherwise neat(ish) evolutionary puzzle. Little is known about their history due to the lack of any closely related living or extinct species from which evolutionary inferences could be drawn. So what is so peculiar about these creatures? Derived from the Malay words for pig (*babi*) and deer (*rusa*), babirusa, pig-deer, are today only found in remote areas of islands in South-east Asia: Sulawesi, Buru, Masbate, Taliabu and Samana. Anatomically speaking they look very different from your average suid (if there is such a thing). Their hairless, wrinkly skin is unique and looks a bit like the skin of the Sphynx cat breed. Their most striking feature, however, is on their snouts, in the form of two rather impressive-looking upper canines. These long teeth, which only the males carry, emerge from two rotated tooth sockets on top of the muzzle – in other words, the babirusa carry these upper teeth in the middle of the face and not in the mouth. The function of the teeth, which can reach lengths of up to 30cm (11¾in),* is not well understood – their inwards curvature makes them useless in fighting or feeding – but it's thought that they may play a role in sexual selection. It has also been suggested that they may act as face protectors when individuals attack each other using the lower, slightly more outward-facing canines.

Another way in which the babirusa is not your typical suid has to do with how its stomach is constructed. Though the stomach is unilocular, that is to say single-chambered, like the stomachs of wild boar and other suids,† it is different in that volume-wise it is bigger and possesses an extra sac, the inner linings of which are covered by a greater number of mucus-secreting glands (up to 70 per cent as opposed to 33 per cent in other Suidae species), which allows for a larger bacterial flora to be sustained there. It has been hypothesised that these features should classify the babirusa as a non-ruminant forestomach fermenter, meaning that it processes its food in a similar way to cows and other ruminants, but it does so with just the one stomach as opposed to four. This is one of the reasons why babirusa are so difficult to classify taxonomically. Despite these peculiarities and their overall differences from pigs, it does, however, appear that a strong link still lurks somewhere deep down in this pig-deer's genes. Even though five pairs of the babirusa's autosomes (numbers 6, 12, 14, 15 and 17)

* They sometimes grow longer than that, so babirusas can get impaled by their own teeth! Nature can be really cruel sometimes.

† The opposite of a single-chambered stomach would be that found in ruminants (such as cattle and sheep), which instead possess a four-chambered organ comprising the rumen, reticulum, omasum and abomasum. The former two allow the animal to form the cud and regurgitate it to be further chewed. Water and inorganic mineral elements make their way into the bloodstream through the omasum, and finally the abomasum plays the role that the single-chambered stomach plays for non-ruminants.

have no direct equivalents in any of the *Sus* species, a male *Babyrousa babyrousa* and a female *Sus scrofa domesticus* did unexpectedly mate and produce five offspring at Copenhagen Zoo in 2006. Three of the piglets survived for several months until they were culled, showing that pig-deer and domestic pigs can easily reproduce. That being the case, this raises the question of what happened in the past to leave the babirusa as such an enigma in our understanding of the evolution of suid life.

Returning to the Miocene, towards the end of this epoch, at some point after ten million years ago, a new subfamily, the Suinae, started to show up in the fossil record. Things must have become a bit out of control with these new kids on the block because by the end of the Miocene, about five million years after the Suinae first made an appearance, the Listriodontinae and Hyotheriinae subfamilies had become extinct. Fast forward another two and a half million years to the time around the Pliocene/Pleistocene transition, and only the Suinae and Tetraconodonotinae subfamilies still roamed the Earth. The Suinae were the most exclusive of the two, only to be found in Eurasia, whereas our Tetraconodonotinae friends were all over the place in Eurasia, Africa and the Indian subcontinent/south Asia. The Suinae waved goodbye to the Tetraconodonotinae shortly after this, and became the Suidae kings and queens of the earthly show; all of the subfamilies except this one were now gone.

This, however, was not a one-suid show, but rather quite the multi-genus cast. There was – and still is – *Hylochoerus*, which is represented by one species, *H. meinertzhageni*, the giant forest hog today found in Africa, which prefers to live in forested environments. It is grey in colour and its large, pointed ears are quite characteristic, as is the spiky hair on its body and tail. *H. meinertzhageni* obviously have a thing for smells judging by the scent glands that the males have in pads on their cheeks, as well as the scent glands in their penis foreskin.

There was also – and again, still is – *Phacochoerus*, of which there are two species: *P. africanus* and *P. aethiopicus*, the sub-Saharan warthogs. *P. africanus*, not to be confused with other *P. africanus*,* is the common warthog, a black or brown creature that lives in open and wooded savannahs, semi-deserts and grass steppes. Its main characteristics are the three pairs of warts on its face (hence its name), and a funky mane that runs from the top of the head and down the spine all the way to the middle of the back. *P. aethiopicus*, the desert warthog, has a greater tolerance for arid conditions than its *africanus* cousin, but it nonetheless prefers savannahs to deserts despite its name. These are big animals, though perhaps a bit smaller than common warthogs, and they too sport funky manes, which can sometimes be white in places, and have warty faces.

Then there was/is *Potamochoerus*, the sub-Saharan bushpig, in its two species forms: *P. porcus*, the red river hog, and *P. larvatus*, the bushpig. The former is now found from west and central sub-Saharan Africa all the way to northern South Africa and even on Madagascar. There are thirteen *P. porcus* subspecies, which means that there is a fair bit of physical variation among them, in particular in terms of their colour: from reddish with a white stripe running along the back to different shades of black and brown. Their most prominent features are their pointy upper (7.6cm/3in) and lower canines (16.5–19cm/6.5–7.5in), their long white

---

* *Panaeolus africanus*, a small brown African, hallucinogenic mushroom; *Paranthodon africanus,* a stegosaurian dinosaur from the Lower Cretaceous of South Africa; *Proconsul africanus,* an extinct primate discovered by Mary Leakey, which lived around twenty-five million years ago and is a common ancestor to both us and apes; and *Pseudoniphargus africanus,* a crustacean.

whiskers, and the warts above the eyes of the males. *P. larvatus* can be found in all sorts of habitats in east and southern Africa, and because it likes to eat agricultural crops – potatoes, corn and sugar cane among other things – it is commonly found close to human settlements. *P. larvatus* tends to be black and its head is usually a different shade from the rest of its body. It has a large bunch of long, bristly hairs running along the back, emerging from a prominent mane starting between the ears. Its hearing and sense of smell are known to be extremely powerful, though its eyesight leaves a lot to be desired; you just can't have it all, can you?

Additionally, there was/is the only *Porcula* species, *P. salvania*, the pygmy hog, which has a bullet-shaped body with a very small tail, and a white stripe above its snout that looks a bit like one of those white moustaches sported by celebrities in that US 'got milk?' US campaign of the 1990s. The pygmy hog is now only found in north-east India and is classified as a critically endangered species. It is, luckily, making a timid comeback to India's grasslands due to a conservation programme started in 1995, which has seen a more than ten-fold increase in its numbers (from six to seventy) since then.

Last but most definitely not least, there is the *Sus* genus comprising ten species, of which four are now extinct (*Sus strozzi*, *S. minor*, *S. peii* and *S. xiaozhu*). Those that are still alive and kicking are *S. verrucosus*, the Javan warty pig living not only on the Indonesian island of Java, but also on Bawean and, until fairly recently, Madura. Though its name kind of gives it away (*verruca* in Latin means wart), the Javan warty pig has, like many of its cousins, three pairs of warts on its face: on its cheek swellings (infraorbital), directly above its upper tusks (preorbital), and on the angle of the jaw (mandibular). These pigs are reddish in colour with their hair turning yellowish towards their undersides.

Like many other suids, Javan warty pigs are the proud owners of a long mane that runs from the back of the neck all the way to the lower back.

Following on from this there is *S. philippensis*, the Philippine warty pig, which has quite funky hair and would have been the envy of all those hair-obsessed people in the 1980s. This pig can be found in all of the Philippine's four major islands (Luzon, Mindanao, Mindoro and Samar). Unlike other warty pigs, it only possesses two pairs of warts on its face: two large ones above its upper canines, and a smaller mandibular duo. *S. cebifrons*, the Visayan warty pig from the Philippine Visayan islands, though first thought to be a subspecies of *S. philippensis*, was recognised as a distinct species in 1997. It used to be endemic to the Philippine islands of Negros, Panay, Guimaras, Cebu and Masbate, but today only survives on the former two and possibly on the latter. The decline in its numbers was due to commercial logging activities, agricultural expansion and hunting pressure. *S. barbatus*, the bearded pig, lives in Borneo, Sumatra, the Malay Peninsula and a few other smaller islands. It sports a rather cool-looking beard resembling those that were in fashion among human males during the Victorian era. Such is the apparent attraction of this species' grey whiskers that even the females grow them despite facial hair being more of a male trait for *Sus* species. *S. celebensis*, the Celebes warty pig, is common in all but the western portion of Sulawesi Island of Indonesia. It is generally black with a few lighter coloured hairs in between, and is the proud owner of three sets of facial warts, which are known to grow with age and reach their full size when the animals are around eight years old.

The last of the still-living *Sus* species is *S. scrofa*, the Eurasian wild boar, the one from which our domestic pig (*S. scrofa domesticus*) descends. It is on these two latter animals that this book focuses, though that's not to say that the others have not been up to much; theirs is just a different story. Now that we have made sense of the origins of the Eurasian wild pig and its domesticated form, we can turn to the weird and wonderful world of this hog, and the origins of our obsession with its pork.

CHAPTER ONE

Once upon a boar

Vela Luka, on Korčula island, Croatia, in the summer of 2007. It was a hot summer afternoon and the thousands of dusty Palaeolithic animal bone fragments from the site of Vela Spila lying in front of me waiting to be identified were not looking particularly inspiring. All I could think of was the cold, crisp lager that I would reward myself with at the end of the day, a drink that I could slowly enjoy on one of the lively bar terraces overlooking Vela Luka bay. Though being an archaeologist is not always (ever?) as adventurous and exciting as the *Indiana Jones* films and popular TV series would have you believe, that particular day was turning out to be especially painful and boring. Each and every one of the hundreds of bone fragments I had analysed from the local cave site of Vela Spila had come from red deer (*Cervus elaphus*). The identifications had all been monotonously 'identical', and I started to wonder if my zooarchaeological identification skills had deserted me and I could no longer osteologically differentiate a red deer from a fox. Now, don't get me wrong, red deer and the part they played in Palaeolithic life and diet are a fascinating subject, and they have taught us a lot about human existence during that period. However, when all the bone fragments recovered during an archaeological excavation look as though they have come from a single species (and a rather common creature of that period at that), the buzz of new discovery can go out of the work.

Things were reaching that point and I was about to give up for the day and drown my archaeological sorrows in not one, but several pints of Croatian lager, when luck intervened and a gleam of taxonomic hope emerged from the heap of bone fragments in the shape of a beautiful, complete incisor; based on its morphology, it could only have once resided in the gums of a wild boar. Unlike other parts of any heavily fragmented skeleton, as was most of the material I had to identify, teeth are usually pretty complete and distinctive. My identification skills would have had to have hit rock bottom* for me not to have realised that the precious lower incisor I was holding was not from a red deer but from a wild boar. My enthusiasm (and self-confidence) restored, I soon identified another two wild boar bone specimens. Based on their morphology and characteristics, the first was a small fragment from the left-hand side of the cranium, specifically the area where the frontal and lacrymal bones meet. The other was part of the shaft portion of a radius, one of the bones in the forelimb.

* Unintended archaeological pun.

The excavation level in which these bones had been found indicated that they were around 18,000 years old, and proof that our love affair with pigs – or in this case their wild ancestors – goes back many millennia.

These Upper Palaeolithic wild boar bones, however, aren't the oldest evidence of our obsession with pig/pork. Going further back in time, to the Middle Palaeolithic, we find various other examples of wild boar consumption, like that taking place at the cave site of Kalamakia on the Mani peninsula in southern Greece. There, butchered wild boar bones alongside those of fallow deer (*Dama dama*), ibex (*Capra ibex*) and red deer were found in deposits as ancient as 100,000 years old. A hundred millennia, it would be fair to say, is quite the long-lasting bond. What is even more interesting about these Greek wild boar remains is that they were found in association with the bones of at least eight Neanderthals – we, in our modern human form, weren't even present in Europe at the time.

If we travel further south, to Israel, we find further proof of this deep-rooted bond at the site of Kebara Cave. Around 60,000 years ago those living there enjoyed wild boar meat treats alongside others from a mixed bag of creatures such as mountain gazelle (*Gazella gazella*), Persian fallow deer (*Dama mesopotamica*) and aurochs (*Bos primigenius*), the mighty ancestor of modern-day cattle. You may think these old dates are impressive enough, but at the site of Medzhibozh 1 in western Ukraine, for example, we know that wild boar were being hunted half a *million* years ago. This was not, however, an isolated case: at the open-air site of Terra Amata in Nice, France, humans were chasing a few wild boar along the Côte d'Azur at some point between 400,000 and 300,000 years ago. At the nearby site of Orgnac 3, humans were hunting wild boar at more or less the same time, and quite a decent number of them, too.

It must be said that the hunting of relatively large numbers of wild boar is slightly unusual for this period; though wild boar featured in these and many other Palaeolithic assemblages, based on the prehistoric faunal data currently available it seems that back then piggies were not as popular a food choice as domestic pigs are today. In most cases humans seemed to have been more interested in the meat of different species of deer, horse, goat and a range of other creatures; wild boar, it seems, were in many cases more of a culinary afterthought. This probably had less to do with human taste preferences and more with this species' availability. Although wild boar are now regarded as pests in many parts of the world, studies have shown that during the Pleistocene (aka the ice ages), *S. scrofa* may not have been as widespread, especially during the colder periods. This is because although wild boar are capable of living and thriving in a wide range of environments, they're particularly fond of open woodland and mixed forests, especially those close to water sources. These wooded environments, however, were much reduced at different times during the Pleistocene, especially during the glacial peaks, so some think that the lessened availability of their preferred habitat may have, in turn, affected their population numbers. Because our ancestors were probably very much into efficiency, it seems that less supply equalled less demand.

Even if there were fewer of them, wild boar were nonetheless living (and being hunted by humans) all across Eurasia, including as far afield as Japan.* It was there that archaeological investigations of the Palaeolithic (40,000–16,000 years ago) and Jōmon (16,000–2,300 years ago)

* This is, of course, from my UK geographical point of view; if you are in Japan this will obviously be close to home.

periods,* revealed new and fascinating insights into how these animals were hunted by people.† It all started with the excavation of the Jōmon site of Kirigaoka in the 1970s, which revealed the presence of 116 mysterious-looking oval pits, all about 1.5m (4ft 11in) wide and 1/1.5m (3ft 3in/4ft 11in) deep. Not only was the discovery fascinating in itself, but an intriguing characteristic was also shared by the pits: they all had small, deep post-holes at the bottom, suggesting that wooden poles or other implements may have filled these gaps at some point in the past. This finding confirmed what many scholars had suspected for a long time: that during prehistory the Japanese used traps to catch their prey.

Hundreds more excavations have taken place since Kirigaoka was first opened up, and these have provided further proof of the existence of such ancient traps. These later works have revealed the presence of many more such pitfalls, of which about 400 date to the Japanese Early Upper Palaeolithic, and some are as old as 40,000 years. Their purpose might have been not to kill the animal, but rather to just stop it from escaping, which makes sense if we consider how wild boar react when hunted today: they either hide or run away. When drive hunts are used, in which hunters and dogs drive and chase the prey in the direction of another group of hunters, wild boar have been seen to run as far as 6km (3.7mi) to escape. Bearing in

---

* *Jōmon* in Japanese means cord-impressed and refers to the characteristic pottery produced by these hunter-gatherers. The fact that they produced pottery is significant as this is generally associated with the adoption of agriculture and the abandonment of hunting and gathering. The Jōmon period is subdivided into the **Incipient** 16,000–11,000 years ago), **Initial** (11,000–7,500 ya), **Early** (7,500–5,600 ya), **Middle** (5,600/4,500–4,000 ya), **Late** 4,500/4,000–3,200/3,000 ya) and **Final** (3,200/3,000–2,800/2,300 ya) **periods**.

† Japan is home to two subspecies of wild boar: the Ryukyu wild boar (*Sus scrofa riukiuanus*) and Japanese wild boar (*S. s. leucomystax*).

mind that they can run as fast as 48km/h (30mi/h), even Usain Bolt, running at his world-record 100m pace, would need a couple more minutes to complete the distance than a wild boar running for its life! I've heard that Russians have a proverb that goes something like this: 'If you go after a bear, take some straw; if you go after a wild boar, drag a coffin with you.' I can see why they would say this, and I totally get why the Japanese of the Palaeolithic would choose to use traps; there is only so much boar-chasing one can do in a lifetime!

The use of traps continued throughout the Palaeolithic all the way to the following Jōmon, and it was during the latter's Middle period that wild boar trapping appears to have taken a new form: in cases where young individuals were caught, these might not have been killed initially, but instead kept alive and fattened up until they were sufficiently big to make it worthwhile to eat them. Apparently this is still a relatively common practice in rural mountain areas of Japan, where people occasionally raise young wild boar they find astray and keep them until they are big enough to eat; or, in some luckier cases, they end up becoming family pets.

The modern practice of trapping and raising wild boar, and the hypothesis that it may have been taking place since the Middle Jōmon (or even earlier), has triggered much discussion among Japanese scholars of the period as to whether or not this represents the earliest evidence of pig husbandry in Japan. Whether this is the case still remains to be seen – more on this in the following chapter – but what is clear is that wild boar held a very special place in the heart of the Jōmon Japanese. This love of all things boar is further attested by the many fired-clay figurines of wild boar that have been found for this period alongside those of *dogū*, the enigmatic humanoid forms also shaped in clay, of which 18,000 have so far been found throughout Japan. The reasons for this artistic inspiration and underlying love affair, however, have yet to be fully understood, especially as the Japanese archaeological record has yet to produce evidence of wild boar representations during the Palaeolithic; as a matter of fact, there is little evidence of *any* artistic activity on the archipelago during this period (or, if there was such activity, it has yet to be discovered).

A lack of creative activity was most definitely not the case in Europe, where an abundance of portable and cave art from the Palaeolithic period has been the focus of study since the late 1800s, following the first discovery of portable art in 1860 (a bear's head engraved on an antler from the cave of Massat in the French Pyrenees), and of parietal art in 1879 (at Altamira cave in Cantabria, northern Spain).

Numerous paintings, made between 20,000 and 15,000 years ago,* cover the walls of the site of Altamira in Spain. When Spaniards think of Altamira's paintings, especially those of its so-called Great Ceiling, images of beautifully depicted red bison tend to come to their minds. Though it is true that there are a lot of red bison decorating the walls and ceilings, the art of this Cantabrian cave is not all bison themed. The Great Ceiling and most of the walls throughout the cave also include depictions of horses, some in motion and some fighting, goats, red deer, human hands and a variety of random shapes. The taxonomic identification of most of the animal representations at the site was assumed to be straightforward when they were first sketched and studied by the French archaeologist Henri Breuil in 1953. There were three figures (numbers 14, 15 and 19), however, which triggered a heated 'boar versus bison' debate in the 1970s and 1980s. Breuil had said that the three figures were boars, but his observations were questioned by the US archaeologist Leslie Freeman, who argued that the boar-ish features described by Breuil are in fact the product of the

* These are the radiocarbon dates. The uranium-series dating of a dot and a red horse at the site have produced two earlier dates: 36,160 ± 610 and 22,110 ± 130 respectively.

undulations in the ceiling. Such natural geological features were commonly used by prehistoric painters to add texture to their paintings, and to give the impression of movement when viewed in flickering fire light. Freeman argued further that the figures were clearly bison and not suids, because wild boars are 'somewhat out of place in the Altamira assemblage' (1987: 81). It's not entirely clear what he meant by this, but could it have been to do, for instance, with how different the diets of wild boar are from those of other ungulates such as red deer, bison and horses?

Wild boar, like us, are omnivores and thrive on all sorts of plant *and* animal foods. Bison, red deer and horses, on the other hand, are herbivores and feed on grasses and other plant foods. Could these different diets (and how similar ours is to that of wild boar) perhaps have something to do with how humans perceived – and depicted – these animals? Who knows. What we do know for sure is that Freeman just wasn't buying that those three figures are wild boar. Though it is true that one of them (number 19) does look very much like the head of a bison (or even that of a musk-ox, *Ovibos moschatus*), Breuil's original interpretations were defended by archaeologist Patricia Rice, who in 1992 published a paper with metrical data that supported the Frenchman's original claims. Rice measured both the lengths and heights of the Great Ceiling figures, as well as those of their limbs. She then used these data to calculate several anatomical ratios,* which would provide information on the shapes of the animals' bodies and the relative lengths of their limbs, which we know are different between bison and wild boar. The results from Rice's ratios showed that of all the figures on the Great Ceiling, there are two that

* Ratio 1: between body length and body height; Ratio 2: between body length and total height; Ratio 3: between total height at hindquarters and length of back legs; Ratio 4: between total height at forequarters and length of front legs.

just aren't quite 'right' in that their ratios are much smaller than those of the other figures. These, Rice said, from an anatomical point of view, are wild boar; Breuil's initial descriptions were, based on her work, therefore mostly spot on.

Despite such academic controversies, in the 1990s two things scholars of Palaeolithic parietal and mobile art used to agree on was that the richness and antiquity of such human artistic representations demonstrated that Europe, with its more than 30,000-year-old sophisticated art, was the cradle of human artistic creativity. For a long time this claim to fame remained unchallenged, with no other region in the world, from the Middle East all the way to Australia, producing that much, and as old, art for that period.

The oldest known depiction of an animal was, until recently, that of a rhino at Chauvet Cave in Ardèche, France, dated to around 35,000 calendar years before the present.* In October 2014, however, the rhino's place on the podium of artistic antiquity became less clear following the publication of a paper in *Nature* by a team of researchers from Indonesia and Australia, which presented evidence from Sulawesi (Indonesia) of what was potentially an even older artistic representation of an animal. That animal was none other than the fierce-looking babirusa, or 'pig-deer', the wild boar's distant Indonesian cousin. The existence of the pig-deer painting at the Leang Timpuseng cave, alongside others of dwarf bovid anoas (*Anoa* sp.),† a Celebes warty pig (*Sus celebensis*), as well as numerous hand stencils, had been known since the 1950s, but it was only recently they were reliably dated.

Cave and portable art are particularly tricky to date, but there was something about the Sulawesi paintings that made it possible to establish their antiquity, and that was

* 32,410 ± 720 (GiF A 95132).

† A kind of midget buffalo.

'cave popcorn'. Much of the better preserved art, the team noted, was covered by a thin layer of coral-type water precipitates. This 'cave popcorn' had not only protected the paintings through the years, but also provided the researchers with the chance to date them. This is because the precipitates can be dated using a technique known as Uranium or Uranium-Thorium series. Generally speaking, the way this dating method works is by comparing the amounts of Uranium 234 and Thorium 230 within a given sample. Because the rate of decay from U-234 to Th-230 is known, by looking at the ratio between the two, scientists can determine the age of a sample. By obtaining a date for the 'cave popcorn', a minimum age could thus be established for the paintings 'trapped' underneath it. The 'popcorn' over the painting of the female babirusa was dated to at least 35,400 years ago. Given that the rhino at Chauvet Cave was dated to around 35,000 years ago, this meant that the painting of the female babirusa from Leang Timpuseng was the oldest known depiction of an animal. Moreover, at the nearby site of Leang Barugayya 2, the painting of a large indeterminate creature, which was thought to probably be a pig, was dated to an even greater minimum age (35,700 years old), providing further evidence that early art in the Palaeolithic was probably more of a global phenomenon than previously thought; it's just a matter of finding (and dating) cave art in other places than Europe.

During the Palaeolithic, babirusa and wild boar were clearly not just sources of artistic inspiration; they were also an important food element in the original palaeodiet, as well as in the following Mesolithic gastronomic repertoire. We know this due to the analysis of faunal remains found at archaeological sites,* such as that of the rock shelter of

* We also owe it to the patience of those identifying the bones, which, as you've probably gathered from the introduction, is many times put to the test.

Les Cabônes in the Jura region, France. The finding and study of sites such as this one has shown, for example, that in this area of eastern France and western Switzerland, wild boar and red deer were quite the popular dishes for those living there during the Mesolithic, between 11,500 and 9,000 years ago. In the case of Les Cabônes more than 1,200 wild boar bones, representing nearly half of the assemblage, were found alongside those of a further 11 species, including red deer, of which 1,039 parts were identified.

In order to gain a better understanding of the diets of our ancestors, those studying the Les Cabônes fauna decided that they wanted to find out more about how wild boar might have been hunted, and they did so by looking at their teeth. This might seem like an odd choice, but teeth can be pretty revealing: generally speaking, within particular species tooth eruption and replacement are known to take place in a sequence with relatively fixed timings, which basically means that the age of an individual can be estimated based on the presence/absence of certain teeth in its mouth. So, for example, whereas the wild boar's lower deciduous (milk) fourth premolar erupts at some point at 11–20 days of age, its upper counterpart only starts making its way through the gums at 1.3–1.9 months. If, say, the skull and mandible of a wild boar were found and only had the lower milk fourth premolars, we would thus know that the animal was at least 11–20 days old, but younger than 1.3 months. So how old were the wild boar at Les Cabônes, and most importantly, what do their ages tell us about how they were hunted by these Mesolithic humans?

Of the 50 sets of teeth analysed, 32 (64 per cent) belonged to individuals less than two years old, whereas the rest were young adults 2–5 years old, and there were also a couple of more 'senior citizens' (seven years old). This age structure, the archaeologists noted, very much resembles that of a typical wild boar herd, aka a sounder, which generally comprises 10–20 individuals, most of which are females with their offspring, all led by a matriarch. Unlike the solitary and dispersed adult males, sounders tend to stick to more restricted areas, where they move about rather noisily and mostly at night. From a strategic and economic point of view, the faunal profiles at Les Cabônes thus make a lot of sense: not only would it have been easier to track down the most predictably located (and noisier) sounders than the solitary, itinerant males, but stalking such a group would allow several prey to be taken at once, even if this meant less meat per individual given the presence of the very young. It was not all females and infants at Les Cabônes, though: the archaeologists also found several fragments of lower tusks, the shape and size of which can be used to distinguish whether they came from males or females. The careful examination of the canines revealed them to be male, showing that the French hunters at times not only had the energy, but also the skills to chase and successfully hunt the more solitary male creatures. The analysis of the canines also revealed the presence of scrape marks and polish to their surfaces, suggesting that they may have been used as tools of some sort, a practice not unheard of for this region or for this time period.

It's no surprise to hear that our Palaeolithic and Mesolithic ancestors were highly resourceful and, you could say, enemies of waste. They not only carefully butchered their prey, making the most of the meat, marrow, tendons, skin and so on, but also made good use of the teeth and bones to create all manner of tools, adornments and, in many cases, grave goods. For example, at Grotta Paglicci in southern Italy, around 17,000 years ago, the bones of red deer, European wild ass (*Equus hydruntinus*), aurochs and wild boar were used many times to manufacture a variety of tools. Wild boar fibulae, the thinner and shorter of the two major hindlimb bones, were carefully fractured and scraped to produce pointy-ended perforating tools such as awls or needles that may have been used to pierce and sew leather and skins. At the Turkish cave site of Üçağızlı I, there is also evidence that wild boar fibulae were used to make bone tools: for example, in its 34,000-year-old Layer F, a worked and polished fibula 20cm (7.9in) in length was found, which the Arizona University team excavating the site believed wasn't a projectile weapon, as some of the other wild boar and fallow deer worked bone specimens appeared to be, but was instead more likely to have been used as a large awl or even a decorative pin.

While worked bone was sometimes used for decorative purposes during the Palaeolithic and Mesolithic, it seems that animal teeth were a more popular choice, though this could, of course, simply be due to a preservation bias.* On the central Russian Plain, for example, a number of sites have produced the pierced teeth of wild boar and those of other species, the circumferences of which were grooved and polished so that they could be used as pendants. At Zvejnieki in Latvia more than 1,900 tooth pendants, mostly made from the incisors of wild boar and elk (*Alces alces*), were found buried alongside the 144 individuals laid to rest at this site during the Mesolithic and the Mesolithic-Neolithic transition. The grave of an adult woman (number 74) even contained a bird figurine carved out of a boar tusk. This placing of such a worked wild boar canine within a human burial is not an isolated find: for example, at the Swedish Mesolithic cemetery of Skateholm II, a man buried in a sitting position,† between 7,700 and 6,700 years ago, was found to be wearing a neck decoration comprising,

* Generally speaking, teeth tend to preserve better than most bones, though there are, of course, exceptions to this rule.

† Although this may seem like an odd thing to do, it was a relatively common practice in many Mesolithic burials across Europe.

among others, roe deer (*Capreolus capreolus*) metacarpals and two wild boar canines.

It is not surprising that we humans have been fascinated by wild boar tusks and have used them for such a long time. The upper tusks, which are big and chunky, curve upwards and outwards, and have an overall rounded body. The lower ones, though thinner and with a more triangular cross-section, are impressive dental pieces (especially those of males), and when they are used as defensive weapons they are not to be messed with. Even though the canines grow throughout a wild boar's life, their size and sharpness are kept in check by the rubbing action that takes place between the canines, preventing the upper ones from growing more than 30cm (11.8in), still a respectable (and scary) length for a tooth with a function that has little to do with eating.

Our fascination with wild boar tusks has continued to the present day and is just as strong as it was back in the Palaeolithic, so much so that the International Council for Game and Wildlife Conservation (CIC) uses the combined length of these tusks in its points system in order to determine the gold, silver or bronze medal status of wild boar hunting trophies. In Britain, where I now live, wild boar hunting and the pursuit of trophies in that field is becoming increasingly popular as the numbers of wild boar continue to increase.

Wild boar first arrived in Britain and Ireland at the start of the Mesolithic, and their butchered remains have been found at archaeological sites such as those of Star Carr in Yorkshire and Thatcham in Berkshire, England, as well as Burry Holms on the Gower Peninsula and Goldcliff in Newport, Wales. They weren't equally popular throughout the isle: wild boar meat was apparently favoured in Berkshire, whereas the inhabitants of Star Carr weren't particularly interested in it and had more of a thing for red deer, present in the area in probably similar numbers to wild boar. The same appears to be true for the site of Goldcliff – given its coastal location its inhabitants had easy access to marine resources, so they ate more of these at the expense of terrestrial species such as wild boar. In any case, soon after this many people didn't have to make a choice about whether or not to eat wild boar meat because the animal is believed to have become extinct in Ireland by the following Neolithic period. It managed to hang on for much longer in Britain, until more or less the fourteenth century, when the last of the isle's populations are thought to have disappeared.

This wasn't to be the end of the British wild boar show though: since the 1600s wild boar have been imported regularly from mainland Europe to be exhibited in zoos and farmed for meat. However, not until the 1990s were they once again seen roaming freely in England, in areas such as Dorset and Herefordshire, and it is thought that there are now more than 1,000 individuals scattered across the country. It is not yet clear how these modern feral populations came about, but their appearance seems to have coincided with an increase in the number of wild boar meat farms, from where it is thought individuals have escaped over the years. Wild boar are also, reproductively speaking, quite prolific, and added to the fact that they have no natural predators (such as wolves and lynxes) in Britain, this could result in their numbers soon growing out of control, and prove damaging to agricultural land and perhaps to other species. This is where human intervention through planned culling and appropriately regulated hunting activities can play a role, and perhaps show whether we have learned from past extinction experiences. Will (pre)history repeat itself in Britain?

While wild boar are today again roaming in Britain, it is not yet clear whether they are in fact true 'pure-bred' boars. This is because over the years a number of the wild boar imported into Britain to be raised for meat have, at different points in time, been crossed with domestic pig sows. The reason for this has to do with productivity and profits – domestic pigs produce bigger litters than their wild counterparts, which results in more meat for sale and greater profits per individual. Crossing them with male wild boars, however, makes the meat retain its 'strong' taste and darker colour, which pleases consumers looking to eat a less 'commercial-tasting' meat.

The practice of cross-breeding wild and domestic pigs is apparently not new, at least according to a 2013 paper published in *Nature Communications* by biochemist and archaeologist Professor Krause-Kyora and his colleagues from the University of Kiel in Germany. Based on evidence from certain Mesolithic and Neolithic sites in northern Germany, they argued that Mesolithic hunter-gatherers in the area had access to domesticated pigs as early as 6,600 years ago. In the world of zooarchaeology, this was quite a statement to make: if true, it would represent the first ever evidence of domesticated pigs at Mesolithic sites, *and* the earliest evidence of domesticated animals in the region, some 500 years earlier than the previously recorded oldest dates for the first domesticated cattle, sheep and goats.

To reach their conclusion, the 11 scholars involved in the project combined data from the sequencing of ancient mitochondrial DNA with the geometric morphometrics (GM) of 63 *Sus* individuals found at 17 Mesolithic (Ertebølle) and Neolithic sites in the region.* The DNA and GM studies led the research team to conclude that the northern European Ertebølle hunter-gatherers possessed the same kinds of domestic pig as those kept by their contemporaneous Neolithic agricultural neighbours, the Stichbandkeramik and Rössen cultures. For example, the genetic analyses of three of the suids found in the Ertebølle sites of Grube-Rosenhof and Poel revealed that they possessed haplotype Y1, a genetic determinate of Near Eastern origin linked to the domesticated pigs introduced into Europe during the

* Geometric morphometrics (GM) is the analysis of biological shapes.

Neolithic. The domesticated status of some of these individuals, living alongside hunter-gatherer, pre-agricultural communities, was further confirmed by analyses of the shape of the individuals' second lower molars, the proportions of which were shown to be more 'compact' than those of wild specimens.*

These 'Mesolithic domestication' claims were challenged a year later by archaeology professor Peter Rowley-Conwy from Durham University in the UK and Dr Melinda Zeder from the Department of Anthropology at the US's Smithsonian National Museum of Natural History, who in their 11-page reply counter-argued that the data from the *Nature Communications* study didn't necessarily represent the first evidence of domesticated pigs being introduced into this region, but could rather simply be showing the presence of wild individuals who, at some point in time, bred with the domestic pigs kept by the Stichbandkeramik and Rössen, or with other wild boar born to wild-domestic parents.

While the Kiel University study is intriguing from an archaeological and zoological point of view, it doesn't necessarily prove that pre-agricultural Mesolithic peoples like the Ertebølle were keeping *and* raising domesticated pigs as did their farming Neolithic neighbours. Domestication, as explained later, is a complex and multilayered process that brings with it many economic and social changes; it's not just about 'keeping pigs', whether these were domesticated (by others) or not. There is a reason why our shift to an agricultural way of life has been described as a 'revolution'; it truly was a drastic and life-changing thing for us to do.

---

* The domestic breeding of pigs led to, among other things, the flattening of the animals' faces. This meant that there was less space available for their teeth and, as a result, these became more compact. More on this in the following chapter on domestication.

WILD BOAR AND RED WINE STEW (CROATIA)

By Anna Colquhoun of *Culinary Anthropologist*

Serves 4–5

This slow-simmered stew for a cold night is based on one of Anna Colquhoun's favourite autumnal Istrian dishes. The Istrian Peninsula today falls mostly in Croatia, but over the centuries has belonged to the Venetian Republic, the Austrian Empire, Italy and Yugoslavia, all of which left their mark on this region's culinary culture. The stew is commonly made using wild boar shot by a neighbour or friend, local red wine made from Teran grapes and juniper foraged from the forest. I was lucky enough to try this stew while on an excavation in Buzet, northern Istria, in 2004. Each evening, after a hard day's work in the field, we drove across the border to Slovenia, where we were served lovely local dishes at a small family restaurant. The restaurant was run by a couple and their two grown-up sons. The wild boar in the stew was hunted by the sons, and we ate it with gnocchi (*njoki*). It was truly hearty and so authentic that it even contained a couple of wild boar hairs! If possible, make the stew a day ahead so the strong flavours have time to meld. Serve with polenta, gnocchi or boiled potatoes.

Ingredients

1kg (2¼lb) wild boar shoulder meat
Salt and pepper
Butter and/or olive oil
200g (7oz) smoked pancetta
1 onion
1 carrot

1 stick of celery
3 fat cloves of garlic
Good sprig of fresh sage
Good sprig of fresh rosemary
1 heaped tablespoon plain flour
2 tablespoons brandy
5 juniper berries, crushed
300ml (10fl oz) Teran wine
200–300ml (7–10fl oz) chicken or beef stock
Dash of red wine vinegar

Method

1. Cut the meat into 5cm (2in) pieces, removing any skin or large pieces of fat or sinew as you go. Leave some fat on. Season well with salt and pepper all over.
2. Heat a knob of butter and a dash of olive oil in a heavy-based casserole or other pot. Over a medium heat, brown the meat on all sides, in batches so as not to crowd the pan. Do not let the meat or butter burn (brown is nice; black is not). Meanwhile, remove the skin from the pancetta and cut it into thin lardons.
3. Remove the meat from the pan and add the lardons. Fry until the fat is rendering. Peel the onion, carrot and celery, roughly chop them, and blitz in a food processor until minced.
4. Add the minced vegetables to the pancetta and cook for another few minutes, stirring, until the vegetables soften. Add more oil or butter to the mixture if it is dry. Meanwhile, peel and mince the garlic, then add it along with the herb sprigs and cook for another few minutes until fragrant and the vegetables are caramelising.

5. Return the meat to the pan and sprinkle over the flour. Cook, stirring, for a few minutes. Add the brandy and let it reduce. Add the juniper berries, wine and enough stock to barely cover.
6. Cover and simmer very gently until the meat is tender and starting to fall apart, about 2 hours. If the sauce is too thin, remove the lid so some of the water evaporates. If possible, leave in the fridge overnight.
7. Reheat if needed, remove the herb stalks, check the seasoning and add a small dash of red wine vinegar to brighten the flavour. Serve with pasta, gnocchi or potatoes.

BOTAN NABE (JAPAN)

By Amelia Ijiri

Serves 4

This hot pot is called *botan nabe* (peony hotpot) because before cooking, the wild boar meat is arranged in the shape of a peony flower on a platter. The dish is popular in rural mountain areas of Japan and is primarily consumed during the cold winter months. In Gifu Prefecture on Honshu, Japan's main island, there is a special train service, Shishi Nabe Ressha, which runs every Thursday between December and February. It travels from Ōgaki to Tarumi, and the trip takes just over an hour. Each of the train's carriages has two long facing tables on which passengers are served *botan nabe* and other seasonal local dishes while they get to enjoy the sights from the comfort of the train. Only in Japan.

Ingredients

650g (1½lb) wild boar meat, cut into bite-sized pieces
Salt and sake, a little of each for pre-seasoning
1 bunch chrysanthemum leaves, cut into bite-sized pieces
200g (7oz) bean sprouts
750g (1½lb) quarter-cut Napa cabbage, cut into bite-sized pieces
1 block tofu, cut into bite-sized pieces
80g (3oz) shiitake mushrooms
1 leek, diagonally sliced into 3–4cm (1¼–1½in) pieces

For the soup base

1 litre (2 pints) dashi soup base
Miso to taste – Hatcho-style preferred
2 knobs grated ginger – adjust to taste

Method

1. Arrange the boar meat in an eye-catching flower shape on a platter. Sprinkle with salt and sake.
2. Add the soup-base ingredients to a pot and heat to a rapid boil.
3. Adjust the soup base by varying the amounts of miso and ginger.
4. Thoroughly cook the boar meat in the broth, constantly skimming off the fat that floats to the top.
5. Cook the other ingredients thoroughly in the same broth, and eat immediately.

BAVARIAN WILD BOAR (GERMANY)

Serves 4

Wild boar are today found all over Germany, except in its southern Alpine region. However, it wasn't until the 1980s that wild boar were first spotted in Bavaria, known for its harsh and snowy winters, which the animals are known not to be too keen on. An interesting fact about these German wild boar is that many, especially those of Bavaria's neighbouring Saxony, aren't fit for consumption due to the radiation in their bodies. Even though Germany is located at some distance from Chernobyl in Ukraine, it's known that the radiation from this city's nuclear disaster made it as far as France, contaminating everything along its way. Because wild boar love to root they are directly in touch with radioactive soil, and they also love to eat mushrooms and buried truffles, both of which are known to store quite significant amounts of Chernobyl's radiation. Tests carried out by the Saxon federal government, for example, found that one in three of its wild boar gave such high radioactive readings that they were not to be consumed by humans. Such is the extent of this problem that since 2012 it has been compulsory for hunters in Saxony to test their wild boar prey before it is sold to the public.

Ingredients

1kg (2¼lb) wild boar
500ml (1 pint) buttermilk
Salt and pepper
2 tablespoons pork lard
160g (6 oz) onion
80g (3oz) carrots

80g (3oz) celery
50g (2oz) bacon
3 tablespoons tomato paste
1 teaspoon allspice
1 teaspoon peppercorn
1 teaspoon juniper berry
1 bay leaf
40g (1½oz) flour
200ml (⅓ pint) red wine
Sugar
Lemon juice

Method

1. Marinate the wild boar in the buttermilk for two days in a cool place.
2. Dry the meat, then rub with salt and pepper and sear all around.
3. Dice and sauté the carrot/onion/celery in the pork lard.
4. Mix the tomato paste in water, and add the spices, bay leaves and juniper berries.
5. Add the vegetables and spiced mixture to the braising dish.
6. Cook the meat in an oven preheated to about 180–200 °C (350–400 °F) for about 1–1¼ hours, turning several times.
7. When the meat is cooked set it aside.
8. Mix the flour with the red wine, add them to the pan juices and deglaze thoroughly.
9. Add the hot meat, and serve with red cabbage and *knödel* (dumplings).

CHAPTER TWO

Old MacDonald had a farm

It was 11 March 2005 and Greger Larson, then a PhD student at the Department of Zoology at Oxford University, was probably beyond excited to have the paper on which he was the leading author published by no other than the prestigious *Science* journal. This genetics paper was revolutionary: the study of the worldwide phylogeography of wild boar, which he had been working on as part of his PhD, revealed that there were not just two (Turkey and China), but rather *multiple* centres of pig domestication. The science behind the study was pretty solid: the analysis of the mitochondrial DNA (mtDNA) sequences of 686 wild and domestic pig specimens indicated that wild boar originated in island South-east Asia (ISEA), from where they then spread throughout Eurasia. Once in mainland Europe and Asia, the wild boar were independently domesticated in many areas across these continents, including India, Myanmar, Thailand, Papua New Guinea, Italy and Sardinia. Moreover, the mtDNA analyses also showed that European domestic pigs are descended from European and not Near Eastern wild boar, as was previously thought.

Given this new scenario, Larson and his colleagues concluded that in order 'To further examine the domestication of pigs, the zooarchaeological records of Europe, India, South-east Asia, and ISEA should be explored in more detail' (p. 1621). This was quite the statement to make, and one that surprised many in the archaeological community, which had been studying pig domestication for the past hundred years and had 'only' been able to pinpoint south-west and south-east Asia as the two centres of pig domestication. Could genetics really hold the key to fully tracking the evolution and spread of domestic pigs throughout the world? Were mtDNA studies the way to go? Would the archaeological analysis of the bones and sites become a more secondary scientific pursuit?

It turned out that although the genetic study was neat, it was in fact showing something slightly different from what Larson and his colleagues first thought it did: the mtDNA data were not showing centres of pig domestication, but rather subsequent admixture with populations not involved in the original domestication, which in genetics is known as introgressive capture. That was the reason, for example, why the European domestic pigs appeared to be descended from European, not Near Eastern wild boar. After Near Eastern domesticated pigs were brought to Europe they soon began mating with local European wild boar. This lead to a 'mixture' of both their genes, and the more the Anatolian domesticated animals mated with the local

European wild ones, the more 'diluted' their DNA became within the resulting piglets, to the point that when Larson and his colleagues looked at the mtDNA of European domestic pigs they got the impression that there was no Anatolian ancestry within them – when in fact it had just been 'watered down'. Though this meant that the multiple centres of pig domestication theory was not entirely right, being able to track the degree to which admixture may have taken place in the past was also in itself interesting: was it intentional on the part of humans? If so, why would humans encourage it? When did intentionality kick in? Was the northern German 'Mesolithic domestication' such an example of intentional admixture?

So many questions – and where to begin? The story of the domestication of pigs is all but a simple and straightforward one. Despite this, it is also fascinating – involving two species and two regions and, of course, a whole load of pork. Before we go into the finer details of where domestic pigs first emerged, let us first look at what we mean by domestication, the different ways in which it can come about and how it is visible in the archaeological record. Even though some people may refer to it as an 'event', the domestication of pigs and other animals was not something that happened overnight. Nor was it likely to have been the result of any kind of 'a-ha! moment' some clever prehistoric chaps had, who thought it would be handy to keep a few pigs, sheep and cows for a year-round supply of food.

Domestication is not a one-off occurrence, but rather a continuum in the evolution and development of a species. At some point during this continuum, animals undergo physical transformations as a result of human selective pressures and the new environments in which they're placed. However, because these don't emerge from the beginning of the domestication process, this makes it tricky for archaeologists to establish when exactly such new human-animal relationships first began to take *place*, which may have been many centuries (or even millennia) before they began to take *shape*. Why is this? Well, one of the results of domestication is that the appearance of animals, both inside and out, changes. This is why, for example, dogs in their various breed forms look so different from the wild form of the wolf, and domesticated pigs, especially those with little hair and fair skin, can be easily distinguished from their wild boar ancestors. Even though skin doesn't tend to preserve archaeologically, bones and teeth do, as we saw for the Palaeolithic and Mesolithic, so it is these that archaeologists focus on when trying to separate the wild from the domestic in the past. An overall reduction in the size of individuals is perhaps the best-known change arising from domestication, but it is perhaps one of the least consistent changes. Not all species, populations or individuals 'shrink' to the same extent, and many studies have confirmed the likelihood of wild boar and domestic pig size overlaps. There are, however, other ways in which the suid skeleton reveals the process of domestication, and these centre around the beast's head.

Perhaps you hadn't noticed this until now, but wild boar have quite prominent faces and snouts. It's because long and sensitive noses help to make finding and rooting for food efficient. Domestic pigs, on the other hand, don't have such prominent nostrils (though their snouts are still pretty impressive), and this has to do with the changes to their diets and lifestyles as a result of human intervention, which resulted in pigs no longer needing to root in order to find food.* As discussed by archaeologist Dr Melinda Zeder † in

---

* Domestic pigs still like to root, though, and can be fairly destructive if left to their own devices.

† The name might sound familiar because she was one of the archaeologists mentioned in Chapter 1 who argued against the 'domesticated Mesolithic pigs' claim.

her 'Pathways to domestication' (2012) paper, it is also thought that this diminution in length came about as a result of the neotonisation of pigs, that is to say, the retention, through human selective breeding, of their infantile characteristics, perhaps as a way of reducing these animals' mistrust of humans and their sometimes aggressive behaviour. It was not only the snout that decreased in size as a result of domestication. A smaller head overall has also meant that domestic pigs have had to make do with a more modest brain size. Of all the domesticates, pigs have suffered the greatest brain-size transformation/reduction: a 33.6 per cent decrease in relation to the size of wild boar brains. The only two other domesticates that get close to this extent of brain-size loss are ferrets (*Mustela furo*) – 29.4 per cent, and dogs (*Canis familiaris*) – 29 per cent.

Not all parts of the pig brain, however, have shrunk to the same extent as a result of domestication. In pigs, as well as in dogs and sheep, it was the limbic system of the brain, the complex structure of nerves and networks in the brain that controls basic emotions such as anger and fear, and drives sex and hunger, that was most affected by the human intervention. This again makes a lot of sense from a human point of view: the more docile the creature, the easier it is to handle and, ultimately, to raise for food. Unfortunately for archaeologists, the brain is a soft-tissue organ and therefore one that is unlikely to survive in the archaeological record. There is, however, the bony case in which it is housed, the cranium, the dimensions of which can be measured in order to determine whether an individual has been domesticated or not. Of course, this is only possible if the skull survives intact, and unfortunately it generally doesn't.

The head has one more part to offer to the archaeological 'wild vs domestic' cause: its (mostly) indestructible teeth. As you can imagine, the flattening of the snout and the shrinking of the head could only mean one thing: less space per tooth. There were two possible solutions to this problem: for the body to reduce the total number of teeth in the mouth, or for it to make the teeth smaller. Pig evolution chose the latter. Though different numbers of teeth in wild boar and domestic pigs would have made the lives of archaeologists infinitely easier, 'nature' thought archaeology should be a challenging subject and opted for the reduction in tooth size, which is a bit trickier to measure as there can be some overlap between the teeth of wild and domestic pigs. Of all of the pig's permanent teeth (36–44 in total),* the one most commonly studied when trying to infer domestication is the lower third molar (the lower wisdom tooth for you and me), as it appears that the shortening of the pig's face affects teeth to a greater extent the further back you go in the mouth. Many studies carried out during the past century showed that the teeth of domesticates in Neolithic contexts were shorter that those recovered from Mesolithic levels. Roughly speaking, these studies found that lower M_3s in domesticated pigs were about 32–40mm (1.3in–1.6in) long, whereas those of wild boar mostly fell in the 40–50mm (1.6in–2in) range.

So it was that this M3 tooth, together with other measurements and kill-off pattern data, was analysed to assess the possible domestic status of the pigs at the Neolithic site of Çayönü Tepesi in the Tigris Valley in southeastern Turkey, thought to be where pig domestication first took place. Length and breadth measurements of the lower third

---

* Dental formula for Suidae (per side): **Deciduous/milk** (upper/lower), incisors 3/3, canine 1/1, premolars 3/3; **Permanent** (upper/lower), incisors 2–3/3, canine (1/1), premolars 3–4/2–4, molars 3/3. Dental formula for Hominidae (per side) for comparison: **Deciduous/milk** (upper/lower), incisors 2/2, canine 1/1, premolars 2/2; **Permanent** (upper/lower), incisors 2/2, canine 1/1, premolars 2/2, molars 3/3.

molar of *Sus* remains from the site showed a *slight* trend towards smaller dimensions through time. The 'slightness' of this trend, however, can't be emphasised enough, as studies have shown that the morphological change to the animals as a result of human intervention was very, very gradual. It was so gradual, in fact, that it actually took about 2,000 years for the pigs to 'transition' from wild to domestic, becoming fully domestic pigs around 9,000 years ago. The teeth of the pigs also showed a gradual increase in a particular dental defect, linear enamel hypoplasia (LEH), a marker of biological stress that appears due to poor nutrition and/or disease, and can be linked to human control over the animals' diets and mobility. It is thought that the domestication of the pigs at Çayönü Tepesi came about via a 'commensal pathway', which basically means that the animals came into contact with humans when they visited their settlements to feed on their garbage, or to prey on other animals also found around these human habitation areas. Through time, the pigs developed a closer bond with the humans, which slowly grew into a domestic relationship between the two. It's little wonder that the whole thing took two millennia.

This kind of domestic scenario is also thought to have occurred for dogs, with the most adventurous wolves making their way close to human settlements to feed on people's refuse, then building a bond with them over time. This commensal pathway is not, however, the most common domestication route: most livestock, including cattle, goats and sheep, were domesticated through what is known as the 'prey pathway'. These animals were once major prey for humans, but it is believed that when local stocks began to dwindle, humans came up with clever hunting strategies to restore prey numbers. Their novel game-management strategies then gradually morphed into a more concrete form of herd management, which later involved more controlled breeding of these animals, ending up with 'full on' domesticates.

A kind of mixture of the commensal and prey pathways is what appears to have taken place at Hallan Çemi, also in southeastern Turkey, and regarded by some to be the oldest permanent settlement in Anatolia, around 11,000 years old. Though sheep and goats were the most common species here, pigs also featured quite prominently, representing up to 25 per cent of the total. Many of the remains found were teeth, and just as had been done at Çayönü Tepesi, second and third molars were measured to assess whether a reduction in size could be noted through time. Unfortunately, the majority fell within the overlap range, so it was not possible to say whether the teeth belonged to wild or domestic pigs. The kill-off patterns based on bone-fusion data, however, were far more informative: at least 10 per cent of the pigs had died before the age of six months, and 43 per cent didn't make it past 12 months. Death due to natural causes of more than 50 per cent of a population before the age of one is highly unlikely, and it points to only one thing: human intervention. The greater number of males killed (11:4 ratio) provides further proof that some kind of selective slaughtering was taking place at Hallan Çemi. All these data have been disputed by many archaeologists who think that they don't necessarily represent the earliest evidence of pig domestication, but rather a kind of management of wild boar, similar in some ways, to how Papua New Guineans raise their pigs nowadays, which involves castrating village male pigs and letting the village sows mate with feral boars that like to get close to the human settlements.

To further complicate this pig domestication scenario, there is also the site of Akrotiri Aetokremnos – not in Anatolia, but actually on the Eastern Mediterranean island of Cyprus. The island, which is 69km (43mi) away from mainland Turkey, has never been connected to the

Asian continent, not even when sea levels were at their lowest during the Last Glacial Maximum, around 20,000 years ago, when they dropped 120m (394ft) and exposed large chunks of land. During this period the distance between Cyprus and Turkey was 63km (39mi), with an islet in between, but Cyprus was still very much an independent mass of land. What has all this got to do with pig domestication, you may ask? Due to the island's isolation, until the end of the Pleistocene it was home to a small number of species: a couple of mice, a genet (*Genetta* sp.),* a dwarf elephant (*Elephas cypriotes*) and a pygmy hippopotamus (*Phanourios minor*), but there were no pigs until 11,700–11,400 years ago. At that point a few suid bones start appearing at Akrotiri Aetokremnos, which could only mean one thing: that the animals were being brought to the island by people (the island, by the way, hadn't been inhabited by humans until a few centuries earlier). Pigs are excellent swimmers, but it is highly unlikely that they would have been able to swim the 45km (28mi) and 18km (11mi) stretches of water separating Anatolia from the in-between islet and Cyprus, especially as sea currents during that period would have been quite strong as a result of the greater temperature gradient between the north and south Eastern Mediterranean.

There was something else that was peculiar about these suid bones: they were all rather small. Could it be that people were bringing domesticates to the island? If so, where were these domesticates coming from? After all, the dates from Çayönü Tepesi and Hallan Çemi are younger than those for Cyprus. Were people bringing Anatolian wild boar to Cyprus and domesticating them there? Or were domestic pigs from somewhere else other than Çayönü

---

* It is thought that the mice and genet were Holocene introductions, but this hasn't yet been fully confirmed.

and Hallan Çemi being shipped to the island and raised there? Well, it turns out that neither of these scenarios is what seems to have taken place on Cyprus. Measurements of the suid bones showed that not only were they small – but they were *really* small compared with the bones of wild boar on the mainland (9–20 per cent smaller). It is probable that this was due to a well-known phenomenon known as the 'island effect', or 'Foster's rule', in which large animals living on islands become smaller over time as a result of these environments' limited food supply and decreased predation pressure. The wild boar introduced to Cyprus from Anatolia were apparently becoming smaller because they were adapting to their new insular environment, not because they were being domesticated here much earlier than on the mainland. In any case, even if these smaller bones didn't belong to domesticated pigs, the fact that people were taking wild boar to Cyprus is quite a cool thing in itself. It also suggests that some of kind of wild-boar management must have been in place like it was, as is believed, at Hallan Çemi. The introduction of wild boar to Cyprus by humans, however, is not an isolated phenomenon during this time period, and later: evidence from, for example, Japan, Flores and New Guinea shows that suids were moved around and managed by humans in a wide range of geographical contexts. Pigs, it seems, were quite the well-travelled sailors.

The domestication of pigs wasn't only a Turkish 'invention': evidence from China has shown that pigs were also independently domesticated in this part of the world. Understanding the evolution of this Chinese human-suid relationship, and detecting it in the archaeological record has, as was the case for Turkey, not been an easy task for archaeologists. Evidence from the sites of Yucanyan in Hunan Province, Xianrendong and Diaotonghuan in Jiangxi Province, and Nanzhuangtou in Hebei Province shows that the domestication of certain crops was taking place throughout China around 10,000 years ago. What is interesting about these sites is that the animal remains found with these first domesticated crops aren't those of domesticated animals, but rather those of wild creatures. From a logistical point of view, though, this makes a lot of sense, which is why it also happened in Turkey: there is no point in keeping animals if you don't have enough of a food surplus, which you directly control, to feed both yourself and your animals. It therefore came as a bit of a surprise when it was claimed that the site of Zengpiyan in Guangxi Province was 10,000 years old *and* possessed the remains of domesticated pigs alongside those of human-managed crops. The non-wild status of the animals had been inferred from their age profiles: 65 per cent of them were one or two years old at the time of their deaths, a distribution that isn't expected in wild populations.

The site's claim to fame, however, soon began to become more and more dubious: for starters, it appears the dates were *a bit* off, by about 5,000 years to be *a bit* more precise. The provenance of the bones was also put into question, with some people saying that they had been excavated from the site's lower deposits, and others claiming that only the upper deposits had been reached. The domestic status of the Zengpiyan pigs just kept getting less and less clear. The straw that broke the domesticated pig's back was the fact that no measurements had been taken of any of the teeth, which (as you've probably gathered by now) is quite a big deal when it comes to pig domestication studies. Many archaeologists weren't convinced by the data presented, and following the analysis of the teeth's morphometry, together with a reassessment of the age profiles, it was concluded that Zengpiyan wasn't, in fact, the Chinese cradle of domestic pigs.

This 'honour' instead fell upon the site of Cishan in Hebei Province, which was dated to around 8,000 years old. Here it was found that the average lengths of the third molars excavated were closer to those of domesticated pigs than those of wild boar. Further proof of human intervention came from the ages of the animals at the time of their deaths: 60 per cent of them were 6–12 months old. This kind of kill-off pattern suggested that meat production was of some importance at Cishan: because body growth and weight gain in pigs slow down when the animals reach maturity,* it makes sense to only keep a few adults for breeding purposes, and to consume animals that are just about mature. Those who studied the site argued that the domestication was not an 'event', but rather a three-stage development, the kind that has been argued for other sites such as Çayönü Tepesi, in which there is first a 'dependence' stage, followed by 'initial exploitation' and finally by full-on 'exploitation'. As we saw at Çayönü, shifts between these phases can take centuries and even millennia, and the 'dependence' stage in particular is very difficult to pinpoint archaeologically. Our special relationship with wild boar may be older than we think, though there's just no way of finding out about this right now.

Other studies have shown that pig domestication also took place independently at other Chinese sites around the same time, about 8,000 years ago: at Kuahuqiao in the Lower Yangtze River, for example, evidence of tooth-size reduction and crowding was shown to represent the presence of human intervention, whereas at the northeastern site of Xinglongwa in Jilin Province, evidence of our special bond came in the form of pig burials within human ones. It doesn't get much more personal and closer than that. But whereas at these sites the evidence is beyond doubt, there are others at which it isn't as crystal clear, so archaeologists

* Although this can vary between individuals, sows generally reach maturity around six months of age, whereas boars do so a little latter, at around seven months of age.

are trying to come up with new and improved methods to better detect pig husbandry in the archaeological bones and teeth of our omnivorous companions. For example, a new geometric morphometric (GM) approach devised by a team of archaeologists in France, UK and China using lower *second* molars was applied to the study of the Early Neolithic site of Jiahu in Henan Province. Looking at 114 lower M_2s of modern and archaeological specimens, the team concluded that the differences between the teeth of domestic pigs and wild boar is in 'the form of an elongation of the crown with a concomitant reduced robustness and a more symmetrical (simplified) organisation of cusp development along the antero-posterior axis of the M_2' (Cucchi *et al.* 2011: 19). Basically, what they mean by this is that as a result of domestication the top part of the tooth, the white chunky bit you get to see inside the mouth, got taller and thinner, and the little peaks within it became more aligned. As they say, it's all in the details.

Whereas it was sheep and goat that are thought to have been Anatolia's first domesticated animals, in the case of China the pig is believed to have been the first ever domesticated animal there. Such has been the special role of the pig in China that the modern Mandarin character for family/home (家, *jia*) is represented by a piggie inside a house. Whereas pig is no longer consumed in Anatolia due to religious reasons – or in most places in the Middle East for the same reason – pork eating in China has continued throughout the millennia, and to a great extent. Of the approximately 1.3 billion pigs slaughtered annually for pork today, half are consumed by China. Economic growth in this Asian nation has resulted in greater consumption of meat, particularly pork, and what once used to be a multi household-farm economy is now mass producing pork to keep up with the ever-growing demand for it. Such is the lust of the Chinese after pork that back in 2013 an agreement was reached between this Asian nation and the UK for regular shipments of frozen and fresh British pig semen to be delivered to Beijing to be used in farms across the country, with the aim of improving the productivity of local pigs. It seems that only a few shipments have made it to China since the deal was signed, but the obsession of the Chinese for pork continues to grow, making this nation the current number one consumer of pork in the world.

Domesticated pigs reached Europe a few millennia after they were first domesticated in Anatolia, and as discussed in the German case study in the previous chapter, whereas some people increasingly raised these newly introduced creatures full-time, others continued their hunter-gatherer lifestyles, while in some cases also keeping a few of the novelty domesticated pigs themselves. Though much research has been devoted to understanding when and how the transition from hunting and gathering to husbandry took place in Europe, the process isn't yet fully understood as there are at least three possible ways in which it may have taken place.*

The first two plausible scenarios concern what is sometimes referred to as the 'Neolithic package'. There is little consensus on the precise definition of this term, but it is generally assumed to mean something along the lines of 'the material culture of these first (Turkish) agriculturalists'. Some scholars argue that this 'Neolithic package' made its way to Europe because it was brought there by people migrating all the way from Anatolia, also known as 'demic diffusion' in archaeology. Others think it reached Europe not because of people, but rather through the transmission

* It may no longer surprise you to learn that here is *yet another* contentious debate in archaeological research. This is the norm for the discipline, and such debates are rather healthy as they foster greater scientific advancement.

of ideas, techniques and so on, along already established trade and exchange networks ('cultural diffusion').

There are others, however, who think that domestication in Europe – including that of the pig – wasn't 'inherited' from Turkey, but rather took place independently, just as it did in China. Greger Larson's 2005 *Science* paper on the world phylogeography of wild boar appeared to confirm this latter scenario, but as discussed at the start of this chapter, he soon figured out that his results weren't really showing a true picture of all the different stages these wild boar and domesticated pigs went through in the past, but rather only the most final product of a long history of admixture. So it was that in 2007 Larson, together with other colleagues, published a new genetics study in which, knowing about the existence of this 'gene dilution', they attempted to understand the (pre)history of domestic pigs in Europe, and to see whether all were Near Eastern in origin or if, perhaps, some were domesticated independently in Europe.

What Larson and his colleagues found this time was a complex yet fascinating story (or rather stories) of domestic pigs in Europe. The DNA samples showed the presence of Near Eastern genes in pig bones found in Neolithic contexts in Croatia, Romania, Germany and France, with the oldest evidence coming from 11 specimens excavated at four Romanian sites dating to around 7,500 years ago. There is therefore no denying that pigs were, at some point in time, brought by people to Europe all the way from Anatolia. Based on the genetic data it also seems that both the people and pigs may have travelled all this way along two – or more – routes, including a northern one through what is known as the 'Danube Corridor', which follows the Danube and Rhine River valleys into northwestern Europe. The novelty of these Near Eastern domestic pigs, however, must have soon 'worn off', because by around 6,000 years ago genetic data from the French site of Bercy in the Paris Basin shows that people there were both breeding Near Eastern pigs *and* domesticating European wild boar.

One thing led to the next and in the space of about 500 years the representation of domesticated pigs descended from European wild boar – as opposed to Anatolian introductions – skyrocketed to a point after which the genetic legacy of pigs of Near Eastern origin becomes invisible in the archaeological record. It's therefore no wonder Larson's 2005 paper got it all a bit muddled up. The relative speed at which this happened in Europe, in contrast to the lengthy process of the domestication of pigs and other species in Anatolia, suggests that in each of these areas these must have been two very different processes, entailing very different relationships with the animals, the plants and among the human communities themselves. The story of pig domestication in Europe, however, doesn't end there.

A 2015 study published in *Nature Genetics* by Laurent Frantz of Wageningen University in the Netherlands (along with colleagues) was able to confirm the presence in Europe at some point in time not only of both Near Eastern pigs and those descended from the European wild boar, but also of a third, so-called 'ghost' population. Some of the DNA found as part of the study didn't match that of any known living wild boar population, so Frantz and his team suggested that another kind of wild boar, now extinct, must have at some point mated with domestic pigs, and this is why its genes are still lurking about. Findings such as this one provide further evidence of the complexity of domestication, which, as mentioned earlier, wasn't an event, but rather a process, and one that may have involved going 'backwards' and 'forwards' between wild and domestic versions of a species. Separating wild from domestic forms, as all of the above have shown, is no easy task, especially if considerable interbreeding was taking place back in the day, and more so if this was with 'ghost' populations we don't even know of.

Against the backdrop of a slide entitled 'How to be very wrong', Greger Larson, speaking at the Pig Out conference in Yale in October 2015, reflected on the findings from his 2005 *Science* paper on pig domestication. He described how they 'went on full scientific rockstar mode' with their conclusions, and how these were 'arrogant', especially considering the many years others had spent studying the topic of pig domestication – and while it is true that his findings were wrongly interpreted at first, they have nonetheless provided archaeology, genetics and other related fields of study with previously unavailable data with which to further test the validity of potential past pig domestication scenarios. They have also shown us what the potential flaws of genetic studies are, and how best to overcome them. The pig domestication jigsaw puzzle is, as you've probably gathered by now, a large and complex one, so the more pieces we can fit together, the clearer the picture will become; let us therefore continue having fun with the tinier mitochondrial DNA and third molar morphology details – every little helps.

PORK *AFELIA* (CYPRUS)

By George Psarias, and Vicki Psarias of Honestmum.com

Serves 4

'*Afelia*' in Cyprus is the name given to pork and vegetable dishes in which coriander (*Coriandrum sativum*) seeds feature prominently. Such is this nation's love of this herb that if a dish has coriander seeds in it it's said to be Cypriot! The Cypriots may claim to be the world's biggest fans of coriander seeds, but based on archaeological finds, they're not the first of its followers. The oldest find of coriander seeds comes from the Neolithic cave site of Nahal Hemar in Israel, and has been dated to around 8,000 years old. *Afelia* is typically served with potatoes or bulgur pilaf, locally known as '*bourgouri*'.

Ingredients

1kg (2¼lb) pork fillet or boneless leg
2 tablespoons coriander seeds
300ml (10fl oz) red wine
2 bay leaves
1 stick of cinnamon about 7cm (3in) long
4 tablespoons sunflower or olive oil
Sea salt and freshly ground black pepper

Method

1. Cut the pork into small cubes each about 2cm (¾in) long, discarding any excess fat.
2. Crush the coriander seeds coarsely with a pestle and mortar, or in a coffee grinder.
3. In a large bowl, mix the pork with the coriander, wine, bay leaves and cinnamon stick, and leave to marinate for at least 4 hours or overnight.
4. Then take the meat out of the marinade with a slotted spoon, and drain on kitchen paper. Reserve the marinade for later.
5. In a heavy-based saucepan, heat the oil and fry the cubes of meat a few at a time until golden-brown. Add the marinade, bring to the boil and add enough water to cover the meat.

6. Add seasoning to taste and cook over a low heat with the pan covered for 30–35 minutes, or until the meat is tender. Most of the liquid should evaporate, leaving a thick sauce.
7. Serve on warm plates and garnish with fresh coriander.

SWEET AND SOUR PORK

By Yuying Qiu

Serves 2

Ingredients

200g (7oz) pork belly
¼ fresh green pepper
¼ fresh red pepper
100g (3.5oz) pineapple cubes
1 tsp cooking red or white wine
¼ tsp salt
2 tsp white sugar
Powdered black pepper
100g (3.5oz) cornstarch
120g (4oz) ketchup
200ml (7floz) + 4 tsp vegetable oil

Method

1. Cube the pork belly and the pineapple, and cut the pepper into medium-sized pieces.
2. Season the meat cubes with salt and pepper and drizzle with cooking wine. Marinate for approximately 10 minutes.
3. Fully coat the meat cubes with the cornstarch and shape them into compact balls.

4. Heat the oil (200ml) to a high temperature and deep-fry the pork balls until they turn golden. Set aside.
5. Set the pork balls aside and begin preparing the sweet and sour paste.
6. To make the sweet and sour paste, lower the heat and add oil (4 tsp), ketchup, and sugar to the frying pan; keep stirring for approximately 30 seconds.
7. Add the pepper slices and pineapple cubes and stir-fry for approximately 1-2 minutes.
8. Finally, add the pork back into the frying pan and mix everything until all is evenly combined.

CHAPTER THREE

Food waste and modern farming

Humans (and pigs) have come a long way since those early small-scale farming days in Turkey and China. The present demand for meat products is outstanding, and pork, closely followed by chicken, is our preferred choice of animal protein. In 2016 a staggering 108 million tonnes of pig meat were consumed across the globe, equivalent to about 14.6kg (32.2lb) for every person on Earth. That's quite a lot of pork to be eating in a year. I wonder what our Neolithic ancestors would make of this. Our current agricultural systems, which of course have little to do with those of Neolithic Turkey and China, have made it possible for us to produce (and eat) food in these vast quantities, but how sustainable is this massive consumption of food in general? Can pigs and our planet cope with such a high demand and all that the production brings with it? Or is time to take it down a notch? It seems that the answers to these questions lie in many interesting places, including our bins and a few too many giant pools of pig excrement. Follow me and you'll soon see why.

According to the Waste and Resources Action Programme (WRAP), in the UK alone an incredible 12 million tonnes of food (the equivalent of around 48 billion steaks) are thrown away by households, hotels and the food-service industry every single year. This represents around half of the country's total food supply. Yes, you read that correctly: *half.* The waste figure for the US is only slightly better and has been estimated to be around 60 million tonnes annually, which is about a third of all food production. That's a lot to be going straight into our bins on top of all the other waste produced from growing this food in the first place. Moreover, according to a 2009 report, 13 per cent of greenhouse emissions in the US are linked to the growing, manufacture, transport and disposal of food. This might not seem like such a big deal in the grand scheme of things until you compare it with other figures: for example, US aviation and marine transportation *combined* are responsible for approximately 5 per cent of total greenhouse emissions. So not only is the growing of the food creating gases, but extra emissions are being produced when getting rid of all the produce we didn't even eat in the first place. Because of this ginormous amount of extra waste, landfills are filling faster than ever, creating not only an environmental problem, but also an economic one. The cost of getting rid of the waste is at an all-time premium and as money talks loudest, those directly affected (farmers, producers, the hospitality industry and the like) are trying to come up with clever solutions to not only reduce the amount, but also make the most out of all this waste. Pigs have the potential to play an active and significant role in this endeavour.

Depending on how old you are you might have, at some point in your life, seen and perhaps used swill buckets. These were buckets in which kitchen waste was collected to be later fed to pigs. In the UK and US this activity was particularly encouraged during the two world wars, when the price of grain soared, making it extremely expensive to feed animals this kind of food. In London, for example, during the Second World War the horse stables in Hyde Park were turned into pens for pigs, which were looked after by the police and fed the contents of swill buckets, many of which could be found on streets throughout the city. The system worked well and not only produced good-quality pork during times of scarcity, but also resulted in less waste being produced. Following the end of the war, the prices of grain fell due to agricultural intensification, making it easier than ever to mass produce pork, and moreover making it fairly cheap to do so. As a result, between the 1960s and mid-1990s swill feeding in the US fell by nearly 40 per cent. A large part of this decline also had to do with the enactment of the 1980 Swine Health Protection Act, the purpose of which was to regulate the feeding of refuse to swine. The US Congress found and declared that, among other things, 'raw garbage is one of the primary media through which numerous infections or communicable diseases of swine are transmitted', and as a result 'garbage may be fed to swine *only* if treated to kill disease organisms' (Public Law 96-468-Oct.17, 1980 – my emphasis). Consequently, in the US, before being fed to pigs food waste must be heat-treated to 100 °C (212 °F) for at least 30 minutes to kill off any potential nasties lurking within it. Although swill feeding is no longer allowed in a number of US states, many farmers and researchers are now, more than ever, turning their attention to this old practice as a way of helping to manage the waste-disposal crisis we currently face.

Of the many waste-management studies and trials underway at the moment, there was one from the Department of Animal Studies at Pennsylvania State University that really caught my eye because it involved the reuse of a rather unexpected product: liquid geriatric formula. Formula, it turns out, isn't only available for babies. Geriatric formula is generally used when an old person is unable to eat solids and can only manage to get the nutrients they need in liquid form. Nutritionally it represents quite a meal, with approximately 83.7g (3oz) of protein, 90.9g (3.2oz) of fat, 217.3g (7.7oz) of carbohydrates and a whopping 2,000 calories per litre (2 pints) prepared. It also contains vitamins A, D and E, as well as calcium, phosphorous, potassium, fatty acids and a number of other nutritional goodies. The problem with geriatric formula, which is commonly sold in tins, is that it has a relatively short shelf life, in part created artificially by the companies that produce it as a way of ensuring consumer confidence in the product. Because of its limited durability, however, many tins are thrown away each year even if the formula they contain, despite being past its sell-by date, is still fit for human consumption. Scientists at Pennsylvania State University had a light-bulb moment when they realised that this geriatric formula could potentially be repurposed and used to make feed for pigs, given their omnivorous ways. However, as one of the main ingredients of the geriatric formula is sucrose, they decided it wouldn't be fed to very young piglets during the trials because other research had shown that this ingredient in particular gives them very bad diarrhoea. A study carried out as early as the mid-1950s at the University of Illinois, Urbana, comparing carbohydrates in synthetic milk diets for baby pigs, noted that pigs aged 1–2 days, when fed sucrose-based milk, suffered severe diarrhoea and rapid weight loss, and failed to thrive, ultimately dying after four days on this milk-based diet. Things didn't get any better for those aged 7–35 days, 40 per cent of which also died as a result of the sucrose. You learn something new every day.

The research team at Pennsylvania therefore chose instead to experiment by giving the liquid formula only to adolescent/fully-grown pigs. As part of the 112-day experiment, a total of 160 pigs were either fed their regular diet (corn, soybean meal, and the required vitamins and minerals) or 2.8 litres (about 3 pints) of the geriatric formula per day in addition to a supplementary dry feed (corn, supplemental calcium, phosphorus, iron, zinc and copper), which they had access to from a conventional feeder located in their pens. Pigs fed the geriatric formula gained weight faster during the first half of the experiment, though by the time of slaughter both groups weighed roughly the same. The researchers also noted that the formula-fed pigs ate *less* of the dry feed, resulting in lower food costs overall. Given that feed costs have been estimated to represent around 60 per cent of the total of factory farming costs, this feeding alternative is sure to be of interest to the farming industry. Moreover, though the carcasses of both groups were similar in weight, those fed with the geriatric formula produced leaner cuts. Given our modern-day obsession with all things low-fat/fat-free, this can also only mean one thing: a higher profit. If farmers need any further convincing about reusing geriatric feed, they just need to take a look at how the pigs reacted to the experiment: most seemed to enjoy their formula-based diet and quickly adapted to the new menus. Only five of the 160 experimental subjects didn't seem at all interested in their new milky diet, and either failed to gain weight or, sadly, died as a result of the trials. This experiment showed that by feeding geriatric formula to their pigs, farmers could be killing not two, but three birds with one stone. They would be reducing the amount of regular feed they have to buy, helping to reduce waste (minus the tins, which, actually, could be recycled), and their profit margins would increase from selling the leaner cuts. The question is: would consumers take to eating pork from a pig that has been fed expired milk formula?

Swill feeding used to be a small-scale affair, but due to the grand scale of today's pork industry, if waste feeding is ever to be as common as it used to be, then not only will a lot of waste need to be processed, but the resulting feed will also need to be manageable and easy to distribute. This is why researchers are also trying to come up with the most efficient (and law-abiding) ways of turning food waste into nutritious *and* compact feed for pigs. For example, a number of projects in the US are aiming to advance dehydration technologies so that voluminous restaurant waste can be turned into tightly packed dry feed. Research carried out at the University of Florida by Professor Myer and his team since the early 1990s has been looking at the nutritional composition, the potential digestibility by pigs, and a number of other health and safety assessments of this kind of potential feed. One of their studies involved collecting food thrown away by two hotels at a resort complex in central Florida, from which a staggering 20 500kg (79 stone) drums full of leftovers were offered for testing and analysis. As part of the trial, the contents of the drums were blended, dried at 170–190 °C (360–400 °F), and mixed with soybean feedstock. The resulting product was a dark brown, greasy dried foodstuff that the researchers said had a bit of a funky smell, combining a mixture of fat, fish and coffee. Sounds like quite a delicious treat, don't you think?

The nutritional analysis of the resulting feed didn't disappoint and showed it to be moderately high in protein, high in fat and relatively low in fibre, all desirable qualities of food to be fed to pigs. The salt content, however, was a bit on the high side of things, so the researchers warned that care would need to be taken if this kind of repurposed food waste was to be fed to pigs, because salt could jeopardise their growth rates. The concoction from the experimental trials was fed to finishing pigs (55–115kg/121–253lb), and just as with the geriatric formula, most seemed to enjoy the food novelty despite its strong smell. The conclusions reached by Professor Myer and his team were that dehydration of food waste produces a safe and nutritious feedstuff for finishing pigs and sows and, as long as it's heat treated appropriately and follows the requirements set out in the 1980 Swine Health Protection Act, it doesn't pose a health threat to either the animals or consumers. Can turning restaurant leftovers into pig feed be a part of the solution to our waste-disposal problem?

In the US, though, dehydrating food waste is not a new thing. For example, in Florida once again, the so-called Sunshine State, known for its orange, grapefruit and other citrus products, citrus pulp has been dehydrated since the 1930s, and fed to dairy and beef cattle. It hasn't, however, been fed as much to pigs despite the many pig farms located throughout the state. This is because studies have shown that dried citrus pulp can only be included in the diet of growing pigs if it represents no more than 5 per cent of their total feed; adding more can compromise their health and growth due to the presence of limonin, a phytochemical that contributes to the bitter taste of some citrus foods, and which is toxic to pigs and poultry. Pigs exposed to relatively low levels of limonin in their diets (about 15 per cent) have, for example, gone on to develop serious health problems such as anorexia and hypothermia.*

* Extreme weight loss as a result of anorexia can also lead to tissue-fat loss. Less fat equals less natural insulation, and therefore a greater tendency to experience hypothermia, the condition of having an abnormally low body temperature. This is why many anorexics develop more hair on their arms and other places – it's the body's mechanism reacting to prevent the body from getting too cold.

The consumption of lime seeds or other limonin-rich foods also tends to produce soft fat in pigs. From a commercial point of view, soft fat is very bad news. For example, soft fat in bacon tends to give it an oily/wet and translucent appearance and makes it oxidise faster so that the meat becomes rancid quicker, which is not ideal from a sales point of view. Soft fat also affects the 'workability' of the meat, making it difficult, for example, to process it into the visually pleasing sausage shapes consumers expect to find at the supermarket. And just in case you were wondering: although we too are omnivores like pigs, it turns out that not only is limonin not toxic to us, but the antiviral properties of this phytochemical, together with those of nomilin, found in Bergamot orange (*Citrus bergamia*), are, for example, currently being considered as part of research on HIV-1 and HTLV-1 (human T-cell leukaemia/lymphoma virus type 1). Limonin has also been shown to reduce the reproduction of colon cancer cells and is being tested as an anti-obesity agent. Who would have thought that citrus fruits had such medicinal potential?

A campaign in Britain, The Pig Idea, considers these kinds of food-waste repurposing initiatives a very good idea. Headed by food-waste expert Tristram Stuart and the Feeding the 5000 group (a coalition of Fareshare, FoodCycle, Love Food Hate Waste and Friends of the Earth), in partnership with chef Thomasina Miers, the campaign aims to fulfil three objectives:

- To restore public confidence in the safety, efficiency, cost-effectiveness and environmental friendliness of feeding pigs surplus food.
- To encourage greater use of already legally allowed food waste unfit for human consumption as pig food (like bread, fruits and vegetables) by raising awareness

of this option among supermarkets, food businesses, animal health officials and pig farmers.

- To change European law to allow food waste, including catering waste such as that from the Florida trial, to be used as pig and chicken feed with a robust legal framework behind it to ensure food safety and prevent the outbreak of animal diseases.

Those behind The Pig Idea think the way farming currently works, especially the large-scale kind, is crazy: for starters, pigs are being fed food that we humans could be happily consuming. Moreover, a large portion of the pigs' diets is soy-based, and this, they argue, is bad news. Deforestation of the Amazon, where a large chunk of the world's soy is grown,* is taking place at an alarming rate. In 1996–2005, in Brazil alone an average of 19,500km^2 (12,116mi^2) of tropical rainforest were cleared *every year* for the sole purpose of growing soy and cattle ranching. To put this rate of deforestation into perspective, let us imagine it in terms of the surface area of Great Britain (209,331.1km^2/1 30,072.3mi^2): if the island was entirely covered in trees, between 1996 and 2005, a staggering 93 per cent of its cover would have been chopped down. Turning all this rainforest into pasture and farmland has also resulted in an extra 0.7–1.4 GtCO2e (billion tonnes of CO^2 equivalents) being released into the atmosphere – *every single year.* That is a lot of pollution and a lot of trees felled for the purpose of cattle raising and pig feeding.

Many researchers have noted the complexity of the dynamics behind deforestation, and that blaming soy

---

* I'm told by Erasmus zu Ermgassen of the University of Cambridge (UK) that most soy is not produced in the Amazon, but in the *cerrado* of Brazil or the dry forests of Argentina. There it is associated with direct clearance of native vegetation, though a lot is also planted on pasture, which is less impactful.

production alone is incorrect. Studies have shown that it is not soy per se, but rather cattle ranching that is the main culprit when it comes to deforestation; it seems that soy is being grown on land that was already deforested or was previously used as pasture. It has also been realised, however, that in some areas, such as Mato Grosso, a state in west-central Brazil, the increase in soy production is displacing pasture north wards, and this in turn is triggering deforestation there. This is therefore a complex issue, but one that needs to be addressed as a matter of urgency.

Research published in 2016 by food-security expert and veterinarian Erasmus zu Ermgassen and his colleagues at the Conservation Science Group at the University of Cambridge argued for the need to identify strategies to reduce the environmental footprint of these current systems of meat production. A life-cycle analysis of European pork production, in which the environmental impacts linked to all stages of the life of a product are assessed, showed that producing a kilo of this meat in Europe represents €1.9 (about £1.60) worth of damage to the environment. The damage is in the form of eutrophication,* acidification, greenhouse gas emissions and so on. This same kilo of pork, however, costs European farmers an average of €1.4 (about £1.20) to produce; the environmental cost is thus higher and a cost pork producers do not have to directly deal with. Much of the environmental damage (75.4 per cent) was found to be directly linked with pig feeding, providing further evidence that it is the food the animals eat that we should be focusing on, and how changing animal diets to low-impact alternatives (such as swill feeding) could provide the most immediate solution to this problem.

* The excessive richness of nutrients in a body of water as a result of run-off from land or the excessive growth of plant matter.

The paper highlights other cases in which swill feeding has proved not only to be safe, but also highly successful. Take, for example, the case of Japan, where the use of food waste in animal feed was not only encouraged, but legalised in 2001, and where now more than 52 per cent of its manufacturing, retail and catering food waste is recycled as animal feed, and the rest is composted, incinerated or ultimately taken to landfills. The food waste is heat-treated by registered Ecofeed manufacturers, which operate under Japanese food-safety law. Such has been the success of these initiatives that by 2010 there were already 259 feed-production facilities in Japan with an Ecofeed certification, partly subsidised by the government under its 'Grant to Create a Strong Agricultural Industry' and 'Urgent Plan to Increase Ecofeed Production' schemes. Food-recycling programmes were also put in place in South Korea and Taiwan in 1997 and 2003 respectively, which have led to a massive reduction in landfill waste there. In the former, based on 2006 data, 42.5 per cent of all food waste – including household waste, which is not used in Japan due to contamination concerns – was successfully recycled as animal feed.

Even though the above examples show the viability and safety* of such swill-feeding schemes, The National Pig Association (NPA) of Great Britain does not consider The Pig Idea initiative calling for such recycling to be a good one for the UK. In a statement released in November 2013, it not only outlined many reasons why a large-scale food-waste feeding programme would not work, but also argued that it would represent a health hazard. First of all, the NPA deems the soy argument to have been greatly exaggerated: it states that over the past ten years the pig

* The foot-and-mouth disease outbreaks in Japan in 2010 and in South Korea in 2010 and 2011 have been proved not to have been linked to the feeding of food waste to animals.

industry has halved the amount of soy it includes in pig diets, choosing instead to use foods such as peas and beans to provide the swine with the protein they need. Besides not relying as heavily on soy products as The Pig Idea seems to imply, the pig industry is, again according to the NPA's statement, already very good at recycling: 43.9 per cent,* of the total pig feed produced in Britain every year, about 1.23m tonnes, comes from 'food waste' (or 'co-product', as it is known among the farming community) such as cake, cereal products and bread, the provenance of which is well known and has passed strict quality controls. The point of such controls is to make sure that these foods have not, at any point, come into contact with animal products such as eggs, fish and especially raw meat, which could lead to serious health and environmental disasters, as was the case with the 2001 foot-and-mouth disease outbreak in the UK.

Foot-and-mouth disease is a highly contagious illness caused by a virus, which affects members of the order Artiodactyla, that is to say, even-toed ungulates (pigs, cows, sheep and so on). Animals become infected through direct contact with a diseased ungulate or by ingesting and/or being near food and other objects that have come into contact with individuals carrying the disease. Although humans cannot be infected by the foot-and-mouth virus, we can unknowingly spread the disease through our clothing, vehicles and similar. Whereas cattle quite often develop blisters on the feet, tongue and mouth, hence the name of the virus, pigs rarely do, which makes spotting the

* Some contest this figure as it includes all co-products, which are not wastes, so the same environmental footprinting does not apply. As zu Ermgassen explained to me, by definition soybean meal is also a co-product (we make both soy oil and soybean meal from soy), but no one would argue that soybean meal is a waste, and therefore environmentally benign.

disease in them trickier than in other artiodactyls. This is what happened in Britain in 2001: the disease was only detected during a routine inspection of several pigs at the Cheale Meats abattoir in Little Warley, Essex. The outbreak is thought to have been triggered when the pigs were fed infected uncooked swill from a restaurant, although the actual route of infection was never fully confirmed. Nearly five million sheep, 700,000 cattle and about five million pigs were culled to halt the spread of the worst foot-and-mouth disease outbreak the country had ever seen, and which cost the UK farming community a whopping £3.1 billion. A smaller scale outbreak also occurred in 2007, but on that occasion it was quickly spotted on cattle and affected far fewer animals. Foot-and-mouth disease is one of a number of diseases that must be reported to the authorities if farmed animals are known to be infected, in order to prevent the spread of the disease, which can be catastrophic if left unchecked. It's therefore understandable that so many farmers are scared of feeding waste to their pigs, but this practice needn't be unsafe if done properly.

Another disease that must be reported is African swine fever, more common in sub-Saharan Africa, but still endemic in regions of Europe such as the Italian island of Sardinia. It is not a human health threat, but African swine fever has pig mortality rates as high as 100 per cent, with death occurring in as little as two days. The fever is caused by a DNA virus of the Asfarviridae family, and is spread through the soft tick *Ornithodoros moubata*, which looks a bit like a tiny raisin with four pairs of legs. Once an animal becomes infected the virus spreads throughout its whole body and makes its way to all of its tissues and fluids, making the carriers highly infectious. Although the disease is not as prevalent in Europe as it is in Africa, hence its name, the 1960s saw a massive outbreak in Spain and Portugal, which nearly wiped out the whole of the peninsula's native pig breed. It was, however, finally eradicated in the mid-1990s, to the massive relief of *Ibérico* ham producers; these pigs, as you will now see, are a pretty special breed.

Ibéricos ('Iberians') are a breed native to the Iberian Peninsula and today are only found in the southwestern portion of Spain, and the Algarve and Alentejo regions of Portugal. These pigs are the *crème de la crème* of the pig world. Within this breed a select few, known as *ibéricos de bellota* ('acorn Iberians'),* spend the final months of their lives in the *dehesas*, vast expanses of grazing land covered by holm oaks. It is all as idyllic as it sounds. Acorns are available in October–March and the pig farmers let their precious *ibéricos de bellota* loose in the *dehesas*, where they can feed on these nuts to their heart's content. The number of *ibérico de bellota* pigs that can be raised for ham in a single year is limited by the natural availability of the acorns: a good year can see around 350,000 pigs roaming the *dehesas*, whereas during bad years only 150,000 or so pigs will be allowed to feast on the acorns. The production of the ham is highly regulated and has a Protected Designation of Origin (PDO) status, which means that only Iberian pigs fed on acorns are allowed to be termed *ibérico de bellota*.

Given the restricted nature of the acorn season, these pigs' life cycles are carefully orchestrated affairs. Sows, which reach sexual maturity at 8–10 months of age, are generally divided into two groups to maximise the rate of Iberian pig production: while one group gestates the other is lactating and vice versa. Pregnancy, like that of other breeds, lasts about 114 days ('three months, three weeks and three days'), and piglets are weaned at around 45 days of age when they weigh about 12–15kg (26–33lb), which is nothing compared to how fat they get even *before* the acorn fattening-up period. Pigs have to be at least a year old before they get to enjoy their own acorn feast, but must not

* They are also commonly known as *pata negra*, which means 'black hoof', due to their characteristically dark-coloured hooves.

weigh more than 105kg (231lb) – most tend to weigh 90–95kg (198–209lb). Iberian pigs *must* gain a minimum of 46kg (101lb) during their three/four-month nut-feasting period in order to comply with the *bellota* PDO rules. The quality of the meat has been shown to improve dramatically when the pigs put on 57.5–69kg (around 127–152lb) of weight, which they can achieve by eating about 10kg (22lb) of acorns per day, an amount not to be sneezed at. Much of this improvement has to do with the oleic acid present in the nuts, which makes its way into the pigs' flesh and contributes to the ham's characteristic flavour and melt-in-the-mouth consistency. Moreover, the high levels of this unsaturated fatty acid in the ham, rivalled only by those found in olive oil, are said to be good for blood circulation and our blood vessels, so much so that the moderate consumption of *ibérico de bellota* as part of a well-balanced diet is claimed to reduce the likelihood of cardiovascular disease.

The production of the *jamón de bellota ibérico* is not only extremely precise but, given its PDO qualification, also strictly regulated, and even more so since 2014 when the law in Spain was modified to specify whether the pig from which the acorn-flavoured ham came was proven to be 100 per cent Iberian, or whether it or any of its ancestors had at some point been crossed with other breeds such as the American Duroc, or the British Tamworth or Berkshire. These crossings were a fairly common practice in the early twentieth century, when attempts were made to improve the productivity of the Iberian breed, which generally produces small litters (6–8 piglets as opposed to 9–11, for example, in the case of the Large White breed). Only those pigs that are 100 per cent genetically Iberian can continue to be generically called *pata negra* and identified by a black label, whereas those fed the acorn and pasture diet but cross-bred at any point in time are now simply known as *jamón ibérico de bellota,* and carry a red label around the ankle even though their hooves, despite the breed intermixing, continue to be characteristically black. So if this is the deal for the *crème de la crème* of the pig world, what is it like for factory-farmed pigs? How does the mass-produced pork that most of us eat today come about?*

To the relief of factory farmers, commercial sows, just like *ibérico* pigs, do not breed according to a seasonal pattern as their wild counterparts do, so pork is, in theory, never in short supply. This year-round reproduction is unusual among polytocous mammals,† which generally only breed at certain times in order to give themselves a break between pregnancies. The length of the domestic sow's oestrous cycle is twenty-one days – this is the time between oestrous periods, the times when the females are on heat. Sows are most fertile during this time, which lasts about 2–3 days, and is longer than that of, for example, a cow (a mere 5–6 hours in winter and about a day in summer), but shorter than that of a mare (seven days). Boars, as you can imagine, are always up for it, but reproductive success lies, alas, in this 2–3-day window. Despite the stallion's reputation, when it comes to semen production, boars give horses a very good run for their money. Whereas stallions ejaculate an average of 70ml (2.4fl oz) at a time, boars produce more than triple that amount: 250ml (8.45fl oz) on average. Some individuals have even been observed to produce as much as 600ml (20.3fl oz). The average for humans, just in case you were wondering, is 2–4ml (0.07–0.14fl oz). This large amount of semen production directly affects how boars and sows 'get jiggy': because so much of it needs to make its way into the sow, both ejaculation and coitus are very, very long – so

---

* It has been estimated that around 95 per cent of pork in EU countries, and 97 per cent in the US, is mass produced, so if you have ever eaten pork in either of these parts of the world it is more than likely that you have consumed factory-farmed meat.

† Animals that produce many eggs or young at a time.

much so that boars have been observed to fall asleep halfway through the fifteen minutes or so it takes them to ejaculate. In order to stop the boar from pulling out too early due to boredom, its penis shaft is shaped in such a way – like a corkscrew – that it burrows into the sow's cervix. This is made up of deep ridges so that the 'corkscrew' makes its way very easily into it, but after a few pelvic thrusts gets 'locked in' and cannot be easily removed until the deed is done. This way, even if the boar tries to pull out/falls asleep/does whatever, every drop of its ridiculously large amount of semen will successfully make its way into the sow's cervix, increasing the chances of pregnancy.

Following on from this, the sow's gestation period is, as we saw earlier, 'three months, three weeks, and three days', after which she gives birth to an average of 9–11 piglets. In many commercial/intensive farming settings pregnant sows are kept in so-called 'gestation crates' (or 'sow stalls' if you prefer to make them sound less horrific than they actually are). These individual metallic stalls only allow the sow to stand up and just about lie down with no possibility of turning around let alone walking/moving freely. The floor on which the sows stand is slotted to allow the urine and faeces to drop down to shared cesspits. Though their use was banned in countries in the EU in 2013, they can still be used between the time the previous litter has been weaned (usually around four weeks of age),* and the first four weeks of the following pregnancy.

Many people in the farming industry try to argue in favour of these contraptions because, they say, it allows them to feed sows according to their individual needs, and also because it prevents the sort of aggression that takes place in group housing settings, where sows are known to fight over the restricted supply of food. These aggressive

* Their British wild counterparts get to enjoy their mothers' milk for much longer than this: between eight and twelve weeks.

behaviours, however, are much less common in large group housing where the sows do not live in cramped conditions and have enough room to move away from potential bullies and, most importantly, where they do not get in each other's way. The EU has strict guidelines on these shared housing units, and in its 'Council Directive 2008/120/EC for the laying down of minimum standards for the protection of pigs' states that 'the total unobstructed floor area available to each gilt after service and to each sow when gilts and/or sows are kept in groups must be at least 1.64m^2 (17.6ft^2) and 2.25m^2 (24.2ft^2) respectively'.

This crating business, however, does not end with the pregnancy: a few days before they are due to give birth, the sows are transferred to so-called 'farrowing crates', the use of which is legal and widespread in pig farming. The cages prevent the sow from turning around and crushing her newborns, but position her in such a way that the piglets can easily suckle from her teats. Close to the farrowing crate is a heated 'creep' area where the piglets gather following their feeds. When left to their own devices, with no farrowing crates involved, accidental suffocation of piglets does take place, but sows have been observed to move the bedding material with their snout to get a feel of where their babies are and to let them know that they are about to lie down. Piglets trapped under their mothers tend to scream, and studies have shown that some sows are more receptive than others to these cries for help. Greater receptiveness is directly correlated with higher survival rates, so there are many who argue that the farming industry should focus on breeding these more receptive females, rather than restricting their movements through the use of cruel farrowing crates. Shortly after the piglets are weaned at around twenty-eight days of age, the sows are once again impregnated so that meat production can be maximised and our global hunger for tasteless pork satisfied.

Other consequences of mass-produced pork are also starting to emerge and it is mostly in the form of bad news. From a human health point of view, a recent study carried out by Cambridge University researcher Dr Mark Holmes showed that minced pork from UK supermarket chains Asda and Sainsbury's contained traces of a strain previously unseen in the country, CC398, of the methicillin-resistant *Staphylococcus aureus* (MRSA) bacterium. MRSA can be contracted from infected meat and contact with infected animals, but proper cooking of the meat is capable of killing the bacteria. This strain of the antibiotic-resistant bug is not as harmful to humans as the 'standard' MRSA found in hospitals and responsible for the deaths of around 300 people each year in England and Wales, but it has nonetheless killed six people and infected 12,000 in Denmark, where its presence is widespread (two of every three pigs carry the bacteria in this Scandinavian country). The reason behind the appearance and increase in CC398 is known to be linked to the unscrupulous use of antibiotics by factory farms. Because of the cramped conditions in which the factory-farmed animals live, coupled with a lack of hygiene, antibiotics are frequently used on them to both treat and prevent the many diseases that their living conditions give rise to, and overuse has led to the emergence of antibiotic-resistant bugs like the CC398 among the animals.

From an environmental point of view, another important consequence of this mass-produced pork is the increase in phosphorous pollution. The cereal grains, soybeans and corn fed to pigs contain phosphorous in the shape of an enzyme by the name of phytate. Unlike cows and other ruminants, pigs do not possess another enzyme called phytase in their stomachs that breaks down the phytate in their feed, so their faeces are very high in phosphorous. This would not be too much of a problem if pigs were not raised in such large numbers, but this high concentration of phosphorous in manure, coupled with the fact that it is used as fertiliser, is becoming a major environmental problem because the phosphorous now present in the soil is regularly leaching, via the action of – for example – heavy rains, into water streams, rivers and freshwater areas. Phosphorous and water are not a good mix as this nutrient is one on which algae thrive, leading to their excessive growth. With the greater presence of algae less oxygen is present in the water, so it is worse in quality and is responsible for the deaths of large numbers of fish and other animals in the wider ecosystem. This major environmental problem was the reason why in the mid-1990s Professor Cecil Forsberg and his team at the University of Guelph in Ontario, Canada, came up with the idea of genetically modifying pigs so that they, like cows, could produce the enzyme phytase, enabling them to digest the phosphorous in their food, which in turn would result in them producing more environmentally friendly excrement. Moreover, engineering such a pig would also mean cheaper feeds for farmers, as they would no longer need to provide the pigs with specially formulated phosphorous supplements to make up for their inability to digest this nutrient from their cereal grain, soybean and cornmeal.

And so it was that the team created the Enviropig, a genetically modified Yorkshire pig that could digest plant phosphorous more efficiently, and would provide a viable solution to the problem of manure-based environmental pollution in the pork industry. The Enviropig was engineered by obtaining a phytase gene from the *E. coli* bacterium as well as some mouse DNA, and inserting this into pig zygotes, which were then implanted into sows. The piglets from these earlier experiments showed traces of phytase in their salivary glands, so those that had the greatest concentrations were further crossed until the optimum version of the Enviropig was born. These pigs could now digest phosphorous, so there would be less of this damaging nutrient in their manure and no need for further phosphorous supplementation. The Enviropig seemed like the perfect solution to the phosphorous-leaching environmental problem.

Concerns were, however, raised by animal welfare experts, who argued that the production of these genetically modified pigs would just result in worse conditions for the animals if they were raised under factory-farming settings: if there was no longer a need to control the amounts of phosphorous in the manure, there would be no need to restrict their numbers. It was not just the animal welfare sector that was worried about these pigs: the public were not convinced by the idea of one day eating genetically modified pigs. Given the lack of public enthusiasm for the idea, in the early 2000s Ontario Pork Producers, which had funded part of this multimillion-dollar research project, withdrew its support and Forsberg and colleagues were no longer able to continue with their Enviropig research. The tenth-generation Enviropigs were slaughtered and the project ended; pigs would have to manage with just the digestive enzymes nature intended for them.

The fact that pigs are still producing phosphorous-rich excrement obviously continues to be a massive environmental problem, and this all has to do with the sheer scale of it; there is just too much waste to handle and dispose of safely. It has been estimated that 50,000 pigs will produce around 227,000kg (500,000lb) of urine and faeces every single day. That is a lot of bodily waste to have to process in a day. Just in case you were wondering, the equivalent number of people would produce an average of 134,000kg (295,400lb) of combined pee and poo.* So what do industrial farmers do with all this excrement? Given the sheer amount of it, and the great cost it would entail to process it thoroughly, many have opted for the cheapest

* Based on an average of 128g of excrement per day and 1.42 litres of urine per day (Rose *et al.* 2015)

'treatment' option: anaerobic/manure lagoons. These are human-built basins into which animal excrement makes its way through pipes connecting the farm with the lagoon. Once deposited in the basin, the poo settles into solid and liquid layers, then several of its compounds, due to a lack of oxygen, gradually turn into methane and other gases.

Keeping all this poo contained within lagoons can, at times, prove tricky, and can get out of control rather easily and quickly. Back in 1995 a manure lagoon in North Carolina, the US's second greatest producer of pork, broke open, releasing around 95 million litres (25 million gallons) of pig waste into the nearby New River. The consequences, as you can imagine, were catastrophic, and around 25km (16mi) of the river were polluted as a result of the burst. It happened again in 1996 following the heavy rains of Hurricane Fran, in 1998 with Hurricane Bonnie, and in 1999 with Hurricane Floyd, which dumped more than 480mm (19in) of rain in the space of a few hours and led to the flooding of many manure lagoons in the state. The worst was feared following Hurricane Matthew in 2016, but it seems that North Carolina's farms did well this time, with only 14 of the state's lagoons overflowing as a result of Matthew. Although 14 may seem like quite a big number of poo lagoons to be bursting uncontrollably, they represent only around 1 per cent of the total number currently being used in North Carolina.

Legislation passed in 2007 prohibits the construction of anaerobic lagoons in new pig farms built in the state, and though many people are relieved by what can only mean the gradual disappearance of these toxic, foul-smelling pools of excrement, others are worried about the costs involved in implementing more environmentally safe poo-storage alternatives, which have been estimated at around $5 billion (£4 billion) for the state of North Carolina alone. It is not all pessimism, though: the latest move by Duke Energy, an electric power company based in Charlotte, NC, has provided pig farmers in the state (and beyond) with a glimmer of hope after it announced that it was going to start using pig excrement to produce energy.* The company made its first announcement in March 2016, in which it said it would be buying methane gas derived from swine and poultry waste and using it to generate renewable electricity at four of its power stations.

This energy-sourcing move was prompted by North Carolina's Renewable Energy Portfolio Standard (REPS) law, which mandates that investor-owned companies in the state must meet up to 12.5 per cent of their energy needs through renewable energy resources or energy efficiency measures; Duke Energy has chosen pig and chicken poo as its preferred source of renewable energy. In order to produce and trap the methane to be used by Duke, Smithfield Foods' pork farms will be using so-called digesters, in which the waste is kept in heated, airtight containers. Keeping the poo under these conditions leads to the growth of manure-eating bacteria, which then release the methane. This gas is in turn collected within the digesters and later taken to the gas power plant, where it is burned to produce electricity. It sounds like a neat solution. The only problem with this kind of technology is that, besides being extremely expensive to run, it only produces small amounts of electricity, which many believe is not worth the effort. In the case of Duke, the pig and chicken excrement methane will only be providing power to around 880 homes every year, which is really an insignificant number considering that Duke provides energy to around 7.4 million customers in the US, and does so mostly from more 'traditional' sources such as coal and natural gas. I guess it's the thought that counts?

* If an electric company can't provide people with at least a glimmer (of hope), I am not sure who can.

Whereas that pork tenderloin on your plate may appear small and, to a certain extent, insignificant, as you've probably gathered by now there's a lot going on behind it. From deforestation in the Amazon to gestation crates, from antibiotic-resistant superbugs to giant pools of pig excrement, our consumption of pork and other meats doesn't shape only our waists, but also the face of our planet. Land is being cleared, trees are felled and space is taken up by foul-smelling artificial lakes for the sole purpose of satisfying our meat cravings. The question is: is this really necessary? Have we gone too far? Is this environmental crisis really worth it just for the simple pleasure of eating pork when we want to?

PORK TENDERLOIN *A LA NARANJA* (SPAIN)

By Marisol Jiménez, a Spanish family friend

Serves 4

There are two places in Spain known for their oranges: Seville and Valencia. You may have heard more of the former as it is the Seville variety that is used to make marmalade. The streets of Seville are full of these orange trees, which produce such bitter fruits that they can't really be eaten raw. This bitter variety was the first to be introduced to the Iberian Peninsula, and it is thought to have made its way from Africa in the fifth century AD. It was not, however, until the Caliphate of Córdoba (AD 929–1031), which spanned all the way from northern Africa (Tanja – now Tangiers) to north of Saragossa (then Saraqusta) and Lerida (Larida), that oranges became popular as food products; until then, orange trees had been only ornamental. In the Catalan-speaking areas of the Caliphate this newly introduced orange was known as '*taronja de llavar budells*' or '*taronja de porc*', which translates as 'orange to wash guts' or 'pork orange'. This is because the bitter juice of these oranges was used to clean and prepare the meat to be used in cured sausages and other pork cold meats. The juice was also used as a condiment, and to polish copper and brass. Despite being under Muslim rule, the Catholics living in the Caliphate were allowed to continue with their traditions, one of which was eating pork, as long as they didn't try to impose them on others of a different faith.

Ingredients

1kg (2¼lb) pork tenderloin
Flour for coating
Olive oil for frying
1 onion, chopped
Juice of 2 oranges
White wine (optional)

Method

1. Slice the pork tenderloin into medallions, and season with salt and pepper.
2. Coat each of the fillets in flour, making sure you get rid of any excess. Heat the olive oil and fry the medallions on a medium-high heat for 2–3 minutes. Once done, transfer to a plate.
3. Use the same oil in which the medallions were fried to gently fry the chopped onion.
4. Once the onion turns translucent, add orange juice, white wine if using and seasoning to taste. Simmer gently for a minute.
5. Blend the sauce and transfer it to the frying pan together with the cooked medallions. Bring to the boil and serve.

PIG TESTICLES (*CRIADILLAS*) IN SAUCE (SPAIN)

By Mar Izvaz of *Mi Bloguico de Cocina*

Serves 1–2

'*Criadilla*' is the Spanish word used to refer to the (edible) testicles of farmed animals. The most popular are those of bulls, lambs and pigs, any of which can be used according to the recipe below. The word '*criadilla*' comes from the verb '*criar*', which in Spanish means to breed, or to raise; a rather apt choice given the reproductive purpose of these organs. '*Criadilla*' may also sometimes refer to a small loaf of bread, around 113g (4oz) in weight, the shape and size of which resembles that of a ram's testicle. Before cooking testicles, as well as other types of offal, these need to be placed in salted water or vinegar for a few hours to get rid of any potential nasties and unpleasant odours.

Ingredients

2 pig testicles
1 onion
2 cloves of garlic
Olive oil for frying
1 laurel leaf
Black peppercorns
White wine (optional)

Method

1. Cube the testicles and place in salted water for a minimum of 2 hours.
2. Slice the onion and garlic, and gently fry in olive oil until the onion turns translucent (be careful not to let the garlic burn).

3. Drain the testicle cubes and add to the frying pan alongside the laurel leaf and some peppercorns.
4. Cover the pan and cook on a low heat. The meat will release a considerable amount of water which, together with the low heat, will gently cook it.
5. The meat will shrink in size when cooked, but will be soft to the touch.
6. If all the liquid evaporates before the meat is ready you can add a little white wine.

CHAPTER FOUR

Fluorescent green pigs

In January 2006, news broke that scientists from the Department of Animal Science and Technology at the National Taiwan University had bred three pigs that glowed green in the dark. Moreover, though earlier experiments by other researchers had managed to produce partially fluorescent swine, this latest experiment had created pigs that were greenish in colour throughout: they had greenish eyes, greenish skin and even their internal organs were green. How on earth did these and other scientists manage to make the pigs fluorescent green? Most importantly, what was the point of doing so?

The answer takes us back to 1928, the year Osamu Shimomura, a Japanese organic chemist, was born. His father had served in the Japanese military, so Shimomura spent most of his childhood and teenage years moving around Japan. In 1945 the family were living in Ishaya, a district of Nagasaki, the city on which an atomic bomb was dropped by the US on 9 August. More than 40,000 people lost their lives that day, and in the months that followed many thousands more died from radiation sickness, burns, and other injuries and illnesses resulting from the explosion. Shimomura was one of the lucky ones: he wasn't permanently disabled by the explosion, though that day did change his life forever, not only as a result of the psychological trauma he suffered, but also because of the scientific curiosity it triggered in him. On that day, a few days short of his seventeenth birthday, Osamu was able to see with his own eyes the flash of light from the atomic blast, which temporarily blinded him, and experience the strong pressure wave and ensuing black rain that took place 12km (7½ mi) away from the bomb's epicentre. This event would mark the beginning of his fascination for all things bright. In 1951 he received a degree in Pharmaceutical Science from Nagasaki Medical College – now a part of Nagasaki University – a branch of medicine that, as he later admitted, he didn't really have a passion for and had followed because it was the only course available to him at the time.* After graduating Osamu became a teaching assistant at the same institution. Four years later, in 1955, Nagasaki University undertook some internal reorganisation, and due to one of his professor's contacts, Shimomura was able to secure further employment as assistant to Professor Yoshihamasa Hirata working at Nagoya University. This institutional transfer turned out to be a life-changing move for Osamu.

---

* Japan was left devastated after the Second World War, and in the years immediately after there were few university places available for study.

Professor Hirata's research required knowledge quite different from the medical expertise Shimomura had; it centred around bioluminescence, the production and emission of light by living organisms. Thinking that Shimomura wasn't that keen on this field or any linked organic chemistry, Hirata gave him a task that at the time seemed nearly impossible and, so he thought, should keep Shimomura entertained for a very, very long time (and presumably also out of Hirata's way). The task was this: to figure out why the crushed remains of *Vargula hilgendorfii*, a kind of tiny crustacean known to the Japanese as the 'sea firefly', produced a bluish light when wet. An American team had been unsuccessfully looking for an answer to this question for quite some time, so it seems odd that Hirata would ask so much from someone as inexperienced in the field as Shimomura was at the time.

A year later, though, and to everyone's astonishment, Shimomura made the breakthrough and was able to explain how the crustaceans are able to glow blue when moist: the light comes from vargulin, a luciferin (a light-emitting compound) specific to *Vargula hilgendorfii*, which, during an oxidation process triggered by the tryptophan, isoleucine and arginine enzymes, emits light for the period until the oxidation is complete and the luciferin has fully decayed. This was quite the discovery and in 1960 Shimomura was awarded a PhD in recognition of his findings. He then moved to the US to work alongside Frank Johnson, professor of biology at Princeton University. Together they studied the bioluminescence of the green jellyfish/crystal jelly *Aequorea victoria*, living off the west coast of North America, a creature capable not only of producing flashes of blue light, but also turning green. By obtaining protein samples from more than 850,000 crystal jellies over a nineteen-year period, Shimomura and Johnson were able to discover how the 'green' jellyfish were capable of producing the disco-like light shows all over their bodies.

It turns out that these medusas have a blue and bioluminescent protein, aequorin, located on the outer part of the body, which, when electronically excited, releases the coloured lights. As a result of these findings and further research into the topic, Shimomura and the Americans Martin Chalfie and Roger Y. Tsien were awarded the Nobel Prize in Chemistry in 2008 'for the discovery and development of the green fluorescent protein GFP'.

Thanks to these three people (and many others), the Taiwanese were able to create green fluorescent pigs by adding genetic material from the jellyfish to pig embryos, a process known as transgenesis, the introduction of a foreign gene, the transgene, into the genome of another animal. Similar Shelleyesque bioluminescence experiments have been carried out on rodents, rabbits, sheep and even fish. The latter turned out to be so popular and attractive that they're now sold to aquarium shops by a company called Yorktown Technologies under the name of GloFish. They are available in various trademarked colours (such as Starfire Red, Electric Green and Sunburst Orange) because, as noted on their website, Yorktown want you to 'experience the Glo!' In the case of the pigs the purpose of introducing the green-glowing protein to their genetic make-up had nothing to do with 'experiencing the glow'; rather, it was a means of proving that this gene, which was originally not present in the piglets, had indeed made its way successfully into their bodies. By knowing that such transgenesis exercises work, scientists could learn how best to introduce beneficial genes into animals. This transfer process has become known as 'pharming', a combination of the words 'pharmaceutical' and 'farming', the purpose of which is to create, in this case, genetically modified pigs that, for example, will one day supply us with insulin-producing cells which can be used to treat diabetes in humans.

As the above examples show, and as you're probably already aware, a large portion of biomedical research relies on animals to model the pathology of human diseases, and to understand how to best treat and prevent them. Much of this testing is undertaken on rodents, including laboratory mice and the guinea pig (*Cavia porcellus*), which, by the way, is neither a pig nor from Guinea. In practice, however, and perhaps not surprisingly, medical experiments carried out on smaller animal models are often not as informative as those involving species that are genetically and physically closer to us. The pig, as you can imagine, is therefore a candidate for this kind of research. But exactly how similar are we to pigs and how does the biomedical community take advantage of this closeness?

Like us, pigs are eutherian mammals – that is, they are placental creatures. They have evolved in a way similar to us, but are still evolutionarily distinct enough from humans and the rest of the primates to allow scientists to better understand the role genetics plays in the development of many of the diseases that currently afflict us. The behaviour of pigs also makes them good experimental subjects: millennia of domestication and interaction with humans have produced extremely social creatures who, if kept in adequate conditions, are rarely aggressive towards familiar people. As we will soon see, they're also rather clever animals, capable of quickly learning tasks given to them. And, although I'm sure many pig owners might disagree with this, pigs' behaviour is, according to scientists, also fairly predictable, so experiments can be planned with known, repetitive behaviours in mind, which is always a plus in any kind of scientific endeavour.

It may not seem so at first glance, but from a physical point of view, pigs and humans are quite the twins: overall, we have the same kinds of muscles, most of which are positioned similarly throughout our bodies, with the exception of a few on the chest and those of the buttocks. In terms of our internal organs, one major difference seems to be the shape of our colons, ours resembling an inverted U, whereas those of pigs are spiral in shape, looking a bit like one of those crazy water park slides! The positioning of the adrenal glands, which produce a range of hormones including adrenaline, is also slightly different: ours rest on top of the kidneys, whereas those of pigs are located close to the aorta. If we make our way down the body, we find two other major organ differences between us and pigs: the first has to do with the vagina and the urethra (the duct from which urine makes its way out of the body). In our case these are two separate openings, whereas in pigs they are neatly fused into one single orifice. The final difference has to do with the uterus, which in pigs is bicornate (it has two 'horns'), whereas ours is not, making it, according to anatomical lingo, 'simplex'.* The horn bits of the pig's uterus (not to be confused with the Fallopian tubes), are what enables sows to produce litters of 8–10 piglets, numbers which, generally speaking, we humans are not capable of giving birth to naturally.†

So, what about the similarities, you may be wondering? Pigs have skin quite similar to ours, making them ideal subjects when it comes to human dermatological research. Rodents, on the other hand, while the preferred choice in biomedical research because of the ease with which they can be obtained and their low cost and easy maintenance, are, when it comes to certain kinds of human skin research,

---

* From my own experience, there is most definitely nothing 'simple' about it.

† The Guinness World Record for the most children delivered by a woman at a single birth to survive was by Nadya Suleman. She gave birth to eight children (six boys and two girls) on 26 January 2009 in Bellflower, California. The children were, however, conceived through IVF. Suleman has fourteen children in total.

rather useless.* Unlike us and our piggy friends, rodents are loose-skinned creatures.† This makes them unsuitable test models in, for example, human wound-healing studies. Rodents and other loose-skinned creatures predominantly heal their wounds by contracting them, whereas we and pigs do so via a more complex set of processes, of which wound contraction only plays a part. The way we do it, just in case you are interested, is by means of four uninterrupted, overlapping and exactly timed stages: haemostasis, inflammation, proliferation and remodelling. If at some point one of these phases is interrupted in any way, however, the healing process may suffer as a result, potentially resulting in chronic and permanently unhealed wounds; as discussed below, this is a massive health problem in many nations.

As a result of this research on pigs we know that haemostasis begins immediately after wounding has taken place, and entails vascular constriction and the creation of a plug or clot over the wound thanks to the mix of fibrin, a protein, and our blood platelets. The presence of the plug and the tissue surrounding the injury then leads to the release of inflammation-inducing cytokines, substances secreted by certain cells of the immune system to affect other cells. Growth factors, substances needed to stimulate growth in living cells, are also released at this point, completing the haemostasis stage. When bleeding is under control, the inflammatory cells make their way into the

* The most common rodents used in biomedical research are laboratory mice, for which there is not a scientific name available as they are not considered a pure species of house mouse (*Mus domesticus*/*M. musculus*); laboratory rats (*Rattus norvegicus*); guinea pigs (*Cavia porcellus*); Syrian/golden hamsters (*Mesocricetus auratus*); and Mongolian gerbils (*Meriones unguiculatus*).

† 'Bingo wings' do not count as loose skin in humans despite what *Cosmopolitan* and *Vogue* may have led you to believe.

wound, triggering the inflammatory phase. During this stage, the injury is invaded by several kinds of white blood cells, whose partial purpose is to clean the wound of any possible evil invading microbes and other bits and bobs that should not be there and might prevent it from healing properly. The proliferation stage overlaps with the inflammatory phase and entails the formation of thin epithelial tissue (that is, the tissue forming the outer layer of the body's surface). Capillary growth and the formation of vascular tissue ensue, leading the wound on to its final remodelling phase, which in some cases can take several years. During this time the wound, among many other things, remodels itself and its structure so that the injury area begins to resemble 'normal' tissue as much as possible.

Injury contraction takes place throughout these four wound-healing stages, but as mentioned earlier, whereas this mechanism is key in rodents (it represents around 90 per cent of the wound-healing process for them), when it comes to pigs and humans it is important, but not as much: in the case of pigs, it represents around 50 per cent of the healing process, and in humans between 25 and 50 per cent. We know that this predominance of wound contraction in rodents is due to the presence of a layer of subcutaneous panniculus carnosus. This rather sensual-sounding layer is quite an interesting one: it is a striated muscle that allows many mammals to move their skin without having to actually move deeper muscles. If you have ever been around horses or cows you will probably have seen the subcutaneous panniculus carnosus in action: their backs sometimes spasm when, for example, insects try to land on them. It's a kind of 'fly shaker' muscle, if you like. In humans and pigs, unlike in other mammals, this layer is only found vestigially, resulting in our different injury-healing processes. In our case, the dartos muscle in the male scrotum is, for some reason, one of the few remaining examples of the subcutaneous panniculus carnosus layer left in our bodies.

Understanding the significance of these anatomical differences and learning how similar we are to pigs (as opposed to rodents) is, in the case of wound-healing studies, helping researchers to determine what factors may facilitate or impair wound healing. This in turn is helping the medical profession and the pharmaceutical industry come up with more effective and long-lasting treatments for skin injuries resulting from accidents such as burns, ailments like bed sores and chronic conditions such as diabetic foot ulcers. For example, in the US alone, 3–6 million people suffer from chronic wounds, and treatment for these has been estimated to cost around $3 billion (£2.3 billion) annually. Diabetic foot ulcers, from which 2 per cent of the country's diabetics suffer, are responsible for most foot and leg amputations in the US, and each ulcer costs $7,000–10,000 (£5,400–7,690) to treat. Developing suitable and effective dermatological treatments is therefore an economic, social and, more importantly, a well-being priority for many nations. Here the pig has once again come to our rescue.

Knowing that our ways of healing are very similar to those of pigs is all very well, but what about the actual structure of our respective skins? How similar are they? Structurally speaking, both pig and human skin have similar epidermal thicknesses and dermis/epidermis thickness ratios. The epidermis is the outermost layer of skin and the dermis is beneath it. It is in the dermis that blood capillaries, nerve endings, hair follicles and sweat glands are located. In terms of the latter, however, humans and pigs are quite different: despite what the popular expression 'sweating like a pig' has led us to believe, suids are not actually very adept at physically cooling themselves down. This all has to do with their eccrine sweat glands, or rather their almost complete lack of them. Eccrine sweat glands in humans are found throughout the whole of our bodies – we have a whopping 2–5 million of these tiny yet vital glands – and they are mostly found on the palms and soles, followed by the head, trunk and extremities. Generally speaking their role is thermoregulatory, meaning that they secrete water to the surface of the skin; the water then evaporates, leaving the skin nice and cool.

In the case of our palms and soles, the role of these glands is slightly different: they are there more specifically to prevent these vital locomotive and tool-use ends of our bodies from drying out, thereby ensuring that our tactile sensibility, which is key when it comes to how we hold objects and move, is not lost at any point. No one wants to have to be walking on hard, crusty and numb feet – though judging by recent summer sandal sightings, one would think otherwise. Pigs, unlike us, have very few eccrine sweat glands, and they are not found throughout their bodies, but only on their snouts (which is why it sometimes seems that they have runny noses) and on their carpal glands.*

What swine have more of all over their bodies, however, are *apocrine* sweat glands – which, by the way, we have too – a type of gland linked to the presence of hair follicles (we have them in our armpits, and around our nipples, ears and a few other hairy areas). Unlike the eccrine glands, the role of apocrine glands is not thermoregulatory per se, and is thought to have more to do with scent communication, for example in attraction/mating; some sweaty armpit smells are, believe it or not, more attractive to you than to others. Pheromones have long been known to draw pairs of the same species together. This was demonstrated in humans in 1995 when Claus Wedekind, a Swiss biological researcher, carried out a 'sweaty T-shirt study' where a number of men wore the same T-shirts for a few days.

* The pig carpal glands are located towards the bottom half of the forelimbs and they are used for scent communication (that is, they produce different smells at different times to, for example, mark territories, for mating or even to communicate danger to others).

Women volunteers were then asked to choose which of the T-shirts they found themselves attracted to. Lo and behold, they chose the T-shirts worn by men who were genetically similar to themselves. So if you are after the perfect mate, perhaps it might be worth waving goodbye to your deodorant and perfume?

Anyway, back to pigs. We've established that even though pigs have apocrine sweat glands, they still cannot really 'sweat like a pig' as we have been led to believe. It makes you wonder why this expression is so popular. Several theories have been put forward to explain the apparent contradiction in this idiom. One perhaps not very convincing theory is that the expression is actually not being used or understood in the correct context: as pigs do not sweat, someone who is 'sweating like a pig' is doing just that, that is, nothing. Another explanation links the idiom to iron smelting. The crude iron first obtained from a smelting furnace, in the form of oblong blocks, is known as 'pig iron'. When the iron cools down the air around it reaches dew point, leading to the formation of water droplets on the metal's surface; the pig iron is therefore 'sweating'. Regardless of the origins of the expression, what is true is that, when it comes to our sweat glands, humans and pigs are quite different. However, there are many other dermatological characteristics that we usefully share. These include our relative hairlessness, especially when compared with other mammals such as dogs and cats or even our closest relatives, the moderately hairy chimpanzees; our tendency to develop considerable amounts of subcutaneous fat, which in the case of pigs can be more significant than on us (though we are not far behind, especially given our modern-day unhealthy eating habits); and last but most definitely not least the ways in which our skins react to prolonged sun exposure.

As we all now know, over-exposure to the sun in humans can ultimately lead to the development of melanoma, a serious type of skin cancer. Only 4 per cent of all human skin cancers are of the melanoma variety, but this type causes the greatest number of skin cancer-related deaths in men and women aged 25–40, clearly exemplifying its very serious nature. Melanoma begins in the melanocytes, the cells that make the skin pigment melanin, hence its name. The abnormal (cancerous) growth of the melanocytes can also occur in many domestic animals such as cattle, alpacas, sheep and, of course, pigs. Spontaneous melanomas are rarer among rodents, except in the case of the Syrian hamster. Melanomas, for some reason, are unusual in cats. Of all these animals, it is the swine's melanoma that has most recently been thoroughly researched because – given our dermatological similarities – it serves as an experimental model for understanding spontaneous cutaneous melanoma in humans. We and pigs are, as we have already seen, similar skin-wise in many respects, so the initial assumption of such scientific studies is that our and pigs' melanomas will potentially develop and behave in similar ways.

The frequency of melanomas in humans in countries such as the US, Canada and Australia is increasing at a faster rate than any other type of cancer (except lung cancer in women for some reason). No one fully understands the reason for the increase. As we all know, exposure to the sun and its UV rays plays an important role in the development of skin cancers, but scientists have also come to the conclusion that approximately 10 per cent of all melanoma cases in humans are hereditary. Though researchers have been able to pinpoint the genes involved in germline mutations,* they have yet to discover the

* A change in the DNA transmitted from parent to child that takes place in a germ cell, a kind of cell that then goes on to become an egg, or in the sperm, during the single-cell stage of embryonic development. When passed onto a child, this kind of mutation then makes its way into every cell of the child's body.

predisposing genes involved in most hereditary melanoma cases. So how can the pig help scientists figure out how key ancestry is when it comes to cancer? Well, studies have shown that all swine melanomas are hereditary, just like the ones researchers are interested in finding out more about in humans. Other similarities between their and our melanomas are their spontaneous appearance, the similar microscopic structure of their tissues (histology), their ability to turn malignant and the way the metastasis takes place.* It probably doesn't get much better than this when it comes to cross-species similarities.

There are two purposefully bred pigs in particular that have a greater predisposition to developing melanomas: the Sinclair and the MeLiM (melanoblastoma-bearing Libechov) mini pigs. Both these breeds do not only spontaneously develop melanomas, but their cancers have also been observed to regress without any external intervention whatsoever. In the case of the Sinclair, these mini pigs can also develop skin lesions early on in their lives, but these too have been observed to spontaneously regress. These breeds are therefore being used to try to understand what favours this automatic and widespread tumour regression that is not seen in humans,† so that an appropriate and effective cure can be developed for our hereditary-type melanomas. Unfortunately, no one has yet been able to fully understand the mechanisms behind the spontaneously regressing melanomas in pigs, but the fact that they happen provides the medical community with hope of one day developing an effective treatment for these

* The development of secondary malignant growths in other parts of the body.

† Spontaneous regression has been observed in human malignant melanomas and basal cell carcinomas, but it is extremely rare and not well understood.

human tumours, which are so highly resistant to chemotherapy, radiotherapy and immunotherapy.

Given that pigs don't develop skin cancer as a result of prolonged exposure to the sun, they are not very helpful subjects when it comes to understanding this kind of cancer in humans. Pigs – or rather their skin – have nonetheless been used indirectly in research testing in this area, for example on the photostability of sunscreens exposed to UVA irradiation. Believe it or not, it turns out that several sunscreens on the market are photounstable, meaning that not all UV filters, which are meant to absorb/reflect/scatter UVA and UVB rays and thereby reduce the amount of this kind of light reaching our skin and damaging it, are made equal. Using pig and human skin, a 2012 study by Crovara Pescia and colleagues from the March Polytechnic University in Italy found certain 'faulty' sunscreens themselves were affected by UV exposure and gave less protection against sun damage than claimed. So though the packaging of brand A and brand B states that they have the same SPF (sun-protection factor), brand B may be more photounstable and is therefore not able to offer protection as effective as brand A. This is not only a consumer trust issue, but also a health one: many people may be increasing their risks of developing skin cancers by using a sunscreen claiming to be more effective than it actually is.

On the subject of sunscreens, let us not forget pigs – especially the lighter coloured breeds – are also prone to getting sunburned. Similarly to us they experience reddening of the skin that, if severe, leads to the formation of blisters and in some cases triggers bacterial infections. Sunburn can also affect pig reproduction: sows with reddened or blistering skin as a result of sun over-exposure are likely to reject boars when it comes to mating, and should the skin damage occur when a sow is pregnant, there is the possibility that she will spontaneously abort or even reabsorb the embryos she is carrying. Over-exposure to the sun in pigs is therefore about more than just damage to the skin.

Obviously, the best way to protect pigs from sunburn is to provide them with shaded areas and mud wallows to roll in. The greater the mud coverage, the better the protection. But this also helps them to keep cool because – as discussed above – pigs cannot sweat and therefore cannot control their body temperature to any great extent, which makes them even more prone to suffering from heatstroke/heat stress. Wallowing in mud is not about them wanting to get dirty, but rather their only way of keeping cool if no other options (like shade or fresh water) are available. Pigs are in fact quite clean animals despite their reputation. Nowadays there are sunscreens specifically formulated with pigs in mind: Pot Belly Pig Sunscreen, for example, 'protect(s) their hair and skin from the sun's harmful bleaching rays and also prevent(s) staining from grass, urine and manure', whereas Sullivan's Sun-Guard Sunscreen 'provides superior protection from the sun's harmful rays, preventing sunburn and other skin damage to all livestock. Sun-Guard works exceptionally well on swine, sheep and slick-sheared cattle.'

Demand for swine sunscreen has increased over the past twenty or so years as a result of the rise in popularity of pet mini pigs, an idea that first started germinating in the minds of US pig breeders back in the mid-1980s, when several micro Vietnamese Pot-bellied individuals were introduced to American zoos. Inspired by these cute and tiny creatures, breeders began playing Frankensteinish games with the different breeds available to them until they were able to create smaller piggies like those in the zoos, which they knew American consumers would want to buy. The fact that celebrities such as George Clooney, Paris Hilton, Miley Cyrus and Megan Fox decided it was trendy to own miniature swine as pets very much helped the breeders' 'cause'. The origins of the idea of creating tiny breeds, however, had less to do with cuteness, fame and glamour, and was more relevant to efficient biomedical research. The development of the first mini pig is not a recent occurrence, but took place back in 1949 at the Hormel Institute of the University of Minnesota. The purpose of breeding a small pig was so that, although small in size, it could be used in exactly the same way as a larger animal, but without all the hassle of managing a larger individual. As an added bonus, the smaller pigs reached sexual maturity earlier, so less time was wasted waiting for them to grow and breed. This made the experimental process quicker, more efficient and, one would assume, less expensive. It turns out that the creators of the experimental mini pig were right on all counts.

Given all of these advantages, since 1949 various kinds of micro swine have been bred, including the Chinese experimental miniature pig, which in 1985 was obtained from a small breed found in the southwestern province of Guizhou in China; the Göttingen, developed in that German city's university in the 1960s by crossing the original Minnesota mini pig with two strains of the Vietnamese Pot-bellied pig and the German Landrace, the latter added to the equation to provide this new mini pig with unpigmented skin (good for skin-cancer studies). Roughly speaking, the Göttingen is 60 per cent Vietnamese Pot-bellied, 33 per cent Minnesota and 7 per cent German Landrace. This breed is now a trademarked piggy (Göttingen Minipig), and is only bred at three centres in Germany, Denmark and the US, from which it is sold as purpose-bred animals for biomedical research. Their production is strictly regulated by the University of Göttingen, and it is only recently that the institution approved the opening of a new, highly controlled breeding facility in Japan, providing the Asian scientific community with a more local source for this mini pig breed.

A Göttingen's birth weight is around 500g (1.1lb), but by the time of its first birthday it weighs 20–25kg (44–55lb). It reaches its maximum weight, 35kg (77lb), at about two years of age. By contrast, some farming breeds can end up weighing more than 400kg (881lb), so the Göttingen is quite the skinny babe by comparison. The boars reach sexual maturity at 3–4 months of age, whereas females do so a month or so later. By comparison, sexual maturity in the domestic pig takes place a little later, at around five, six or seven months of age in both males and females.* Given their earlier maturity, Göttingen pigs therefore represent an advantage for farmers time-wise.

As George Orwell might have said, however, not all mini pigs are created equal, especially if ruthless breeders wanting to make a few bucks are involved in the process. As we saw with the Göttingen Minipig's weight data, these 'mini' pigs do not stay mini for long: 35kg (77lb) is not a weight figure to be sneezed at; an adult Labrador dog, for example, weighs about the same. So this pig breed is not quite the teacup-sized creature people have in mind. Moreover, not all mini pigs sold are in fact mini; some are just regular farming breeds advertised shortly after birth, but described as mature individuals. The lack of public awareness of the not-so-smallness of even the smallest of pig breeds, coupled with the fraudulent ways of some pig sellers, results in many people buying a pig in a poke. That in turn leads to more than 300,000 pet pigs being abandoned annually in the US; a Canadian TV report noted that only 5 per cent of pet pigs in the country are kept by their owners past their first year. These are grim statistics. Luckily, many of these pigs are rescued and cared for by animal sanctuaries; the rest, unfortunately, end up being euthanised.

Coming back to the experimental side of things: not all biomedical research concerning pigs, mini or otherwise, centres on the (human) skin. One of the best-known

---

* Data for the Swedish Landrace and Yorkshire breeds from Reiland (1978).

examples of other ways in which pigs are used is in human heart-valve replacements. So how do these work and what have they to do with pigs? Before getting into the details of this, we need to immerse ourselves in the subject of cardiology. The role of the heart is to pump oxygen-rich blood around the body so that our cells are well fed and can prosper. Blood always travels through our heart in the same way: it comes in from the body through the right-hand side, then moves on to the lungs to receive oxygen, then makes its way back into the heart, this time through the left-hand side, before being 'released' back into the body. The heart's left and right sides are each further subdivided into two chambers: the left and right upper atria, and the left and right lower ventricles. The role of the atria is to collect the blood flowing in from the body and lungs, whereas that of the ventricles is to eject it out to the lungs (right ventricle), and to the aorta and out to the body (left ventricle). This blood movement is controlled by four valves (aortic, tricuspid, pulmonary and mitral), the important functions of which are to open correctly so that the chamber can empty, but also to close themselves at the right moment in time to prevent blood from flowing in the wrong direction. Though the mechanisms behind these valves are worthy of anatomical admiration, unfortunately they sometimes stop doing their job properly (becoming narrower or leaky) and this is bad news for their owner. Known as valve disease, this open-close failure does not necessarily produce any symptoms, though the most common are chest pain, light-headedness and shortness of breath. Fortunately, if someone is suffering from this disease there are various ways to treat it, but it is the valve-replacement option that interests us here, since many of the valve replacements are carried out using valves derived from pigs.*

---

* They can also be made of cow's tissue.

Many different types of heart valve have been developed and tested since the 1950s, when they first became available for implantation. Valve replacements can either be prosthetic or made from animal or even actual human tissue. In the case of human tissue, aortic or pulmonary valves are obtained from cadavers, or even made from the patient's own pericardium or their pulmonary valve. Those of other animal origin are derived from either cattle or pigs; in the case of the latter the aortic valves are used to make replacement aortic *and* mitral valves for humans. Each kind – prosthetic or animal – provides its own set of advantages and disadvantages: in the case of the former, though they are extremely durable to the point that they can outlive the patient, they are, unfortunately, not well tolerated by our blood, so the recipients of these valve replacements need to take anticoagulation medication for life. Porcine/bovine heart-valve replacements, on the other hand, are well tolerated by our circulatory system, *but* (there is always a but), unlike prosthetic ones, have limited durability. As a matter of fact, porcine-derived heart-valve replacements in general tend to have relatively high failure rates. For some reason, after a period of time they begin to get stiff and thicker overall, rendering them less flexible and mobile. This is most definitely not good news for a body part, the purpose of which is to open and close to let the blood flow in and out of the heart. Studies have found that after a short period of time these porcine replacement valves also begin to develop a number of bumps to their surfaces, which further decreases their overall effectiveness.

The art of heart-valve replacement is yet to be fully perfected, and many researchers worldwide continue to work on how to best and most effectively combine the advantages offered separately by prosthetic and porcine/bovine heart valves. This is something that, for example, Jacob Brubert worked on as part of his PhD in biomedical engineering at the University of Cambridge. His doctoral work centred around assessing the extent to which a flexible polymer* can be used in prosthetic heart valves to achieve the durability offered by these kinds of valves and, at the same time, have the blood compatibility of the porcine/bovine ones. Although Brubert's work has yet to provide a significant contribution to this area of cardiac surgery research – testing of his doctoral findings is still ongoing – he has already had his fifteen minutes of fame after he won the 2016 'Dance your PhD' video competition organised by the American Association for the Advancement of Science (AAAS), in which students dressed up as pigs, cows and polymers dance to the tune of Miriam Makeba's (Mama Africa) 'Pata Pata' to explain why porcine and other heart-valve replacements still need many improvements.†

There are currently about 120,000 people in the US and 7,000 in the UK waiting for an organ transplant. In 2015 in the UK alone, more than 1,300 people died or became too ill to be able to receive a transplant due to this shortage of donated organs. However, while 95 per cent of Americans – and probably similar figures in the UK – are in favour of organ donation and transplant, as the figures quoted above show, it is clear that we are facing an organ donation shortage crisis. Around half a million people die in the UK each year, but based on NHS data, only 1.5 per cent of them can provide suitable organs for donation; and this percentage figure does not take into account the fact that not all of these potentially suitable donors will have consented to having their organs donated in the first place.‡ As a result of this shortage, the biomedical community has

* A molecule mostly or completely made up of a large number of similar units bonded together.

† The link to Jacob's winning video can be found in the references section.

‡ If you have not already done so, please consider joining your national organ donor register.

for many years been investigating the possibility of using pigs (and other animals) to both harvest *and* create specifically tailored organs for human transplant. But the idea of transplanting pig organs into humans is not a novel one.

In the 1960s, several attempts were made to transplant kidneys from our close cousins, the chimpanzees, and those of baboons into humans, but the patients only survived for a few months before their immune systems rejected and attacked these foreign organs. Though the patients died as a result of these first experiments, the failures did not put a stop to xenotransplantation research. On the contrary, they provided the biomedical research community with a clear challenge: find an artificial transplant solution that will end organ donation shortages worldwide. Thus in the 1990s an ever-growing flow of research began to be published on why the human body rejects non-human organs. One of these studies, published by a team at the University of Pittsburgh in Pennsylvania, was able to show that when using pig organs for transplant most of the human immune rejection responses were triggered by one of the carbohydrates, α1,3-galactose (α-Gal), present on the surfaces of pig cells. The team also discovered that pigs possess a specific enzyme for the production of this carbohydrate molecule; learning of the existence of this sugar-producing enzyme was a breakthrough for the scientific community. By eliminating the gene behind its production, pigs' cells, and consequently their organs, could be freed from the element that makes them unsuitable for human transplant. This knowledge was soon put to the test in pig-to-baboon transplants in which the enzyme had been suppressed. All, however, failed miserably and the baboons died as a result. Perhaps the immune system was not as neat and straightforward as the team from Pennsylvania first thought? Enthusiasm for xenotransplantation died down a lot after that and even Novartis, the Swiss pharmaceutical company that was keen for the xenotransplantation investigations to advance and had plans to fund around $1 billion's worth (around £800 million) of such investigations, decided it was no longer interested in this avenue of research and withdrew the money. That was very bad news for the scientific community, which relies heavily on big pharma company funding to advance its knowledge.

Coincidentally, it was at about this time that a shift in researchers' ways of thinking about the problem appeared: instead of focusing on the organs themselves, which had proved so tricky to transplant given our bodies' 'sensitive' immune systems, how about looking at the smaller parts within them? Are these of any use? Well, it turns out that they are, and work carried out using pig corneas (minus their conflictual cells) and pancreatic islet cells,* is proving that pig-to-human xenotransplantation may become a reality sooner than we think. Other plans include creating genetically modified pigs whose livers and lungs would produce their own antibodies against the human/primate immune cells that would attack them post-transplantation. A US biotechnology firm, United Therapeutics, has even gone as far as buying land in North Carolina to build a sort of 'lung factory' where around 500 pigs would be raised annually for the sole purpose of having their lungs removed and donated to humans.

Another research avenue being pursued in organ-transplant studies is that of growing *human* organs inside pigs (and other animals). This is not just a fantasy – a team at the University of California, Davis is already attempting just that: to grow human pancreases inside pig bodies. How do they expect to achieve this? The plan is to remove the bit of DNA linked to the growth of the pancreas from a pig

---

* Hormone-producing cells that detect the presence of sugar in the blood and, as a result, release insulin to maintain adequate blood-sugar levels.

embryo. Human stem cells will then be injected into the pig's embryo, which should, in theory, result in the growth of a human pancreas inside the pig's body, leaving the rest of the pig organs unaffected by this DNA tinkering. Researchers argue that the pig-grown organs will not only help with the human donor shortage problem, but might also assist in producing better organs because, as they are made using the stem cells of the person needing the transplant, the organ produced would not be rejected by the patient's immune system as it would really be his/her own. Further gene tinkering of these real-life chimeras might also enable more disease-resistant pancreases and other organs to be made, further increasing the life expectancy of the organ recipients. For the moment, these pig-human embryo chimeras are being destroyed after one month of growth, so that the team at the University of California, Davis can assess the extent to which the human cells may have made their way into other pig organs. No results are available yet, but what if this does happen? For example, what if the human cells make their way into the pigs' brains? What if it all goes horribly wrong and we end up with part human, part animal creatures? Mary Shelley, I am pretty sure, would be both fascinated and horrified by all this.

Medical experiments on pigs, however, are not a modern phenomenon. In the year AD 129, Aelius Galenus, Galen to English-speaking people, was born in the ancient Greek city of Pergamon (now Bergama in Turkey). Galen, who at first did not have much interest in medicine and was only encouraged to pursue it as a career after his father had some weird dream about how that was to be his son's destiny, went on to become one of the greatest doctors of the Roman Empire, where he lived most of his life. Moreover, his biology and medicine teachings remained very influential throughout Europe until the sixteenth century, and were still being cited as late as the nineteenth century.

Galen owed a great deal of his expertise to medical experiments carried out on Barbary macaques (*Macaca sylvanus*), cattle (*Bos taurus*) and, of course, pigs.* He had to make use of animals because dissection of human bodies was not allowed at the time. Perhaps the best known of Galen's animal experiments was that of the 'squealing pig', which led him to realise that it was the pig (human) brain and not its heart, as was the belief at the time, that controls actions and thoughts. This may seem obvious to you and me now, but it was not so in the Roman Empire during Galen's lifetime. Despite all their other attributes, it seems the Romans had little interest in ancient texts because, for example, if they'd an interest they would have come across the Hippocratic Collection of early ancient Greek medicine texts, compiled mostly in the fifth and fourth centuries BC, which highlighted the role the brain plays in how we think, move and feel, and completely contradicted their way of thinking.

You may be wondering how Galen got to his conclusion of a brain-body connection by performing a vivisection on a pig. It turns out that during one of his tests, which involved a squealing pig strapped down to the table where the vivisection was taking place, Galen accidentally cut through the animal's laryngeal nerves, and as a result the pig stopped squealing *but* continued moving. That was a surprise to Galen and prompted him to study these nerves in greater detail, looking at their location and function in a variety of creatures, including those with very long necks. What he found was that the laryngeal nerves emerge from the vagus, one of the brain's nerves, making their way down past the larynx, then taking a tour of the aorta and the subclavian artery (the artery below the clavicle, hence

* Apparently Galen preferred to use pigs instead of macaques for vivisection because their facial expressions of pain were less unpleasant to look at.

its name). Vocalisation in this case was controlled not by the heart, as commonly thought at that time, but by the brain. This was quite a revelation for the Romans, so much so that Galen was asked to perform the experiment again, but this time for the public. Many people at first doubted that such a thing could indeed be the case, but his first public and subsequent experiments proved the brain's central role within the body. A new conceptualisation of the human body emerged as a result and the rest, as they say, is (medical) history.

Even though it may appear so from the examples given above, not all past and present experiments involving pigs have been of the physiological variety. There have been many others that focus, for example, on understanding pig behaviour and intelligence. There is the case of the pig mirror tests carried out by Cambridge University Professor Donald Broom and his colleagues at the Department of Veterinary Medicine. The aim was to assess the extent to which, in this case, pigs can learn about complex aspects of their world and their degree of awareness. Are pigs clever enough to realise what a mirror is/does? If so, are they capable of using the information displayed on it to their advantage? In order to figure this out Broom and his colleagues observed the behaviour of several 4–8-week-old Large White and Landrace pigs. Having never seen a mirror in their lives, the pigs were left to explore it for a period of five hours. After this time, a bowl was placed in the pen containing the mirror; the pigs, however, could only see the food bowl reflected in the mirror as it was physically placed behind a screen. Would the pigs be clever enough to figure out that the food bowl reflection was just that and that the actual bowl had to be somewhere behind the screen? It turns out that they were. Seven of the eight pigs used in the experiment soon realised that the bowl of food was not in the mirror, and quickly made their way to the other side of the barrier so they could feast on its contents.

The mean time that it took these seven piggies to figure it all out and find the food was twenty-three seconds! That's twenty-three seconds after only a five-hour mirror familiarisation period. According to Broom this is quite advanced behaviour, and is slightly more advanced than that of three-year-old humans. They say 'if pigs could fly'; I say, give them time.

Other studies involving pigs have also shown that they can fulfil the role of 'emotional support animals' (ESAs). These animals provide therapeutic benefits to their owners through their affection and companionship. Unlike service animals, traditionally dogs, but in some cases mini horses and even capuchin monkeys, ESAs are not trained in any way; it is their presence that helps a human. US legislation, however, requires the person benefiting from the companionship of an ESA to have a letter from a mental health professional in which the role fulfilled by the animal is clearly explained. Only then can ESAs be allowed to be in places that animals are not normally allowed to enter. Twenty-eight-year-old Megan Peabody, who suffered from anorexia in the past, possesses such a letter, which allows her to fly with Hamlet, her pet pot-bellied pig. Megan relies on the company of her Shakespearean-named friend to overcome situations that might trigger anxiety in her, like flying does. In 2013 the US Department of Transportation updated its *Policy Guidance Concerning Service Animals in Air Transportation* to include the statement that 'animals that assist persons with disabilities by providing emotional support' now qualify as service animals and are therefore welcome on board; Hamlet and Megan are therefore two of the beneficiaries of this legislative change.

Pigs can provide more than just emotional support. While living in Spain, Jo Bailey-Merritt started to notice unusual behaviours in Sam, her two-year-old son, which quickly began deteriorating to the point that he became completely withdrawn and reverted to being non-verbal.

After many visits to specialists and tests, a diagnosis was made: Sam was autistic. Following the split from Sam's Spanish father, Jo, Sam and his little brother Will moved back to the UK. It was here that, a few years later, Sam would meet Chester, a ginger piglet being raised at a miniature pig farm in Devon.* On seeing the animal, Sam sat next to it and stroked it until it fell asleep. This sort of behaviour was unusual in Sam, and then and there Jo decided that Chester would be the family's newest member. As detailed in Jo's book, *Sam & Chester: How a Mischievous Pig Transformed the Life of My Autistic Son*, the presence of Chester at the Bailey-Merritt household for the past eight years has led to huge changes in Sam's behaviour and social skills: for example, he now interacts and plays with his brother Will, which he did not do before. Sam can also relate to Chester's feelings and needs, and cares for him accordingly; this represents much progress given that Sam's empathy had very much been impaired before Chester came along. Many studies over the past couple of decades have shown the positive influential role animals can have in the lives of people with autism, and how beneficial animal-assisted therapy can be for them and also for those suffering from mental health issues. Though anecdotal evidence like that of Sam and Chester, and of others, has shown how effective pigs (and other animals) can be in this area, many people in the fields of psychology and medicine are asking for more rigorous research to be carried out in this field so that the best possible animal-human therapies can be developed, suitably tested and applied to those who will benefit from them the most.

When Galen was carrying out his experiments on squealing pigs back in the second century AD, he could never have imagined not only how relevant his work would

* Chester turned out *not* to be a miniature pig – he currently weighs around 114kg (252lb) and is 1.67 (5.5ft) long.

be to future generations of medics, but also how important pigs would become in our understanding of human physiology and disease. He would probably have been very surprised to hear of Shimomura's work with the green florescent pigs, and the extent of animal testing today. He would probably also be greatly puzzled by the idea of people dressed up as pigs dancing to the tune of 'Pata Pata' to explain heart disease to the masses, and by the fact that pigs provide emotional support to humans and can now, thanks to us, fly. How times have changed.

ASIAN-INSPIRED PORK UTERUS WITH GREEN ONION AND GINGER (US)

By Carly Morgan of *Ever Clever Mom*

Serves 2

Ingredients

400g (1lb) pork uterus
Salt brine (4 tablespoons salt to 1 litre/2 pints of water)
Dash of vegetable oil
Grated ginger (to taste)
Chopped green onion
Soy sauce

Method

1. Chop the uterus into small pieces following the organ's natural morphology.
2. Place in a salt brine for about 24 hours, then rinse with plenty of cold water. Add more brine than specified if necessary, using salt/water ratio given above.

3. Heat up some oil and gently fry the ginger and chopped green onion. Add the pork.
4. The pieces will quickly turn white and start shrinking and hardening. Some of the blood from within the pork might come out at this point – you may drain it if you like.
5. After a while the pork pieces will start to look like macaroni; add soy sauce at this point and cook for a few more minutes. Be careful not to overcook it as it can become very hard.
6. Serve and enjoy. Its smell is similar to that of liver, but with strong pork undertones. The taste is like rich, salty, pork-flavoured calamari.

FIG-FED PORK (*FICATUM*), AND WINE SAUCE FOR FIG-FED PORK (*IN FICATO OENOGARUM*) (ANCIENT ROME)

From *Apicius's* Book VII, Sumptuous Dishes (*Lib. VII. Polyteles*)
Edited and translated by Joseph Dommers Vehling

This recipe is one of the many contained within *Apicius*, a collection of Roman recipes thought to have been compiled at some point in the late fourth century/early fifth century AD. The book's authorship has often been incorrectly attributed to Marcus Gavius Apicius, believed to have been a gourmand of the first century AD living during the reign of Emperor Tiberius (42 BC–AD 37). Book VII of Apicius is dedicted to 'Sumptuous Dishes', including the fig-fed pork (Chapter III) here described, as well as other pig delicacies such as 'sow's womb, cracklings, bacon, tenderloin, tails and feet' (Chapter I), sow's belly (Chapter II) and pork shoulder (Chapter IX). Note that the Italian word for liver, *fegato*, has nothing to do with the Latin word for liver, *jecur.* This is because the modern-day name for this organ is instead derived from the Latin *ficatum*, meaning 'stuffed with figs' (*ficus*), a popular gastronomic practice during Roman times, as exemplified by the preparation above.

Fig-fed pork liver (that is, liver crammed with figs) is prepared in a wine sauce with pepper, thyme, lovage, broth, a little wine and oil. To attain fig-fed pork liver, pigs were starved, and the hungry animals were then crammed with dry figs, and suddenly given all the mead they wanted to drink. The violent expansion of the figs in the stomachs, or the fermentation, caused acute indigestion that killed the pigs. The livers were very much enlarged. The technique is similar to the cramming of geese for the sake of obtaining abnormally large livers.

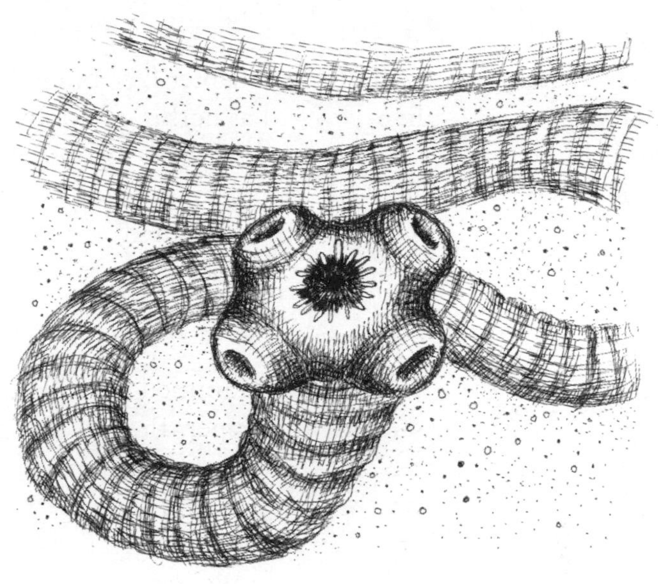

CHAPTER FIVE

What doesn't kill you...

... makes you stronger, or so they say. As we saw in the previous chapter, pigs are in many cases useful animal models when it comes to understanding human disease. Pig parts are even modified and used in the manufacture of elements and medicines to help keep us alive. But whereas pigs often provide a medical solution to many of our ailments, they can also be their source. Take the case of the fifteen-year-old girl who we shall refer to as 'María'. She lived in the Peruvian Andes and, for three months, had been suffering from headaches, nausea and vomiting. Things got progressively worse and her speech soon became incoherent, she was confused, and she began experiencing visual and auditory hallucinations. No one really knew why her health had declined so drastically in such a short space of time, so medical help was sought to try to understand what was causing all this. An MRI scan revealed a rather disturbing image of what was going on in her head: her brain, to put it mildly, looked a bit like a geological map of the moon; she had tons of cysts scattered throughout it. Tests on María's stools soon confirmed the reason behind her decline and the cysts on her brain: she had been infected with *Taenia solium*, the pork tapeworm, and as a result had developed an infection known as neurocysticercosis.

Neurocysticercosis is just as scary as it sounds, and involves the infection of the human central nervous system by *T. solium*. Though you may have never heard of it before, this pork tapeworm invasion is actually the number one cause in the world for adult-onset epilepsy. As a matter of fact, the World Health Organization (WHO) and Food and Agricultural Organization (FAO) recently stated that *T. solium* is the food-borne parasite of 'greatest global concern'. It is most prevalent in developing nations, but the number of infections has been growing in the US over the past thirty years. Much of it has to do with eating tapeworm-infected pork. Epilepsy isn't the only 'side effect' to having these tapeworms living inside your body and brain: their presence has also been linked to the appearance of brain tumours, depression and even dementia, which in most cases can be reversed if its source is an untreated case of *T. solium*. When María first started suffering from headaches she probably didn't give it much thought (who doesn't get headaches from time to time?), but research being carried out at, for example, the Hospital Clínica Kennedy in Guayaquil (Ecuador) has suggested these are triggered by small bits of the calcified bodies of the tapeworms making their way into different parts of the brain, triggering inflammation and therefore headaches. I'm not sure about you, but *this* is the kind of stuff nightmares are made of in my world.

So how does the infection happen and spread? It all starts when an infected piece of pork (raw or undercooked) is consumed by a person. Once inside the body, the larva of *T. solium* gets digested out of the meat and attaches itself to the upper small intestine of the human, where it matures over the following 5–12 weeks. The resulting worm can grow to be up to 7m (23ft) long, and live undisturbed for up to 25 years; taeniasis is, after all, symptom-free. The fully mature worm, however, soon starts producing large numbers of proglottids, that is to say, the bits of the tapeworm containing complete sexually mature reproductive systems, with more than 30,000 eggs each. These proglottids then break loose and are excreted by the human, or in some cases little worms will crawl their way out of the poor person's anus. Imagine the shock. The eggs then make their way into the environment, ending up on vegetation on which the pigs feed. The pigs eat the eggs, which pierce through the walls of their intestines and make their way to different parts of the body. If a human eats undercooked pork from infected pigs the whole cycle begins again.

There is also the human auto-infectious route, in which a person ends up ingesting the eggs from their own faeces. In these cases embryos from the ingested eggs behave just like they do in pigs: they pierce through the intestine walls, making their way into different parts of the body via the circulatory system. Depending on where the cysts end up, the person may or may not develop symptoms. In María's case the symptoms were pretty obvious and severe, because the brain is a rather sensitive area in which to be hosting pig tapeworm cysts; but having a few in, say, the liver, will most likely not give rise to any symptoms. There are several ways in which infection can be prevented: first and foremost, always make sure you cook pork thoroughly. The larvae can also be killed by freezing the meat at -5 °C (23 °F) for four days, –15 °C (5 °F) for three days or -24 °C (-11.2 °F) for a day. It may sound a bit patronising and like something your parents would tell you, but personal hygiene is a must: washing your hands after going to the loo is key to preventing the auto-infectious route. As you now know, ingesting the eggs you're hosting might mean that you end up with cysts in your brain, and I'm sure that's something neither you nor anyone else is keen to experience.

Then there is the more familiar case of trichinosis – also known as trichinellosis – which many argue is the reason behind the pork taboo in the Jewish and Muslim religions (more on that later). Trichinellosis is acquired by eating raw or undercooked meat that is infected with, most commonly, the cysts of the *Trichinella spiralis* parasite, though there are several other species of it that are known to be able to infect humans. The parasite is mostly present in wild animals such as wild boar, rodents and bears, but it is known to still persist in farm-raised pigs. The first signs of trichinosis are of the upset-tummy variety and include diarrhoea, vomiting, nausea and abdominal pain, and they usually emerge one or two days following the infection. It is a fortnight or so later that the more 'classic' symptoms emerge, which include swelling of the face, especially around the eyes, muscle pain, fever and an itchy skin that can later develop into a rash. Because many of the symptoms are so similar to those of flu, for example, many mild cases are undiagnosed and usually clear up by themselves in the space of a few months. In any case, around 10,000 cases are confirmed every year, and some can even turn out to be fatal. Numbers have, however, been declining since the early twentieth century, especially in Europe and the US, and this is as a result of a number of complaints from a few disgruntled customers.

In 1879, Italy and the then Austro-Hungarian Empire had had enough of trichinae-infected pork making its way into Europe from the US, so decided to ban it from within their borders. A year later Germany and Spain followed suit, and the US found itself with a whole load of pork it

Above: Clockwise from top left: a pot-bellied pig (*Sus scrofa domesticus*); a Visayan warty pig (*Sus cebifrons*); the Oxford sandy and black or 'plum pudding' British pig breed; a Bornean bearded pig (*Sus barbatus*).

Below: A babirusa (*Babyrousa babyrousa*).

Left: Some of the thousands of prehistoric animal bones from Vela Spila (Croatia) that I sorted and identified during my doctoral research.

Below: Too close for comfort? An example of canine morphology and tusk-rubbing in a modern wild boar.

Above: Illustrations by French archaeologist Henri Breuil of some of the animal depictions at Altamira cave in Spain: a wild horse (top left), two bison (bottom), and one of the controversial wild boar figures (top right).

Left: Site of Akrotiri Aetokremnos in Cyprus where small suid bones were found. This photo was taken when the site was discovered in 1960.

Above: Ibérico pigs feeding on acorns in the Extremadura dehesa, Spain.

Below: Sows in farrowing crates. The cages prevent the sow from turning around and crushing her newborns, but position her in such a way that the piglets can easily suckle from her teats.

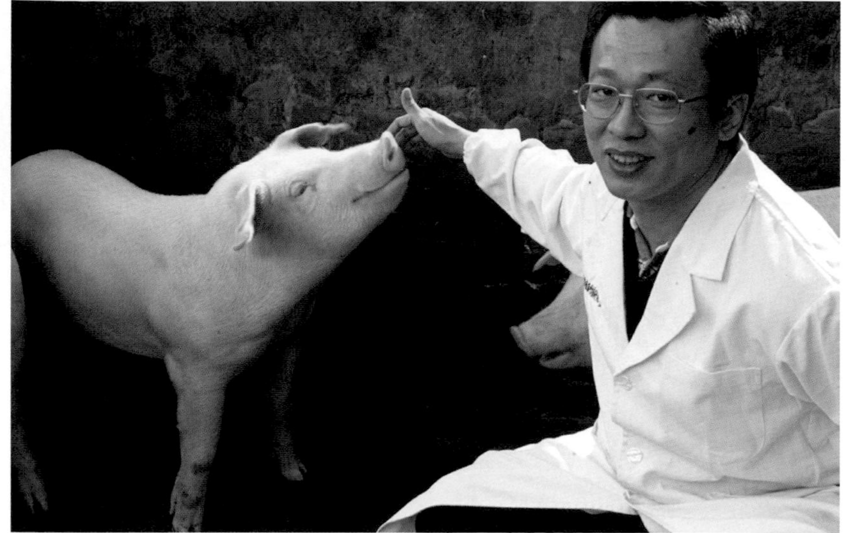

Above: Professor Wu Shinn-chih, who led the research team at the National Taiwan University that bred transgenic fluorescent green pigs, playing with a transgenic pig in Taipei.

Left: One of the pigs taking part in the mirror tests carried out by Cambridge University's Professor Donald Broom and his colleagues at the Department of Veterinary Medicine.

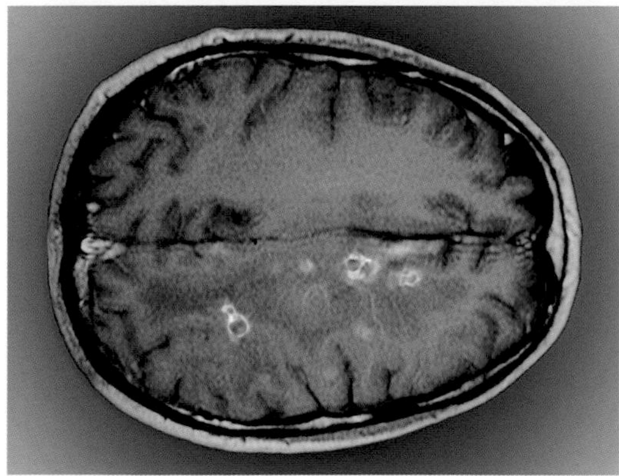

Left: MRI scan showing patient with tapeworm cysts in their brain as a result of ingesting the eggs of *Taenia solium* (pork tapeworm). María's case was more extreme than the one depicted here.

Left: *Tiết canh*, traditional blood dish from Vietnam.

Below: A roasted suckling pig. Such is the tenderness of its meat that in Segovia, Spain, where suckling pig is a speciality, the roasted animal is cut using only the edge of a plate.

Left: Legs of ham on display (and for consumption!) in a bar in Madrid, Spain.

Below: The expulsion of the Jews from Spain by Isabella and Ferdinand, 31 March 1492. Portuguese rabbi Isaac ben Judah Abravanel pleads before the queen for the revocation of the edict, but the Grand Inquisitor Thomas de Torquemada, crucifix in hand, convinces her not to.

Above: The village of Colonnata in Italy where lardo is produced. This photograph was taken from one of the marble quarries used to make the *conche* in which the lardo is cured.

Left: 30 September 1946: 'Pig 311' and 'Goat BO Plenty' arrive back in Washington from Bikini Atoll in the Pacific Ocean, where they were exposed to radioactive fallout during US atomic weapons testing.

was unable to export. It therefore decided to do something about its supposed infected produce, and the US Department of Agriculture began looking into it in 1881. It must have realised something was going on, because three years later inspection laboratories were set up in Atlanta, Boston, Chicago and Washington DC, where pork was inspected manually with the use of a microscope to detect the presence of trichinae before export of the meat. In 1898 Germany was still complaining about trichinosis infections from US-imported pork, so a representative from the US Department of Agriculture was sent to Europe to assess the trichinosis claims being made by the Germans. It was there that the inspector realised that of the more than 6,000 German trichinellosis cases for the 1881–1898 period, about a third had been caused by pork that had been deemed safe by microscopic inspection. It was therefore decided that this *Trichinella* identification method was not good enough, as there was more to this parasite than met the eye. This realisation prompted the department to look into the life and death of the parasite further and, among other discoveries, in 1913 it was found that trichinae in pork can be destroyed if the meat is kept at -15 °C (5 °F) for three weeks; the days of widespread trichinosis in the US and Europe would soon be a thing of the past.

Sometimes it's not the eating of the meat of pigs that makes us sick, but rather the drinking of their blood that does. Take the case of the northern Vietnamese dish *tiết canh* made using fresh animal blood and cooked meat. Though the most popular version is made with duck, it is the pork variety that interests us here. To prepare the dish, a pig must first be bled. A small amount of a saline solution (salt and water or diluted fish sauce) is added to the blood to stop it from coagulating. The pork cuts, which vary from region to region, are then boiled, roasted or fried, and mixed with roasted ginger and onion. This meat mix is then plated and the blood, to which extra water has been added, is poured around it. The blood is left to set, and once coagulated, roasted peanuts and chopped onions are sprinkled over the dish. It can be served with lemon and/or herbs such as basil. Though it may not be to your taste – it definitely isn't to mine – it's quite the popular dish in many parts of Vietnam. It is also 'popular', or rather of interest, in the medical community due to the diseases associated with its consumption: meningitis triggered by *Streptococcus suis*, and trichinosis.

Streptococcus suis is a bacterium that can be found in the upper respiratory tracts of adult pigs, the presence of which doesn't cause them any problems. In young piglets it can be pretty serious: meningitis, septic/infectious arthritis and septicaemia are common signs of infection, the development of which represents a major source of agricultural loss throughout the world. But whereas this was thought to be a pig-exclusive pathogen following its discovery in 1954, a few years later it was realised that it could also find its way into humans, as attested by the first human case recorded in 1968 in Denmark where, as we saw in Chapter 3, they have quite the problem with pig-to-human disease transmission. The number of *S. suis* cases in humans has been increasing steadily since then, and there are currently more than 700 cases recorded annually, around 90 per cent of which are found in Asia. As a matter of fact, such is the prevalence of *S. suis* meningitis in Vietnam that a lot of medical research is focusing on different aspects of this national consumption of raw pig's blood, mostly in the form of *tiết canh*. These studies are aiming to identify human risk groups and their practices, as well as their awareness of the likelihood of developing various very serious conditions from consuming such a raw pig product.

Surveys carried out among different demographic groups in Vietnam in 2012/3 by the Oxford University Clinical Research Unit and Hanoi Medical University showed that overall there is little awareness of the risks associated with consuming raw blood from pigs; as a matter of fact, many of the respondents believed that eating such a product was not only safe, but also good for one's health because, among other things, it helps prevent anaemia. These surveys, however, also highlighted an important aspect relating to the consumption of *tiết canh,* and that is mostly to do with traditional family celebrations, weddings in particular. The slaughtering and bleeding of the pigs represents a shared happy experience during which families slaughter their own home-raised pigs so they can be consumed communally. Based on responses to the surveys, the fact that there is a family tie to these pigs, and that their pork and blood are shared among the group taking part in the celebration, provides those taking part in the celebrations with reassurance of the food's safety. This underestimation of the risk involved, neatly described by the Oxford and Hanoi researchers as 'optimistic bias', is far from the truth: pigs that appear healthy may, in fact, be carrying the bacterium because, as noted earlier, it's mostly asymptomatic in adult pigs. Because the consumption of *tiết canh* is so closely tied to special social occasions, the researchers came to the conclusion that simply banning the dish or lecturing people on the health risks associated with its consumption would be useless if it didn't taken into account the human traditions associated with it. Easier said than done.

Another bacterium that doesn't cause clinical disease in pigs, but which has quite a nasty effect on humans if consumed in undercooked pork, is *Yersinia enterocolitica.* In the US alone this bacterium affects more than 110,000 people every year, of whom over 600 need hospitalisation, and 35 or so die as a result of the infection. Children are most vulnerable to infection, and the most common signs of yersiniosis in them include fever, abdominal pain and bloody, loose stools. Older children and adults, on the other hand, tend to develop more of a right-hand abdominal pain as well as a high temperature, symptoms that are often confused with those of appendicitis, though the two ailments have nothing to do with each other. The most common route of infection is through eating undercooked or raw infected pork, but yersiniosis can also arise from handling pork or coming in contact with someone who has handled it without washing their hands. There is such a high risk linked to the manipulation of infected pork that the website for the US's Centers for Disease Control and Prevention has a page devoted to explaining the risks involved when preparing chitterlings/chitlins, otherwise known as pork intestines. This is a popular winter dish in the south of the US, and has strong historical links to the times of slavery, when the 'less desirable' parts of the pigs, the 'leftovers', were given to the slaves to eat. The dish continues to be popular among African-American families, though many refuse to eat it given its links to slavery. Such was the extent to which pork intestines were thought of as food for slaves that between the early nineteenth and mid-twentieth centuries, venues throughout the US where African Americans could safely perform and which they could attend were known as the 'Chitlin' Circuit'.

The consumption of chitterlings is not solely an American tradition, but very much a global phenomenon: in France, for example, they go by the name of *tricandilles*, and they are particularly popular in the southwestern department of Gironde. There they are first boiled, then grilled, and are generally enjoyed as a crunchy snack accompanied by a glass of local Bordeaux wine. In the Philippines, pork intestines, which are known as *isaw* or *bituka*, are used in a traditional dish by the name of *dinuguan*, which is very similar to the Vietnamese *tiết canh* discussed above. *Dinuguan* is a stew made with all sorts of pork offal (intestines, kidneys, heart...) simmered in pig's blood, garlic, chilli and vinegar. This rich stew is very often accompanied by *puto* (steamed rice cakes) or white rice, and is generally a main-course dish. The dish has many fans, but I must say the idea of it doesn't sound at all appealing to me.

Hepatitis E is a disease of the liver triggered by the hepatitis E virus (HEV). It is thought that around twenty million infections take place every single year across the globe, three or so million of which are symptomatic and lead to nearly 60,000 deaths. Common symptoms include tiredness, nausea and vomiting, fever, abdominal pain and jaundice. Though most people recover from it without much of a problem, acute cases, especially in pregnant women and those with compromised immune systems, can lead to what is known as 'fulminant hepatitis', or acute liver failure, with 20–25 per cent fatality rates among women in their third trimester. It is known that the virus is transmitted via the faecal-oral route, especially due to the drinking or accidental ingestion of contaminated water, which is why the disease is most widespread in developing areas of the world with poor sanitation systems. Researchers were therefore puzzled when they started finding that over the past decade cases of hepatitis E were on the rise in places like the UK, US, France, the Netherlands and Japan, where drinking water is assumed to be uncontaminated.

Though it was thought that a number of these infections may have taken place abroad and were then diagnosed back home, the increase appeared abnormal. Several studies were therefore carried out to try to determine the source(s) behind the increases. In France, for example, it was found that many of these unexpected HEV infections were taking place due to the consumption of *figatellu*,* a traditional Corsican pig liver sausage commonly eaten raw. This sausage was also responsible for a trichinellosis outbreak in

* From the Italian word for 'liver', in turn derived from the word 'fig' (see Apicius' recipe in the previous chapter).

southeastern France in 2015, when three people became infected with *Trichinella britovi* after consuming raw *figatellu* from the French island. In Japan, the source of a number of the infections was traced back to the consumption of infected wild boar and sika deer (*Cervus nippon*). In the UK, where in 2003–2013 a 550 per cent increase in hepatitis E cases was reported, tests carried out on sausages and processed pork-meat products in 2014 revealed that one in ten had traces of the hepatitis E virus. The authorities therefore recommended that sausages should be cooked for at least twenty minutes so that an internal temperature of 70 °C (158 °F) is reached, which is, according to UK cooking safety guidelines, hot enough to kill the virus. The pork cooking temperature recommendations by the US Department of Agriculture (USDA), however, are slightly lower than those recommended in the UK. It was initially recommended that pork be cooked to 71.1 °C (160 °F) in 2011. However, following research commissioned by the National Pork Board, Pork Checkoff, the internal temperature recommendation was lowered to 62.7 °C (145 °F),* after studies showed that pork can be consumed safely when cooked to this internal temperature, followed by a three-minute resting period. Pork Checkoff funded this research because they felt that Americans were overcooking their pork when it wasn't necessary to do so, and therefore missing out on the true and juicy flavours of a less-cooked meat. This new recommendation, they argued, is both safe and provides the most ideal cooking conditions for the kind of pork being produced today: one very lean in nature, with 27 per cent less saturated fat than two decades ago, and which will easily overcook and dry out.

* These new guidelines, however, only apply to cuts such as chops and roast; the advice is still to cook ground pork to 71.1 °C (160 °F).

It's not all bacteria and viruses in our pork, though: back in 2012 China rejected a 90,000kg (200,000lb) pork shipment from the US after it found traces of ractopamine (ractopamine hydrochloride) in the meat delivery. Ractopamine, an adrenaline-like drug originally developed to treat asthma but which was deemed unsafe for humans, is now fed to finishing pigs and turkeys in the US to make the animals up to 10 per cent more muscular in their final weeks before slaughter. As described in a promotional poster for Paylean, one of the brands selling ractopamine to the US pig and turkey industries, 'Now, more than ever, Paylean, pays: Meatier pigs, heftier profits'. The use of ractopamine as a feed additive is legal in the US, but is banned, among others, in EU countries, Russia and China, hence the reason why the latter rejected the US pork shipment. The US's National Pork Producers Council has reassured American consumers that any traces found within the meat are well below the 'safe levels' established by the UN's Codex Commission.* Others, including US physician and world nutrition expert Dr Michael Greger, have been quick to point out that these 'safe levels' were only approved by a one-vote margin, and those voting against any kind of levels did so because there are 'outstanding safety concerns' over exposing humans to this product, as well as for the health of the animals being fed ractopamine.

The only clinical trial involving humans when the failed asthma medication was being put to the test involved giving six men different doses of ractopamine. When given the higher doses (40mg), the men reported strong palpitations and increased heart activity; one of them found his heart racing to such an extreme that he withdrew from the trials.

---

* The CODEX Alimentarius, or 'Food Code', was established in 1962 by the Food and Agriculture Organization (FAO) of the United Nations, together with the World Health Organization (WHO) 'to develop harmonised international food standards, which protect consumer health and promote fair practices in food trade'.

When the men were given the lower dose (5mg), cardiac activity remained the same, so these data were used to set the maximum, human-safe level of ractopamine residue that could be legally found in pork: fifty parts per billion. Many have argued that the fact that the men did not show altered heart activity when taking the lower doses is statistically insignificant, and that a minimum of sixty people would have needed to take part in the trial for any significant cardiac activity anomalies to be fully picked up, before setting minimum safe levels for humans. Ractopamine does not only trigger tachycardia in humans: pigs regularly fed the drug have been observed to suffer from chronic faster than average heart rates and a more stressed disposition, and find it difficult to move. These motionless pigs are known to suffer from 'downer' or 'fatigued pig syndrome', caused by, for example, the use of such feed supplementation, genetics or the result of stress. The pigs are viewed as a burden by the industry as they are difficult to transport to abattoirs, especially as the US Humane Slaughter Act prohibits farmers from dragging their animals onto trucks, which many are known to do illegally using metallic chains. The use of ractopamine therefore presents many drawbacks to the industry, and to the pigs themselves, but surely it's worth the farmers' while? After all, as Paylean says, 'Meatier pigs, [equal] heftier profits'. Well, a 2012 study carried out at the Department of Animal Sciences at Ohio State University found that using doses of 5–10mg/kg for a maximum of 35 days before slaughter only provides an extra 1 per cent pork yield for the farmers. Seems like quite the health price (and risk) to be paying for what can only be a small increase in farmers' profits margins.

As the above examples have shown, what doesn't kill you may, in many instances, not only *not* make you stronger, but could actually end with you in a hospital feeling very sorry for yourself. From larvae cysts in your brain, through liver disease, to drug-derived tachycardia, eating pork – or any other meat for that matter – can be a risky business, especially when eaten raw. Cooking, that great human invention, is capable of killing most of the bacteria and viruses in our food, and though this may seem like an easy and straightforward solution to preventing diseases such as hepatitis E, meningitis or yersiniosis, there is more to food than just calorie fulfilment. Partly raw dishes like the Vietnamese *tiết canh* are not only traditional foods for special occasions, but also create and maintain important social bonds – consuming the raw blood of someone else's pig shows trust and respect, and offering it provides social status. Many social occasions and group affiliations across the globe centre around the consumption and sharing of pork in its numerous forms. As we will soon see, though, it is not just the consumption and sharing of pork that can take many shapes, but also the way pork is cooked, and what this all means in terms of what ends up on our plates. Cooking and the science behind it is more than just pots, pans and a little bit of heat. Time to put our aprons on.

HOW *FIGATELLU* ARE MADE (FRANCE)

WARNING As noted in this chapter, the consumption of raw pork can lead to various health problems. The consumption of raw *figatellu* is known to be a risk factor for infection with hepatitis E, so its production and consumption are undertaken at your own risk. The sausage can be fried, thus reducing the risk of contracting the disease. The recipe below is provided for illustrative purposes only.

The main ingredients of *figatellu* are blood-impregnated pork, pig liver and pig fat. These are coarsely chopped, precisely seasoned and mixed with ground cloves. The mixture is then well kneaded and left to rest overnight in a cool, dry place. Good-quality red or rosé wine is then strained through a paste of crushed garlic cloves. The garlic-infused wine is added to the meat, blood, liver and fat mixture until it is well moistened, but avoiding making the mix too runny. This mixture is inserted into pork casings and smoked for several days. Given the raw nature of the product, it is recommended that the *figatellu* are consumed no more than 20 or so days after they have been made.

CHITTERLINGS/CHITLINS (US)

By Linda Stradley of *What's Cooking America*

Serves 6

WARNING As noted in this chapter, the preparation of chitterlings/chitlins entails a potential health risk due to the possible presence of the bacterium *Yersinia enterocolitica* in the pork intestines. If you do decide to prepare the dish, make sure you handle the raw intestines as little as possible, and always wash your hands with warm water and soap after handling them, especially focusing on the area under your nails. Also wash any surfaces the chitterlings come into contact with. Keep children away from the area where the chitterlings are being prepared, and do not touch any baby bottles, toys and so on before thoroughly washing your hands. Making this recipe is done at your own risk.

Ingredients

4.5kg (10lb) fresh or frozen chitterlings
Cold water to cover

1 cup cider vinegar
5 bay leaves
2 large onions, coarsely chopped
2 large potatoes, peeled and coarsely chopped
1 green or red bell pepper, cored, seeded and coarsely chopped
3 cloves of garlic, minced
Salt and freshly ground black pepper, to taste
Hot pepper sauce

Method

1. Cleaning chitterlings: soak the chitterlings in cold water throughout the cleaning stage. Each chitterling should be examined and run under cold water, and all foreign materials should be removed and discarded. Chitterlings should retain some fat, so be careful to leave some on.
2. Using a small, soft brush, clean the chitterlings thoroughly; rinse in several changes of cold water. Cut into 4–5cm (1½–2in) pieces.
3. Place the cleaned chitterlings in a large pot; cover with water and vinegar. Add bay leaves, onions, potatoes, green or red pepper, garlic, salt and pepper.
4. Bring to a boil, then turn the heat to low and simmer for about 2½–3 hours, or until the chitterlings are tender. Remove from the heat and drain well.
5. Serve with your favourite hot pepper sauce.

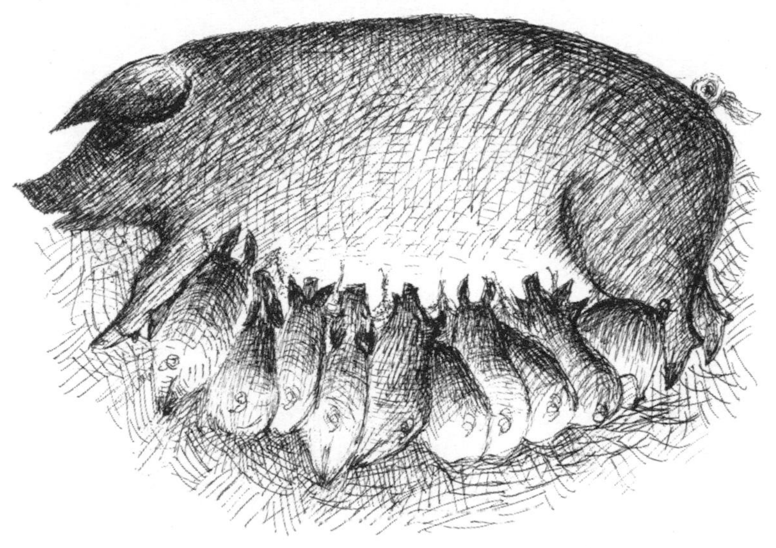

CHAPTER SIX

Pork cooking science

When Max Ferdinand Perutz arrived in Cambridge in 1936 to study crystallography for his PhD at the Cavendish Laboratory, he soon found out that not having a college affiliation was a bit of an impediment to his scholarly pursuits.* After being turned down by a number of the colleges, Peter Wooster, also working at the lab and a

* All undergraduate and graduate students at the University of Cambridge are required to be affiliated to one of its thirty-one colleges while pursuing their studies at this ancient institution. Although lectures take place in departments, students live, eat, socialise and also benefit from small-group teaching at their respective colleges.

Fellow of Peterhouse, suggested that Perutz apply to his college because it had, according to him, the best food in the city.* And so it was that Perutz applied, got in and became a member of Cambridge's oldest college, where, by the way, he was required to take the college's delicious meals in hall several times a week. This gastronomic-driven decision to apply to Peterhouse, however, would only become significant years later, in 1962, when Perutz, together with another Petrean, John Cowdery Kendrew, were awarded the Nobel Prize in Chemistry 'for their studies of the structures of globular proteins'. Though at first sight their research may not sound very food related, its ramifications were huge – and its relevance to pork has to do with a particular globular protein: the mighty myoglobin.

Whereas most people will have heard of haemoglobin, myoglobin is its lesser known sister, even though their functions are similar. On the one hand, iron-containing haemoglobin is what makes blood red and helps carry oxygen from the lungs to the muscles; on the other, myoglobin, which also contains iron, is what helps the muscles store oxygen. Having oxygen stored in the muscles allows us and other animals to move them instantly. If we didn't have these reserves, demanding activities would not be possible as the muscles would soon run out of oxygen, and would have to wait for new vital supplies to arrive. The amount of myoglobin stored in muscles varies from species to species. It also varies in muscles in different parts of the body, based on their individual movement requirements, and the amount of myoglobin stored in muscles increases with age.

Myoglobin and its iron content are also responsible for the meat colour spectrum we see at the butcher's: from

* Being an alumna of Peterhouse myself I can say that its food isn't bad!

mostly white in chicken breasts, through the pink of pork and light red of lamb, to the cherry red of beef. The greater the amount of myoglobin there is in a muscle, the redder it will be: pork, for example, on average has 2mg of myoglobin per gram of muscle, whereas beef has four times that amount, which is why a raw beef sirloin steak is red, whereas its pork equivalent is pink. You may have noticed that when you buy meat, it doesn't stay the same colour for long; again, this is most obvious in redder meats like beef, but it also happens in pork, a pink-coloured meat.* When first cut the meat will be dark in colour, and may in some cases even appear to be purple-blue,† not a colour we consumers tend to associate with freshness. Cutting the meat, however, exposes it to oxygen in the air, and the oxygen then makes its way into and binds with the central iron atom in myoglobin. The oxygen plus the iron result in the oxygenation of the myoglobin, which in turn triggers the formation of oxymyoglobin. This oxygenated version of myoglobin is what gives pork its bright pink colour and beef its cherry red colour, which consumers associate with fresh produce.

Because meat producers are aware of our slightly incorrect 'bright pink-red equals fresh' association, nothing is left to chance in meat-packaging departments, where factors such as the porosity of the packaging material as well as its ability to harbour gases within its microstructures are considered at length to prevent the meat from being exposed to too much oxygen. A small amount of oxygenation is, from a meat appearance point of view, good for pork sales, but too much of it can be disastrous.

---

* Although we have been led to believe that pork is a so-called 'white meat' like chicken, and therefore is a 'healthier' alternative to the red variety, it in fact falls more in the latter category.

† This is why a rare steak in France is referred to as *bleu* – as fresh and as raw as they come!

This all has to do with myoglobin's and oxymyoglobin's ability to lose an electron, which leads to oxidation. Moreover, whereas oxidation results in rust forming on your iron garden furniture when you leave it exposed to the elements, pork turns brown due to the presence of metmyoglobin, the oxidised cousin of myoglobin. Brown meat, as you can imagine, is a meat seller's worst nightmare – people are not too keen on it as they don't perceive it to be fresh. The truth of the matter is that brown meat is not necessarily spoiled, and it should really be up to our noses to figure out whether brown-coloured pork is fit for human consumption or not. Though this is difficult to achieve, it is at times possible to reverse metmyoglobin back to oxymyoglobin to give pork a fresh appearance once again, and the same is also true for an oxymyoglobin-to-myoglobin reversal. As a matter of fact, some vacuum-packaged fresh meat has a purple undertone to it not because it has just been cut and prepared for sale, but because oxygen has been extracted from the package, which has reverted the oxymyoglobin in the meat back to its bluer myoglobin state.

Unless you're a super fan of steak tartare and only consume this kind of meat as part of your diet, it is more than likely that you've also noticed how pork changes colour when it's cooked: from pinkish-red, progressively getting less and less pink, all the way to a rather unappealing white(ish)/tan tone. This colour change during cooking has to do with the denaturing of the myoglobin. Basically, what this means is that the characteristic properties of this protein are being destroyed by, in this case, the heat, which in turn is disrupting the myoglobin's molecular conformation. The breaking down of these secondary and tertiary structures in myoglobin during cooking also makes our digestion of pork much more efficient, as the cooking does much of what our body would have to do if we ate the meat raw.

When cooking pork, besides the progressive change in the colour of the meat, you will have noticed that browning of its outer surface also takes place. This browning is known as the Maillard reaction, and it was discovered in 1912 by a French chap by the name of Louis Camille Maillard. The reaction not only browns pork, but also helps in the development of its flavour. It gives rise to so many different flavours and aromas that according to chef Nathan Myhrvold, founder of The Cooking Lab and leading author of the six-volume *Modernist Cuisine: The Art and Science of Cooking*, it should not be called the browning, but rather the 'flavour reaction'. So how does the reaction work? Generally speaking, the Maillard reaction is the reaction between the sugars and the denatured proteins found on the surface of pork, which recombine – combining differently – and give rise to a differently coloured and flavoured meat. For this to happen, temperatures above 120 °C (250 °F) need to be reached, which is not always as easy as you would expect it to be. The reason for this has to do with moisture: if a piece of pork is very wet (for example due to having been defrosted), it will be difficult for it to undergo a Maillard reaction because the water within it will only reach boiling point, which is 100 °C (212 °F). Only after the moisture has evaporated will the pork's temperature be able to rise above 100 °C (212 °F) and get closer to undergoing a Maillard reaction – by which point the meat will be too dry to enjoy and probably tasteless, wholly defeating the point of getting to this stage in the cooking process.

In order to reduce the amount of moisture present on meat and prevent the above cooking mishap from happening, many cooks pat meat with a clean cloth or kitchen paper to dry the surface as much as possible before cooking. This must be done gently, as the natural juices within the meat should be retained as much as possible to prevent dryness. The Maillard reaction continues to take place up to around 180 °C (355 °F), after which point it turns into a new kind of reaction: pyrolysis. If you're not really sure what this reaction is all about, but the name rings a bell, this might have something to do with those self-cleaning pyrolytic ovens that burned off dirt, which were so much in vogue a few years ago. That's what pyrolysis is all about: it results in the decomposition of something brought about by high temperatures, like the charring on a pork chop. Some people may like their meat to have a bit of charring here and there, but any charring should really be minimal: not only does this charring add bitterness to the meat, but its regular consumption has been linked to the development of cancer.

Polycyclic aromatic hydrocarbons are a group of a hundred or so different chemicals that are released, among others, when rubbish is burned, through tobacco smoking, and when burning wood or coal. Of all the PAHs, fifteen have been classed by the US National Toxicology Program as 'reasonably anticipated to be human carcinogens', and these can be found in all sorts of foods. A 2012 survey of PAHs in food products by the UK's Food Standards Agency (FSA) found that though concentrations were generally low, there were a number of smoked products that exceeded the current safe limits for benzo[a]pyrene (BaP), which results from incomplete combustion at 300–600 °C (572–1,112 °F). The FSA was not surprised by these findings; PAHs are, after all, released through burning, so it is entirely logical that there are more of them in smoked and charcoal-grilled products. The findings did, however, alert the food manufacturers to the high readings, and recommended ways in which they could be reduced, as humans should be exposed to PAHs as little as possible. For example, a 2005 study by researchers at the US National Cancer Institute, Harvard Medical School and John Hopkins Bloomberg School of Public Health found that the frequent consumption of smoked and grilled meats is correlated with a high incidence of colorectal cancer, a disease that is the fourth most common cause of cancer deaths in the world, with nearly 700,000 people dying as a result of it each year.

Other studies have shown that cooks regularly exposed to the fumes of meat cooking are at an increased risk of developing cancer of the respiratory tract, while separate research has found that there are fewer deaths due to respiratory disease and lung cancer among vegetarians than among meat eaters. It's not only about what you cook, though, but also about what others are preparing around you. A 2012 study by researchers at the Cheng Shiu University in Taiwan found that those living next door to restaurants from which meat-cooking fumes regularly emanate are at an increased risk of developing cancer due to this exposure when compared with the health of those not living near such restaurants. The consumption of barbecued meat by pregnant women has also been shown to potentially affect the development of their unborn children. Research carried out in Poland involving the study of 432 pregnancies showed that prenatal exposure to PAH as a result of the women's diets, which included the consumption of grilled meat, may have potentially had a negative effect on the birth weight, length and head circumference of the children at the moment of the birth. Who would have thought that cooked meat could lead to so many health troubles?

Several studies have shown that one effective way of reducing the amount of PAHs formed when chargrilling pork is to marinate the meat before cooking. However, not any kind of marinade will do: research carried out by scholars at the Universities of Porto in Portugal and Vigo in Spain studied the effectiveness of different marinades, and found that though marinating meat in red or white wine, tea or beer reduces the levels of heterocyclic aromatic amines (HAs),* the beer marinade was the most effective and also the most flavoursome. Further research into these types of marinade also showed that not all beers were created equal, and that different amounts of PAHs are released from chargrilled pork loin steaks previously marinated in Pilsner beer, non-alcoholic Pilsner beer and stout (black beer).† The greatest PAH inhibition was noted on the pork marinated in stout, and several explanations were put forward to explain this, including its different fermentation – compared with lager – and the presence of food colourings, flavourings, sweeteners and a range of other additives found in this beer type. In addition, it has been shown that the food colourings in stout provide it with a higher antioxidant capacity than that in lager beers, and this in turn also has an effect on the PAH protective properties of stout marinades. Surprisingly, the second most effective marinade was that made using the non-alcoholic Pilsner beer. Its effectiveness, as in case of stout, had much to do with its antioxidant properties, stemming from the variety of additives contained within the beer, including a number of added flavours and even glucose-fructose syrup.

Marinades are not only good for reducing our exposure to PAHs, but are also (as you probably already know) flavour enhancers. Traditionally they generally comprise two or three of the following components: some kind of

---

* Whereas PHAs are produced as a result of the fat and juices from meat grilled directly over an open fire dripping onto it and therefore causing flames, HAs are formed when proteins, sugars and creatine react at high temperatures. Though their origins are different, both are known to be mutagenic, meaning that they trigger DNA changes in humans that can ultimately lead to cancer.

† Marinating time was four hours at 5 °C (41 °F) and the meat to marinade ratio was 1g of pork loin steak for every millilitre of beer. The cooking took place on an outdoor kind of grill over a bed of charcoal, at a 15cm (6in) distance from the flames.

acid (like lemon juice), oil (like olive oil), and a variety of herbs and spices (such as rosemary, cumin or black pepper). Each of these ingredients plays a different role in the creation of new flavours within the meat. The acid helps to partially denature the proteins found in the meat, which leads to the opening of small passages along the fibres of the muscles along which the herby, spicy and oily flavours of the marinade make their way, aided by the lubricating action of the oil. Because the density of muscles varies from species to species, marinating times differ depending on the kind of meat that is being cooked. Muscles on a chicken's breast, for example, are not as well developed as those in steak, sourced from a cow's back, so marinades will act faster on the former. Chicken should therefore not be marinated for too long, as the acid within it could end up actually curing (that is, cooking) its outer surface!

Pork is generally speaking a dense meat, so most of its parts can be marinated for hours with no ill effects on its flavour. In the case of the beer marinade study, the pork loin steaks were marinated for four hours before cooking, and the flavours were still reported to be pleasant by those sampling the cooked products. Because pork is so dense, it is recommended that the meat is divided up into small(ish) pieces to allow the marinade to penetrate the largest possible surface area and therefore maximise its flavour-enhancing action. The parts of the pig best suited for marinating are the fillet or tenderloin, and pork leg (ham). Leg steaks are known to be particularly dry and greatly benefit from a marinade. The meat can be further tenderised by beating it with a rolling pin or meat mallet before cooking, which helps loosen the long muscle fibres in these rear-limb cuts.

Another way to enhance moisture retention in dry cuts such as pork tenderloin is to brine the meat, that is to say, to soak it in a salt-water solution, before cooking. However, this technique has divided the cooking world for two reasons: firstly, because there is disagreement about how brining actually works; secondly, because even if it does improve moisture retention and meat texture, the flavour is not as effectively enhanced by this cooking technique as by others. So what is it about the chemistry of brining that people don't quite agree on?

Many people say that brining adds moisture to meat through osmosis, which is a process by which molecules of a solvent pass through a semi-permeable membrane from a less concentrated solution into a more concentrated one. When it comes to pork, some argue that this means that when the meat is submerged in brine, the fluids in the meat's cells are less concentrated than the salt water, which triggers the flow of these molecules out of the meat cells, and enables the salt from the solution to flow in. As a result of the presence of the salt some of the proteins are dissolved, making the cell fluids more concentrated and drawing more water back in. Others explain this tendency of water to move from a low-solute area to a high-solute concentration area by arguing that the cells are a high-solute concentration given all the compounds (like proteins) found within them, and therefore attract the water from the brine solution. Many cooks have pointed out the basic flaw in this osmosis-brine explanation: if osmosis was really at play here, then a pure water solution would work even better because it would result in the cells in the pork being even more concentrated by comparison, and would therefore draw more water in, resulting in a juicier cooked meat. By this same rule, a brine with super-high concentrations of salt would draw moisture out of the meat. However, tests on turkey carried out by chef J. Kenji López-Alt, author of the *New York Times* bestseller *The Food Lab: Better Home Cooking Through Science*, have shown this not to be true, even in 35 per cent salt solutions: these were just as effective at retaining moisture as the more moderately concentrated solutions

(6 per cent). The only notable difference was in the saltiness of the meat, which was mostly inedible in the former case. So how, then, does brining help with moisture? Contrary to the above view, other people argue that diffusion plays a part – that is to say, the intermingling of the meat, water and salt through the natural movement of their particles. The water and salt flow into the meat, making it nice and juicy.

Regardless of whether brining helps to moisten meat through osmosis or diffusion, what is true is that this technique does in fact add quite a significant amount of juice to meat – and not only that, but the juiciness stays put throughout the whole cooking process. However, what many cooks don't like, including J. Kenji López-Alt, is that this added moisture is just that: plain and simple. It doesn't really add flavour to the meat, which just oozes tasteless H_2O when eaten. The added plumpness might help us with the chewing and swallowing of the meat, but besides that brining doesn't really add much more to meat dishes.*

Would it help to add a little flavour to the brine to make the extra juices in the cooked meat tasty? Would a stock-based brine work? Not really, and once again it all has to do with food chemistry. Making a basic vegetable stock involves gently boiling a variety of vegetables, such as leeks, carrots, fennel and celery, and once cooked, pouring the stock through a sieve and reserving the vegetables for later use. It may not seem like it at first sight, but, as López-Alt pointed out during his turkey brining trials, the stock will be chock full of tiny solids, which though small will still be bigger than the salt molecules. We know that salt can make its way easily through the meat cells' semi-permeable membranes, but what about the solids in the stock? Well, it turns out that they can't do this because they are too big to

* Many will disagree with this; I guess it's all a matter of taste!

pass through the meat's membranes, and this can only mean one thing: if the vegetable molecules aren't making their way into the cells of the meat, the flavour isn't either. So no, brining meat in flavoured solutions doesn't impart flavour to it. If, in any case, you wish to try your hand at brining your meat, make sure to first check that the pork you are about to brine has not been 'enhanced'. This is because, as already noted a couple of times, factory-farmed pork is so lean and tasteless that many producers have resorted to injecting a briny solution into their meats to make them appear juicier than they actually are. Check the label before experimenting with brines to avoid cooking an excessively moist but tasteless pork dinner.

The tenderness and juiciness of meat is also affected by other elements, including the amount of collagen and fat present within different parts of an animal's body. Collagen, which is the main component of connective tissue including the skin, tendons and ligaments, reacts to heat by breaking some of its hydrogen bonds and heat-sensitive cross-links, subsequently turning into gelatine. The collagen present in the connective tissues of younger individuals contains fewer and weaker cross-links than is the case in adults, so that it gets more easily converted into gelatine and gives the meat a relatively tender texture and juiciness.

Take, for example, the case of suckling pigs, unweaned piglets that are slaughtered at some point between two and six weeks of age. They are generally roasted whole and anyone familiar with this type of pork will tell you how straightforward it is to cook these young animals, and how difficult it is to overcook them. Such is the tenderness of this meat in particular, that in Segovia (Spain), where suckling pig is one of the regional food specialities, once roasted the animal is cut using only the edge of a plate; the meat breaks up when subjected to just the lightest of touches. The cross-links found in the collagen of older individuals, on the other hand, are very difficult to break through cooking; in fact, many never actually come apart, which is why their meat is much tougher than that of younger individuals.

Cooking this kind of meat in moist heat – as opposed to dry – helps break down the tough, old connective tissues, and assists with the gelatinisation of the collagen, all of which makes the meat less chewy and more of a pleasure to eat. Moist heat cooking entails either braising, that is to say lightly frying the meat, then slowly stewing it in a closed container, pressure cooking it or simply cooking it in a liquid (for example as part of a stew). However, whereas moist heat cooking is ideal for collagen-heavy cuts and the meat of old animals, it is not well suited to pig parts with small amounts of collagen, such as the ribs and loin steaks. These low-collagen parts are best cooked quickly and to a medium-rare stage following the USDA's pork-cooking temperature guidelines discussed in Chapter 5. Fat content works in the opposite way to collagen: the more of it there is, the more tender the meat will be. This is because the fat contained within the pork will melt as a result of the cooking heat, lubricating the muscle fibres found within it and therefore adding sponginess and tenderness to the meat. As a rule of thumb, fat is found in the areas of the body a pig uses the least, including its shoulders and ribs. Fat on pork, as you're probably aware, is easy to spot: just look for the marbling or whole white bits; the more of these there are, the tenderer the meat is.

What do Italian salami, Spanish chorizo and French saucisson have in common? Yes, they are all sausages, and though we tend to think of them simply as cured meat – which, by the way, they are too, but more on that later – their flavour, texture and colouring in fact also have much to do with a slightly different process: fermentation. Chemically speaking, fermentation is the breakdown of a particular substance through the action of, most typically, bacteria. What this is all means when it comes to salami, chorizo and saucisson, however, sounds less than appetising: fermentation is, plain and simple, the spoiling of the meat. It may not sound very appealing when you first think about it, but spoiled meat full of bacteria is not necessarily a bad thing; salami and company are all good – and tasty – proof of this. Fermentation is activated by the presence of what are known as lactic acid bacteria (LAB), or lactobacilli, found in a meat mix comprising, in most cases, about 80 per cent lean meat and 20 per cent pork fat. The LAB can either be added to the mix as commercial starter cultures, or they may be found naturally within the meat. Even though many 'sausage purists' are against the idea of commercial starter cultures, the truth is that their use is very widespread because not only do they produce good levels of lactic acid, but mixing and matching them gives rise to specifically sought-after and predictable meat tastes, textures and appearances. Replication, even in the world of sausages, is key to returning customer palate satisfaction.

Of the various genera of lactic acid bacteria found out there, commercial starter cultures contain mixtures of at least two bacteria in particular: *Lactobacillus*, which you have probably heard mentioned in yogurt adverts, and their cousins *Pediococcus*, also commonly added to various dairy products due their probiotic properties. Depending on the kind and size of sausage being made, different LAB mixes can be created on an individual basis to optimise the fermentation process in each case. The use of *Lactobacillus*, for example, is known to lead to a quick acidifying of the meat, so more of it might be used in starter cultures added to mass-produced sausages. *Pediococcus*, on the other hand, works in a more relaxed fashion, and is therefore a good starter culture for products being fermented over a long time. The possibilities are endless.

The lactobacilli feed on the sugars present within and/or added to the meat, in turn producing lactic acid.* The rate at which lactic acid production takes place is temperature dependent: the warmer it is, the faster the rate of fermentation. It will, however, stop if the meat mix is placed in room temperatures above 50 °C (122 °F), or below 12 °C (53.6 °F). The more the amount of lactic acid increases in the meat, the more acidic the mix becomes, leading to the 'cooking' of the meat. This process is also good from a food safety point of view, as the acidifying of the mix kills off the less-resistant and nasty bacteria such as *Staphylococcus aureus* wanting to spoil the meat.† Lactic acid continues to be produced and acidification continues to rise until there is no more sugar present in the mixture for the LAB to happily munch on.

Lactic acid is not only produced during fermentation, but can also be found naturally in pork and other meats. In this case the lactic acid is derived from the carbohydrate (sugar) glycogen, which is found in the muscles of animals, and the function of which is to act as a form of energy storage. Muscle movements in animals take place due to the protein filaments found inside each of these tissue's cells. In order for the movements to take place, energy is sourced from a molecule that goes by the name of adenosine triphosphate (ATP). Oxygen is needed to produce ATP and therefore to make muscles move, and as you can imagine, this process no longer takes place once an animal dies as there is no more oxygen being pumped through the

---

*You may have heard of this acid before. It's the one we build in muscles when we exercise and which make us feel sore a few hours later.

† *S. aureus* is, if you remember from Chapter 3, the bacterium of which an antibiotic-resistant strain was found in minced pork being sold at UK supermarkets. Though not as dangerous as its hospital counterpart, it can give you a nasty case of food poisoning and, in some very rare cases, it can be deadly.

system. Muscles, despite the deaths of their owners will, however, still 'feel the urge' to pump some ATP, and they will do so through a process known as anaerobic glycolysis (or how to make ATP from the muscles' glycogen stores when your now-gone oxygen supply can no longer lend you a hand). This final production of ATP leads to a contraction of the muscles and also produces lactic acid, which then builds up in these tissues because there is no blood circulation happening that would help take it away to somewhere else in the body. More lactic acid results in more calcium build-up in the muscles, and before you know it they are hard as rocks. This is why bodies stiffen up (undergo rigor mortis) shortly after death. The amount of glycogen present in the muscles of animals at the time of their slaughter will greatly affect the quality of the meat because, as we saw above, lactic acid alters the pH of meat, so having too much or too little of it in the meat directly impacts its appearance, texture and, most importantly, taste. Research has shown that stored glycogen levels in animals are very much affected by the animals' overall fitness and amount of stress: the sicker and more stressed an animal is, the less glycogen its muscles will have. Long-term glycogen depletion can arise from, for example, transporting pigs over long distances with little or no food. This is known to be the leading cause of 'dark, firm and dry pork', or DFD for short, which is very unappealing from a consumer point of view and therefore difficult to sell. Ending up with this sort of unattractive pork, however, can easily be prevented by simply feeding, resting and keeping pigs calm. Short-term glycogen depletion, on the other hand, gives rise to 'pale, soft and exudative pork', or PSE, which, just like DFD, is not the kind of meat average consumers would like to eat.

Returning to the business of fermentation, the process is further boosted by adding salt to the meat mix, which helps lower water activity, which in turn reduces the amount of moisture present in the meat and helps with the drying/curing of the sausages (more on this a little later). Both reducing their level of pH and eliminating part of their moisture help to make these raw fermented sausages safe to eat. Raw meat, let's not forget, will always contain some nasty bacteria, and however small their number, their aim will always be to proliferate and spoil the fermentation's party. This is why commercial producers of raw sausages, besides regularly testing the meat for potential pathogens, also add chemicals such as citric acid,* or Glucono-delta-Lactone (GdL),† to accelerate the rate at which acidity increases as quickly as possible and therefore stop the unwanted spoilage bacteria from taking over the show. Next time you're at the supermarket, check out a chorizo sausage's label – it's bound to have at least one of these acidifying chemicals among its ingredients. If not using chemically based acidifiers, the best way to promote the growth of the friendly fermentation flora, and to suppress that of nasty spoilage bacteria, is to keep the meat at a relatively low room temperature (around 20 °C/68 °F) throughout the process. This is the reason why pig slaughter traditionally took place in the winter so that, among other things, sausages and hams could be fermented and cured at a consistent low temperature without spoiling.

As noted earlier, adding salt to the meat mix plays an important role in preventing the growth of unwanted bacteria. The use of salt, however, is more often associated with the curing of the meat, a process in which this mineral plays an important part through osmosis. Earlier we established how osmosis had nothing to do with the brining of meat, but this process is, in this case, the very reason why sausages and hams have the right level of moisture within

---

* $C_6H_8O_1$ – it occurs naturally in citric fruits such as lemons and limes, hence its name.

† This is one of those 'evil' E numbers everyone keeps talking about (E575) – $C_6H_{10}O_6$.

them, and can be air-dried successfully; the salt just sucks them dry (sort of). When making sausages the salt also helps bring out the salt-soluble proteins present in the particles of the lean meat. These gelatinous-like proteins, once freed by the action of the salt, act as a natural sort of glue, gradually sticking together the lean and fatty portions of the meat mixture. So what is the result? It's a progressively firmer sausage that will continue to tighten up throughout the whole drying process, leading to that perfectly chewy consistency consumers of raw fermented sausages are so used to and enjoy so much. In order for this binding process to take place, a minimum of 26g (1oz) of salt per kilo (2.2lb), or 2.6 per cent, of ground pork and fat are required for the process to kick off, though most sausage producers add 2.6–3 per cent salt content just to be on the safe side. Salt is also used as a carrier of sodium nitrite ($NaNO_2$). Adding nitrite to the mix not only helps with the curing side of things, but can also aid in fixing the red-pinkish colour of cured meats, giving them extra flavour and stopping them from turning rancid. If you have ever had the misfortune of eating a super-rancid cured sausage, you will appreciate how important nitrite is when it comes to preventing this kind of flavour. Even the tiniest bit of rancidity goes a long, long way flavour-wise, and it's just not pleasant.

The best examples of cured pork are perhaps those of Italy's Parma ham and its *Ibérico* counterpart, discussed in an earlier chapter. All that is required to produce these succulent meats is salt, the correct temperature and humidity, and a whole lot of patience. In the case of Parma ham, on arrival from the slaughterhouse the pork legs are salted by what is known in Italian as a *maestro salatore*, or salt master, because of the skill required to get the correct amount and perfect coverage of salt that will draw out the right amount of moisture for the curing process to take place successfully. Whereas the skin on the leg of the ham is covered in damp sea salt, the exposed muscle parts are sprinkled with dry salt.

The reason for this is mostly a practical one. A wet salt paste will stick more firmly to the skin, which, because of its rugosity, cannot keep dry salt permanently attached to it.

So meticulous is this salting business – and so important in terms of the curing process – that Ferrarini, one of a number of producers with the license to call their products by the name Parma ham,* has even patented a method that enables the *maestro salatore* to use the right (and minimum) amount of salt required based on the size of the leg and a few other technical considerations. Once salted, the legs of ham are placed in cold, humid chambers. The reason for placing them in a chilled environment is to prevent them from absorbing too much salt, the drawing up of which – as noted – takes place through osmosis, a process that helps make the hams similarly salted throughout. Cold chambers are also used in the production of *Ibérico*: the hams are kept in so-called salt mountains for around nine days, one for every kilo (2.2lb) of a leg's weight, at 0–5 °C (32–41 °F).

As we all know, adding salt to food helps enhance its flavour, and when it comes to cured hams, this is no exception. In the case of Parma ham, the salt drawn into a leg brings out its cheesy undertone flavours, stemming from the pigs' diets, which are centred around whey, a by-product from the production of Parmigiano Reggiano (Parmesan cheese) that takes place nearby. Now you know why this ham has a slight odour of feet (or at least that's what it smells like to me)! In the case of the Iberian hams, the salt helps bring out the nuttiness of the acorns from the *dehesas*, on which these black Spanish suids, as we saw earlier, are encouraged to pig out on. The salt paste and mountains are not there throughout the whole curing process, though – if they were, the resulting ham would probably be too salty to

* Parma ham has a protected designated origin (PDO), which means that only hams produced in Parma following a strict set of rules based on the ancient tradition of ham making can be so called.

be fully enjoyed. This is why both kinds of ham are washed and brushed after their 'cold-chamber experience', following on from which they are taken to so-called 'maturing rooms'.* This is where the rather unglamorous-sounding 'sweating' stage of the curing process takes place. The 'sweating' refers to the slight natural melting of the legs' outer fat and the oozing of some of the inner juices, triggering the development of friendly flora on the outsides of the hams, which is why they end up with crust-like patches on the exterior. These patches are a kind of edible mould, if you like. Sausages also grow these covers when left to cure, and they are perfectly safe to eat so don't be put off by their rather unattractive appearance.

Unlike in the cold chambers, the temperature in the curing rooms is pleasant. It is gradually increased, and the humidity is regulated in the old-fashioned way: by opening and closing the windows at different points during the day. Because environmental factors play such an important role in this 'sweating' stage of the process, it is not surprising that the origins of these hams are protected through protected designated origin (PDO) status. In the case of Parma ham, for example, production within the designated region is not allowed to take place more than 900m (30ft) above sea level, because everyone living there knows that winters at such high altitudes are too cold and too long for the first stage of the ham curing process to take place successfully. Every tiny detail of these ham curing processes, as you can see, has been assessed and fully monitored to produce the most unique and high-quality products.

Parma hams are kept in the 'sweating chambers' for three months, after which *signatura*, a mix of lard and pepper, is manually added to the uncovered surface of the meat in

---

* Actually, after washing Iberian hams are hung to dry in cold chambers, where they are left to 'settle' for just over a month. It is after this that they are moved to the 'sweating' chamber / 'maturing room'.

order to protect it. Following on from this, the hams are moved to so-called *cantinas*, or drying cellars, where they are left to dry for a minimum of five months. The trajectory of *Ibérico* legs, however, is slightly different in that they are made to 'sweat' at least twice, so they get to spend a couple of summers in the rooms ventilated the old-fashioned way. In both cases, however, the final quality of the hams is also tested using an ancient tradition involving a similar implement for both ham types: a horse-bone needle in the case of the Italians (*ago d'osso di cavallo*), and a cattle-bone needle in the case of the Spaniards (*cala*). The needles are inserted into three different parts of the leg (femoral vein exit point, hock joint and hip bone). They are then sniffed by the PDO inspector to check that the curing process has taken place satisfactorily; even the subtlest of funky smells will be picked up by these ham-smelling experts, which could lead to the hams not getting their prized certification. This choice of implement, just in case you were wondering (I did when I first came across it), has to do with how the bones are good at *not* retaining the aromas to which they have been exposed, so that following their use a quick clean with a cloth removes all traces of the previous ham's smells, leaving them odour free for the next inspection.

From those tiny proteins responsible for the colour of meat, through to the protective properties of beer marinades, all the way to the fermenting and sausage-making power of those milk-sounding bacteria, making pork edible is all about chemistry and the tiny, tiny details lurking within it. The research carried out by Perutz, Kendrew and many other scientists has opened up a whole new world of gastronomic discovery, and one we should be making the most of. As you've just seen, when it comes to cooking pork, or any other kind of food for that matter, there is so much more than meats the eye.*

---

* Sorry, I had to do it!

BEER-MARINATED PORK CHOPS

By Ashley of *Kitchen Meets Girl*

Serves 4

Ingredients

4 boneless pork chops
330ml (11fl oz) bottle of your favourite beer (use stout if you're looking to reduce the amount of PAHs released during cooking as much as possible)
2 cloves of garlic, minced
1 teaspoon salt
½ teaspoon black pepper
85g (3oz) blue cheese or Feta cheese
2 green onions, chopped
60g (2oz) chopped pecan nuts

Method

1. In a Ziploc bag, combine the chops, beer, garlic, salt and pepper. Seal the bag and allow to marinate overnight in the fridge.
2. In a grill pan, over a medium-high heat (Ashley cooks hers on a charcoal grill), cook the chops until they are no longer pink and the juices run clear.
3. Just before removing the chops from the heat, top them with the cheese and onions, and heat further until the cheese has melted. Scatter the chopped pecan nuts on top just before serving.

CÁNDIDO-STYLE SEGOVIA SUCKLING PIG (*COCHINILLO ASADO*) (SPAIN)

By Cándido López of the *Mesón de Cándido*, Segovia

Cándido López Sanz (1903–1992) was a Spanish cook who, as a young man, worked at the *Mesón de Azoguejo* in Segovia, Spain. There his specialty was roasted suckling pig, which soon became a favourite of customers. Following his marriage to the owner of the restaurant, it became known as the *Mesón de Cándido*, and such was its popularity that in 1941 it was included in the city's list of 'artistic monuments'. Throughout his life Cándido López was awarded many distinctions, including that of *Caballero de la Orden de Isabel la Católica* ('Knight of the Order of Isabelle the Catholic Queen'), equivalent to the Queen's Honours in Britain – and all because of his roasted suckling pig...

Serves 6–8

Ingredients

1 suckling pig (4–4.5kg/9–10lb in weight) – in Segovia the piglets to be cooked this way are slaughtered at 15–20 days of age
Few bunches of fresh rosemary
250ml (8fl oz) water
100g (3½oz) lard
Salt to taste

Method

1. Cut open the piglet along the backbone, from the head to the tail. Season to taste.

2. Place on a clay pan, on which some fresh rosemary bunches have been placed beforehand. The piglet must be placed with its insides facing up.
3. Add the water to the pan.
4. Place the pan in an oven preheated to 180 °C (356 °F). Bake for 1 hour.
5. Remove the pan from the oven, and turn the piglet upside down so that the skin faces upwards. Use a fork to poke some holes in the skin, then spread the lard over the skin with a baking brush.
6. Add more water to the sauce if necessary.
7. Bake for a further 45 minutes at a slightly higher temperature. The meat must be crunchy enough to be carved with the edge of a plate.

CHAPTER SEVEN

The swine; he is unclean to you

On 18 July 2012, the controversial American hip-hop rapper and actor Snoop Dogg – known for his love of cannabis smoking, drug and gun possession, and for being banned from several countries – officially notified the world via Twitter of his new identity: Snoop Lion.* The reason for this canine-to-feline name change and supposed selfhood transformation was, he claimed, a religious one: a 'spiritual reincarnation' to Rastafarianism, a religious movement that developed in Jamaica in the

* At the time of going to press, the singer has two active Twitter accounts (@SnoopDogg and @SnoopLion), though his latest album, *Coolaid* (2016), has been released under the name of Snoop Dogg.

1930s, which was greatly influenced by the Bible and symbolised by a lion, hence the new name. The main tenets of Rastafarianism include the belief that its followers are the chosen people of God, and a conviction that God will bring back to Africa those torn from their original homeland by slavery. Given his very public drug-taking record, it is perhaps not surprising that one aspect of the Rastafarian religion that Snoop Lion quickly embraced was the smoking of marijuana (*ganja*) during religious ceremonies to enhance spiritual awareness; however, it seems that while Snoop was happy to puff his way to religious plenitude, he had trouble embracing another important tenet of the Rastafarian faith, namely diet (*ital*) and giving up the consumption of pork.

While Rastafarians are encouraged to embrace vegetarianism, many interpret the *ital* rules in their own way, though it is thought that most do respect the dietary prohibitions set out in Leviticus 11: no pork, no shellfish, no camel, no raven, no bat, no vulture, and no to a number of other animals. It seems Snoop chose to ignore some of the teachings of Leviticus because, as he argued in an interview with *Rolling Stone* magazine: 'me and Porky Pig, we agree with each other. You gotta understand, I was fed this shit from a baby [sic]'.

Rastafarians are not the only Christians forbidden to consume the flesh of this omnivore and other earthly creatures. Seventh Day Adventists also follow the dietary instructions in Leviticus, as they believe this will lead to wholeness and overall good health, as do Ethiopian and Eritrean Orthodox Tewahedo Christians. But it is the dietary laws of Judaism and Islam that contain the most widely known prohibitions on eating pork. In the case of Orthodox Judaism, the origin is the *mitzvot* or commandments of the Book of *Vayikra* in the Torah (Latinised as Leviticus in the Old Testament), the code of behaviour set out in *Devarim* (Deuteronomy in the Bible), and the *kashrut* dietary laws interpreted from those sources in the Talmud. Leviticus singles out the pig from the other forbidden non-*kosher* or unclean living things listed because, while it is cloven footed, it does not graze, and is not a ruminant animal like a sheep or cow – two of the qualifying characteristics for meat to be classified as *kosher* and therefore fit to eat.

Muslims, on the other hand, guide themselves by the teachings of the Qur'an which, in Surat Al-Baqarah 2: 173, specifically states that 'He has only forbidden to you dead animals, blood, the flesh of swine, and that which has been dedicated to other than Allah. But whoever is forced [by necessity], neither desiring [it] nor transgressing [its limit], there is no sin upon him. Indeed, Allah is Forgiving and Merciful.' *Halāl,* or the religious laws of what is permissible for Muslims in daily life, considers pigs as scavengers and therefore unclean.

Numerous reasons have been suggested to explain these ancient pork taboos, but the most frequently cited is disease transmission. Pigs, many argue, are dirty animals that like to feed on rubbish and waste, and thus become the focus of numerous diseases transmissible to humans, especially trichinosis. This is a disease caused by consuming under-cooked meat that contains the larvae of the roundworm *Trichinella.* Its symptoms in humans include abdominal pain, diarrhoea, fever, weakness, severe pain and tenderness of the affected muscles and, in cases where the brain is infected, a real possibility of death. Until recently it was thought that animals and humans were only infected by one species, *Trichinella spiralis*, but recent studies have shown that several other *Trichinella* species (such as *T. pseudospiralis* and *T. nelsoni*) are also responsible for infecting thousands across the world every year. Although pork consumption is the major source of *Trichinella* infection in humans, pigs are not its only source. Other potential carriers of this roundworm include bears, foxes, rats, dogs, crocodiles and horses, the consumption of which is, funnily enough, also prohibited by Leviticus.

The trichinosis-Leviticus connection has attracted and been debated by many scholars over the ages, but it seems unlikely, though admittedly not impossible, that the specific health risks associated with consuming undercooked pork or meat from other animals could have been properly understood around 800–600 BC, when the Book of Leviticus is believed to have been compiled. First, the *Trichinella* roundworm was only discovered and formally recorded by James Paget, an English medicine student, in 1835.* Furthermore, it was not until a few decades after Paget's discovery that three German scholars, Rudolf Virchow, Rudolf Leuckart and Friedrich Albert von Zenker, were able to demonstrate indisputably that the symptoms of what is now known to be trichinosis were, in fact, caused by the *Trichinella* roundworm.

We will never know whether the ancients truly understood the potential parasitological risks associated with the consumption of certain meat products, but what is certain is that, to different degrees, these religious pig taboos have been highly effective. Even with modern refrigeration and freezing systems, powerful cooking appliances and, most importantly, our awareness of the disease's transmission mechanisms, countries with majority Muslim and/or Jewish populations have much lower rates of *Trichinella* infection.

In Egypt, for example, where a majority of the population are *Halāl* followers, only one human outbreak of trichinosis has ever been officially recorded. This single infection took

* Paget would go on to become one of the best surgeons of his time. He was Surgeon-Extraordinary to Queen Victoria, discovered Paget's disease – the disorder that affects bone renewal and repair cycles leading to bone weakening and deformation – and was one of the founders of scientific medical pathology.

place in 1975 after a group of French tourists consumed infected pork meat. A similar event occurred in Senegal, also a predominantly Muslim nation, when nine Europeans visiting Dakar were infected by *Trichinella* after eating warthog. In Israel, the world's only Jewish-majority country, trichinosis outbreaks are also extremely rare – data available up to 2007 showed only six human outbreaks for the whole country, and these have all been largely among Christian Arab and Thai immigrant communities.

On the other hand there is the case of Spain, where 70.9 per cent of the inhabitants define themselves as Catholic. Catholicism, unlike Judaism, Islam, Rastafarianism, Seventh Day Adventism or the Ethiopian and Eritrean Orthodox Tewahedo Churches, does not prohibit the consumption of pork, or any other kind of meat for that matter, except during Lent, the six-week period preceding Easter. To say that Spaniards have happily embraced this culinary liberty is an understatement considering that Spain was, until very recently, the world's number one consumer of pig meat. In 2012, the average Spaniard's annual per capita pork consumption was estimated at 51.6kg (114lb), more than twice that of the UK. This astronomical figure represents, to put it into perspective, 172 x 300g (660lb) packets of pork-fillet medallions, or 516 trays of sliced chorizo. Such a massive consumption of pork, however, comes at a cost: 50–100 outbreaks of trichinosis in humans are recorded in Spain *every* year. The same is also true for other Catholic-majority countries such as Croatia, where 30–50 trichinosis cases are reported annually.

While a ban on pork has the potential to reduce disease transmission, this does not appear to be the sole reason why it is a forbidden food for many of the world's religions. British Professor Dame Mary Douglas, one of the most influential social anthropologists of the twentieth century, in *Purity and Danger: An Analysis of Concepts of Pollution and*

Taboo (1966), tried to find other possible reasons for the pig prohibition. In Chapter 3, 'The Abominations of Leviticus', she argued that human rational behaviour involves classification, and the act of classifying is a human universal. The world, she noted, can be divided/classified into three environments – land, water and air – and all three are found in the creation story in the Book of Genesis. Each of the Earth's species can be categorised into one of these three environments, which it shares with similarly adapted creatures. While studying the laws set out in Leviticus 11 concerning animals forbidden and those allowed for consumption, she found the same environment-based classification pattern for the species being described. Cloven-hoofed ruminants, such as cattle, goats and sheep, for example, form a neat terrestrial group, but how does the pig fit in among them? It is, like them, a cloven-hoofed creature, but it does not 'chew the cud'; nor is it a strict herbivore. In fact, it is quite the opposite, as it is as unfussy an eater as can be. According to Douglas, this makes it largely unclassifiable in this world order of things, especially in relation to other 'land' creatures, and it therefore cannot be considered in the allowable food categories according to Jewish (and Islamic) laws.

Although *Purity and Danger* was generally well received when it was published and continues to be an influential social anthropological study of food taboos, Douglas has received much criticism for the above theory because, as scholars noted, the argument is not robust enough. It also fails to take into account, for example, the fact that Leviticus makes no mention of the consequences of breaking this particular dietary law, which one would expect to find associated with such a taboo. Rather it is the consumption of pork that is in itself the sin. In the preface to the 2002 edition of the book, Douglas confessed: 'I was out of my depth when I wrote Chapter 3 nearly forty years ago. I made mistakes about the Bible for which I have been very sorry ever since.

Longevity is a blessing in that it gave me time to discover them.' (Douglas 2002: xvi). There continue to be many theories as to why pork is a taboo food in many religions. For example, a 2015 publication by Professor Richard W. Redding from the Kelsey Museum of Archaeology at the University of Michigan puts forward another interesting idea to explain the pig prohibition, and it has to do with another animal, the chicken. Before discussing the poultry connection, there is a bit to be said about the ecology, behaviour and human management of pigs that is key to understanding Redding's rather interesting theory.

The analysis of many Middle Eastern zooarchaeological assemblages has shown, as we also saw in Chapter 2, that pigs were domesticated early there. The domestic pig continued to be a common species – in certain cases comprising up to 50 per cent of archaeological faunal assemblages in some places in the Middle East – until the Late Bronze Age (1550–1200 BC) and was a favoured animal (for example by the Assyrians) even in the Iron Age. Redding argues that pigs may have persisted in areas of Israel after this time, and points out that even today a kibbutz in Lahav in the southern part of the country raises pigs, though it does so, it claims, for medical research purposes. Since 1963 the raising of pigs for meat has been illegal in Israel except in the Arab-Christian area in the north of the country. Pigs therefore, despite the religious ban, have never actually disappeared from the wider Middle Eastern area.

Although the zooarchaeological record shows that pigs were present and consumed in the Middle East, they were rarely mentioned in textual records, or depicted as much as cattle, goats and sheep, especially in the case of ancient Egypt, which is the focus of Redding's research. Before the more recent zooarchaeological analysis of Middle Eastern archaeological assemblages, this lesser textual and pictorial focus on pigs led Egyptologists to believe that pigs were not depicted/referenced as much because they were creatures not to be consumed, and were therefore avoided in every shape and form. Redding, however, argues that the lack of representation and mention of pigs was not due to their avoidance, but rather to a lack of interest from the central authorities in this species, which (due to a number of its characteristics) was not part of the wider redistributive economy, and was only of importance at the local village or urban subsistence level. As such, the production of pork was not taxed and was of no interest to central governments.

What are the characteristics that would have made the pig more of a household product than a state staple? Well, a major issue concerns their mobility (or rather lack of it). Pigs, unlike sheep, goats and other earthly creatures, are quite useless when it comes to walking long distances. Not only do their short legs make it physically difficult for them to travel for extended periods of time, but they are also generally rather uncooperative when it comes to being driven by humans. Having said this, there is ample historical and ethnoarchaeological data to show that pigs can be moved over relatively long distances, even though this is not the norm as it is, for example, for sheep. A 2011 ethnoarchaeological study of pig herding in central Sardinia by Dr Umberto Albarella of the University of Sheffield and his colleagues showed that, though pigs are herded here between the lowlands and highlands at different times of the year, if left to their own devices they rarely travel more than 10km (about 6mi), which is not far in animal range terms. So, because these animals cannot be moved easily, in pre-refrigeration and pre-modern transport times surplus domestic pigs could not be traded/exchanged over long distances, and were therefore unattractive within the wider subsistence system.

Another issue that may have influenced the pig's role in these Middle Eastern economies would have been this species' water requirements. Pigs, as previously discussed, do not sweat and thus rely heavily on water and mud to cool themselves, especially in hot climates such as those found throughout the Middle East. Hot weather, however, is not an impediment in itself to pig survival *as long as pigs have access to sufficient water.* This is generally not a logistical issue when groups are permanently settled in areas with good access to water, but it may have been a significant problem for nomadic groups like those of Abraham and Jacob, two of Judaism's patriarchs. Could the water issue, coupled with pigs' little love for covering long distances, be the reason behind their lack of appeal to Jews and Muslims? Well, this may have been the case, but it is also worth noting that though pigs need water to cool themselves, in terms of their water consumption they are actually quite efficient water consumers. They 'only' require 6,000 litres (1,350gal) of water to produce 1kg (2.2lb) of meat, whereas cattle require a whopping 43,000 litres (9,460gal) and sheep a staggering 51,000 litres (11,220gal). Pig rearing, despite its limitations, therefore still appears to have been a viable subsistence option for people in the Middle East. All this, of course, fails to explain the pig prohibition, and it is at this point that we can turn our full and undivided attention to the small size yet what appears to have been influential role of chickens in all of this.

The chicken (*Gallus gallus domesticus*) is not native to the Middle East. Its origins have been traced to South-east Asia, and it is believed to have been introduced into the Middle East by nomadic and seafaring groups, an introduction that some argue took place several times and was not just a one-off event. The earliest recorded possible evidence of chicken found thus far in the Middle East comes from Iran: a single bone fragment in deposits that yielded finds between 3900 and 3800 BC. More robust zooarchaeological evidence has been recovered from Turkey, Syria, Jordan, Israel and other places, yielding a range of dates: 2900 BC, 2400 BC, 1200 BC and 1650 BC.

However, the vast majority of these are only isolated finds, some of which are disputed in the literature. Not until the Iron Age do we see extensive exploitation of chickens in the Middle East. If we put the dramatic appearance of chickens in larger numbers into perspective, their numbers increase at the same time as pig frequencies decrease. It is really not until the Late Bronze Age (1550–1200 BC) that, based on the current zooarchaeological data shown in the notes to Redding's paper, their numbers may have started declining in the Middle East. It seems from these and other dates, which are supported by other findings as well (of which there are too many to discuss here), that *perhaps* the chicken, to some extent, began replacing the pig in the local village or urban economy subsistence systems.

Coming back to the point of how efficient pigs are when it comes to water consumption and meat production: pigs, compared with cattle, sheep and other animals, need relatively 'small' amounts of drinking water to produce a kilo of meat. Chickens, however, are even more efficient: they 'only' require 3,500 litres (925gal). Moreover, chicken meat averages 19g (¾oz) of protein per 100g (3½oz), whereas pork provides much less: 13g (½oz) on average. In addition, chickens produce an extra source of protein in the form of eggs (a secondary product), which pigs obviously do not, adding a further 12.8g/100g (½oz/3½oz) of protein to their yield per individual. It seems therefore that eating chicken was a water and protein win-win situation. The only way that pigs could compete was in the fat and calories departments.

Chickens are also somewhat easier to manage than pigs, even though the latter do not require much labour input when kept at the local economy level. In most cases chickens can be left to their own devices as far as feeding is concerned, whereas pigs require some level of control when left to roam close to crops, which they will happily root/destroy if left unsupervised. Another important advantage of the chicken is its size, which makes it an ideal single-serving portion for a family because there are no leftovers (a problem in pre-refrigeration times). A pig provides more than a single meal, so in the past leftover meat would have needed to be preserved in some way (such as smoking), adding further labour and overall costs to pig raising. Having said this, pig rearing can be a multifamily affair, so nothing need go to waste. In Papua New Guinea, for example, where pigs are a very important part of the community, pork isn't preserved, just gifted to other members of a group, and the favour is returned at the next feast. The smaller size of chickens was also an advantage if they were traded, as they could easily be transported over relatively long distances in cages carried by horses or donkeys,* or simply by tying the chickens' feet and placing them over a horse or donkey's back, something that, for obvious reasons, would have been more difficult to do with pigs.

As Redding argues in his concluding remarks: 'with the introduction of the chicken in semiarid and arid areas of the Middle East that did not include extensive woodlands or marshes [where pigs would have easily thrived], humans had a decision to make' (Redding 2015: 358). Chickens used less water to produce the same amount of meat, provided more protein than pork, supplied an extra source of protein in the form of eggs, required no labour input, provided single-family meals thus eliminating waste, and could be easily transported. The pig's role in the local economy could thus be fulfilled more efficiently by the newly arrived chickens, and pigs fell out of favour; perhaps their prohibition was not a prohibition at all, but instead the result of food-production efficiency? The *Sus-Gallus* connection theory is an interesting one, but as Redding

* Chickens, like pigs, are not keen long-distance walkers, so herding them is mostly impossible.

points out more zooarchaeological data are needed to explore this idea further, especially from around the time when chickens were introduced to the Middle East and began spreading in the area. Perhaps an archaeologist out there will provide the missing piece to the pig-prohibition puzzle?

In the case of Catholicism, pigs (or rather pork) played an important role, for example, in the Spanish Inquisition. Even though the Roman Catholic Church's Inquisition set up to fight heresy had already been in place since the twelfth century, Ferdinand and Isabella, the Catholic monarchs of Spain, established their own – and more brutal – Spanish version, the Tribunal of the Holy Office of the Inquisition (*Tribunal del Santo Oficio de la Inquisición*) in 1478. Though Muslims and Jews had been living alongside Christians in relative peace for hundreds of years, Ferdinand and Isabella took exception to the presence of Christians of Jewish origin within their Castile and Aragon kingdoms. The extent to which these 'New Christians' or *conversos* ('converted') had truly turned to the Christian faith was routinely doubted by both the Church and 'pure-blood' Christians, and many times *conversos* were the subject of anti-Semitic hate and name-calling. One such name was *marrano*, which was used to describe converted Jews who continued to secretly practise Judaism (Crypto-Jews). The Spanish's equivalent to the *Oxford English Dictionary*, the *Diccionario de la Real Academia Española* (DRAE), notes that the word can also mean a dirty and grubby person, a wicked or excommunicated person, a rude individual lacking in manners or a person who misbehaves. None of these adjectives is the kind of description you would want to have associated with your name, but there is a fifth meaning to *marrano* that may have been particularly hurtful to Jews and Muslims, and that is 'pig'. It has been argued that *conversos* were labelled *marranos* because of Judaism's prohibition on the eating of pork, but there are etymological disagreements about the extent to which this link is true. Some people have argued that it could simply be derived from the verb *marrar,* meaning to fail or to go wrong; whereas the DRAE places its origins in the (Hispanic) Arabic word *muḥarrám*, meaning 'forbidden thing'. Regardless of whether the origins of the word *marrano* had anything to do with resembling a pig, pork did play an important role in helping inquisitors track down Crypto-Jews (and Muslims) and bring them to trial.

In the Iberian Peninsula during this period, meat in general was an important food source, but it was the ways in which meat was sourced and prepared, the customs linked to its consumption and, most importantly, the kinds of meat consumed that were the most useful evidence to inquisitors and their informants when tracking down those they believed to be traitors to Christianity. Among the items on the Inquisition's 'Jew- and Muslim-spotting' list were cooking with olive oil instead of lard. The preparation of *sofrito* (typically onion and garlic fried in olive oil) as the base to a number of dishes was, according to inquisitors, a clear giveaway of someone's Jewishness or Muslimness, to the extent that many 'pure-blood' Christians who regularly used olive oil to cook stopped doing so for fear of being mistaken for Jews or Muslims. Funnily enough, modern-day cooking in Spain is olive-oil based, and *sofrito* is a basic starting point to many dishes, whereas lard is most often used for baking. Such is Spain's obsession with *sofrito* that when David Beckham moved to Madrid in 2003 to play for Real Madrid FC., his wife Victoria reportedly said that 'Spain smells of garlic'. Although during an interview with *Vanity Fair España* (February 2014) she denied having ever made such a remark, it is indeed true that at lunch and dinnertime many streets in Spain are redolent with the fragrant smell of bubbling olive oil slowly cooking juicy onions and garlic.

Such was the obsession with pork eating among the inquisitors that *conversos* were forced to prove their change of faith by publicly eating pork at least once daily (Anderson 2002: 101). This well-founded paranoia still continues to be felt by some descendants of Spanish Crypto-Jews, especially in South America and parts of the US, where many families took refuge after escaping inquisitorial Spain. For example, in a 1990s study of several Latino now-Catholic families living in Arizona, Colorado, New Mexico and Texas (US), one woman recounts that while growing up in Mexico, 'we didn't eat pork, but my family always made sure that there were pigs in the yard because you didn't want to let the neighbours know that you don't eat this meat' (Liebman 1996: 108).

Appearances played a vital role in Crypto-Jewish lives, and it was not uncommon for households to have ham legs on display and sausages hanging from the ceiling should visitors turn up unannounced. If you've ever been to Spain you will have come across the sight of hanging meat quite often, as many bars and shops have pig body parts conspicuously on display, as they probably did during the Inquisition, when they would have announced that the occupants were pig eaters. Another way of giving the impression of living in a Christian-abiding household was to have something distinctively porcine-smelling cooking in the background for visitors to get a sniff off when dropping by. Surprisingly, it was the adaptation of a traditional Shabbat dish, *adafina*, that saved many Iberian Crypto-Jews from suffering at the hands of the ruthless inquisitorial torturers.

The Sabbath – Shabbat for Sephardic Jews – is a day of religious observance and abstinence from work, kept from Friday evening to Saturday evening, and requiring Jews to cook whatever they will be eating on Saturday to be prepared before Friday evening. An easy way to overcome this logistical obstacle is to prepare a dish that can either be left cooking overnight or eaten cold on Saturday. *Adafina*, a popular Shabbat casserole and dish in fifteenth and sixteenth century Spain, represents just that. Derived from the Arabic word *dafīnah*, meaning 'buried', the *adafina* pot was covered with embers and ashes and left cooking overnight. There were several varieties of the dish, depending on the availability of ingredients in each region and the financial means of the families, but lamb and beef were generally the meaty base to this Shabbat dish, which included, among other ingredients, chickpeas, carrots, hard-boiled eggs, and a number of herbs and spices.

Consumption of *adafina* on Saturday evening sent a clear signal to others of one's Jewish identity, so the dish was modified to include the Christian-friendly ingredient par excellence: pork. The eggs in the recipe were replaced by pork, and pig fat was sometimes used instead of olive oil to distance the dish as much as possible from its true Jewish origins. This survival strategy on the part of Crypto-Jews ultimately gave rise to one of Spain's (and Portugal's) staple dishes, the *cocido* (*cozido*), of which there are several regional varieties, such as the *cocido montañés* (Cantabria), *cocido galego* (Galicia) and the capital's *cocido madrileño*. Not many Spaniards and Portuguese are aware of the Sephardic origins of the ridiculously pork-rich dish that they so much enjoy during the cold winter months. If you fancy trying *adafina* or *cocido madrileño* at home you will find recipes for both at the end of this chapter.

Deceiving the inquisitorial authorities did not always require the consumption of pork, but rather the pretence of doing so. Legend has it that this was the case for *alheira*, a smoked sausage typical of the Trás-o-Montes northeastern region of Portugal, first produced by Portuguese Jews at the end of the fifteenth century. *Alheiras* were made to physically resemble the pork sausages so much loved by Christians, but instead of containing pork they were filled with chicken and flour. Over the centuries these smoked sausages have become popular throughout Portugal, and as a result their composition has been modified and now contains other meats, such as rabbit, red deer and, of course, pork.

As a result of the modification of their eating habits, their close-knit communities and other behaviour traits, many Iberian Crypto-Jews were very successful in hiding their true religious identity from the Christian authorities, but some of these *marranos* paid a high price health-wise for doing so.

In 1917, Samuel Schwartz, a Polish Jewish mining engineer, originally from Galicia (Spain), visited the then remote Portuguese town of Belmonte as part of a survey exercise. It was there that he discovered a community of Crypto-Jew descendants who not only still practised many Jewish rituals, but were isolated to such an extent that they also thought they were the only Jews left on Earth. According to accounts described in Cecil Roth's *History of the Marranos*, when the Belmontese Crypto-Jews first met Schwartz they did not believe he could be a Jew like them because he was not able to recite any of their traditional Portuguese prayers. It was not until Schwartz recited the *Shema Yisrael* (שְׁמַע יִשְׂרָאֵל/'Hear, [O] Israel'], a central prayer in morning and evening Jewish services, that they finally accepted that they were not the only Jews around. This was because the prayer contains the word *Adonai* (The Lord), the only Hebrew word they continued to use and were therefore able to recognise. The community were able to maintain their Crypto-Jewish isolation through very strict endogamy. The lack of 'fresh blood' within the community for centuries had unfortunately also given rise to a unique type of autosomal recessive retinitis pigmentosa (RP) among the descendants of these Portuguese Jews, the mutation probably having taken place 200–500 years ago, shortly after their forefathers settled in Belmonte. RP is a group of inherited conditions of the retina that progressively reduces vision. Its first symptoms often include worsening night and peripheral vision, and an increasing difficulty to read. The degeneration is, for most people, a slow and gradual one, and can happen at different ages depending on the genetic cause and the inheritance route it has taken. Approximately one in every 4,000–5,000 people is affected by RP, with around 1.5 million people across the globe suffering from this retinal degeneration, which is currently the leading cause of inherited blindness.

Health troubles of another kind have been noted in a different population of Crypto-Jews, the *Chuetas* or *Xuetes* from the island of Majorca in Spain. This tight-knit community is thought to descend from *converso* Sephardic Jews living on the island at the time of the start of the Spanish Inquisition. A recent study noted the high prevalence of familial Mediterranean fever (FMF) among many of the *Chuetas*, when no such cases have ever been recorded in the rest of the populations of the island. FMF is a hereditary disease commonly found among Jewish, Armenian, Turkish and Arab populations. It is characterised by recurrent short episodes of inflammation and serositis (inflammation of a serous membrane, such as the peritoneum), including fever, pleuritis (inflammation of the pleurae,* which impairs their lubricating function and causes pain when breathing), peritonitis (inflammation of the peritoneum, typically caused by bacterial infection either via the blood or after a rupture of an abdominal organ), and on rare occasions meningitis. The study found that a third of the *Chuetas* possess the mutations known to cause FMF, confirming that at least a part of this Majorcan population shares a common origin with other non-Iberian Jewish populations.

* Pairs of serous membranes lining the thorax and covering the lungs.

Treating many if not most illnesses such as these involves pigs. As discussed in Chapter 4, much of the medical research behind the treatments developed to deal with these types of illness have used pigs as human models. Pigs, however, are not only involved in the medical research side of things, but are also physically present in hospitals all around the world in the form of the drugs and implements used by doctors to treat patients. Porcine-derived ingredients are widespread, for example, in both the hard and soft capsules of most medicine tablets, which are usually made of gelatine obtained from the skins and bones of pigs and cows. Pig gelatine can also be found in those little sponges regularly used in surgery, especially in ear and maxillofacial operations. These small, foam-like, highly absorbent sponges are capable of soaking up many times their own weight in blood, and can be left inside the body after surgery as they dissolve in 4–6 weeks.

A number of low molecular weight heparins such as Enoxaparin sodium, Dalteparin and Bemiparin, used to prevent and manage blood clots by thinning blood, are derived from pigs' intestinal mucosae. Insulin, which is used in the treatment of diabetes was, until the 1980s, mainly obtained from the pancreas of pigs and cows; though animal insulin is still available on prescription, the use of lab-grown human and human analogue insulins has taken over since the early 2000s, and these are now the most common hormones used to control the disease. Porcine dermis/skin is used in breast reconstructive surgery. It is the main component of, for example, Strattice, an acellular dermal matrix (ADM), a kind of surgical mesh resembling a thin white piece of leather, which is attached to the pectoralis muscle to create a small pocket inside the chest and on which the implant is placed. This support acts as a kind of in-body bra, giving the implanted breast a more natural shape and droop. ADMs are not just used as implant supports, though; they can also provide collagen structures on which human tissue can remodel itself while healing. ADMs are used, for example, in the treatment of diabetic foot wounds, chronic venous leg ulcers, and to repair inguinal hernias and injured or collapsed abdominal walls. These ADMs are also derived from pig skin or can be made using living tissue obtained from pigs' and other animals' small intestine submucosae, pericardium (the membrane enclosing the heart) and other body parts. In some cases acellular matrix products are obtained from human sources such as donated human cadaver skin.*

The list of pig-derived medicine products is endless. The need to use such medical products obviously represents a religious dilemma for many people. Muslim and Jewish religious leaders suggest that non-animal alternatives should be sought first; if unavailable, medication obtained from pig sources can then become an acceptable means of treatment because the preservation of human life is always of greater importance than blindly following Jewish or Muslim laws, a concept known as *Pikuach Nefesh* in the former. As the Surat Al-Baqarah 2: 173 in the Qur'an notes: 'whoever is forced [by necessity], neither desiring [it] nor transgressing [its limit], there is no sin upon him. Indeed, Allah is Forgiving and Merciful'.

As you can see, pigs are in hospitals and in drugs – they are *everywhere*. This fact was highlighted by Dutch photographer Christien Meindertsma in her 2007 photography book *Pig 05049*, where she investigated what happened to the pig with ear tag number 05049 from the moment it left the farm in the Netherlands where it had

---

*These are known as allografts: tissue obtained from and transplanted to members of the same species. In the case of cross-species transplantation these tissues are referred to as xenografts.

grown up, to the moment when its many parts were made into a surprisingly large number of everyday and not-so-everyday products. As Meindertsma noted, she 'tried to draw connections to all products for which parts of pig 05049 were used – not to promote the pig as a widely varied supplier but to show how little we, as consumers, know about the products that surround us'. Meindertsma traced a total of 185 products made from parts of pig 05049, including make-up foundation, biodiesel, toothpaste, anti-freeze and fine bone china, the latter not just a fancy name for a type of crockery, but rather a description of its main component, bone. Bones, as a matter of fact, can be used in all sorts of ways: the extra calcium in some yogurts, for example, is derived from pig and other animals' bones; a number of train brakes in Germany are manufactured using a combination of pig bone ash and other materials; and the glue that keeps many cardboard products stuck together is obtained from pig and other animals' – mostly horse – skeletons. Perhaps most surprisingly, however, is the fact that pig 'bits' can also be found in wine. Did you know that more often than not wine is, despite its grape base, actually *not* vegan?

Wine makers in America, Australia and Europe are allowed to use a variety of substances to filter and improve the quality of their wines, and many of these are animal in origin, including albumen (egg whites), casein (milk protein), chitin (fibre obtained from crustacean shell) and isinglass (a type of gelatine extracted from fish-bladder membranes). Another animal-derived additive commonly used in wine production is pig or cow trypsin, a digestive enzyme secreted by the pancreas of many vertebrates, the main function of which is to break down proteins in the small intestine. Its use in the wines of EU countries is prohibited, but the US Food and Drug Administration (FDA) does not have a problem with it, and states that pig or cow trypsin can be used for the purpose of reducing or removing heat labile proteins in wine.* The FDA also lists porcine or bovine pepsin, one of the main digestive enzymes found in many animals' (and our own) stomachs, as another approved wine additive, so many US wines are quite the fruit-animal cocktail. If this has got you thinking about whether your wine and/or beer is more than just a fruit-based concoction, you can check its vegan friendliness on www.barnivore.com.

Meindertsma's most extraordinary finding was the discovery that pig blood was being used in the manufacture of some cigarette filters. Not pig blood per se, but rather its haemoglobin, the oxygen-transporting protein found in blood, had been used since 1997 by a Greek cooperative cigarette manufacturing company, SEKAP, to produce so-called 'biofilters' that would apparently lead to safer cigarette smoking. The advertising of such health claims was unsurprisingly banned by the Greek government in 2002, but SEKAP continued to promote the biofilter by claiming it 'would change the history of smoking'.

A study on how tobacco smoke leads to oxidative damage, cancer and a range of other health troubles carried out at the Free Radical Research Group at the Department of Chemistry of the University of Athens in Greece concluded that: 'Filters (so called "bio-filters") with antioxidant compounds impregnated in active carbon *can affect only marginally the composition and toxicity of solid and gaseous phases of cigarette smoke*' (my emphasis – Valavanidis, Vlachogianni and Fiotakis 2009: 457). So, in other words, the biofilter works, but to an insignificant degree. Pig haemoglobin, I'm afraid, is really not going to make lung cancer less likely.

---

* Different levels of protein in wine affect its stability, and hence need to be 'regulated' to prevent, for example, the formation of crystalline deposits in already bottled wine.

In late March 2010, the Australian media was made aware of the presence of 'pig blood' in cigarettes via a press release by Dr Ross MacKenzie and Professor Simon Chapman from the School of Public Health at the University of Sydney in Australia. MacKenzie and Chapman had been told about Meindertsma's *Pig 05049* publication earlier that month and were keen, after consulting her and doing a bit of research of their own, to use her and similar findings to highlight the tobacco industry's concealment of cigarette ingredients. Their press release, entitled 'New book on pig products reveals problems for Islamic, Jewish and vegetarian smokers', had an immediate impact. Soon hundreds of thousands of Google searches were being made on pig haemoglobin cigarettes, pig blood cigarettes and similar search strings. Then, of course, came journalistic distortions, and soon organisations like the South African National Halaal Association (SANHA) were warning (and issuing leaflets in this particular case) that cigarettes are *haram*, that is to say, forbidden by Islamic law: 'Beware!!! Pig Extracts & Wine in Cigarettes. Muslim Jurists have for long time condemned cigarette smoking. In addition, the use of PIG HAEMOGLOBIN, COGNAC & RUM (WINES) in its manufacture has now also been confirmed. MUSLIMS ARE URGED TO ABSTAIN!!!'

Things got a bit tense in late July 2010 when Associated Press globally shared information coming from the semi-official Iranian Mehr news agency (owned by the Islamic Ideology Dissemination Organization), which was quoting Mohammad Reza Madani of the Society for Fighting Smoking as allegedly saying that contraband Marlboros in the country had been deliberately contaminated with pig haemoglobin *and* nuclear material. He went further than that by supposedly stating that Philip Morris International, which produces well-known tobacco brands such as Marlboro and Chesterfield, is 'led by Zionists' who purposely sell these polluted tobacco products to Muslim smokers such as those in Iran. These claims were, of course, denied by Philip Morris, and a number of other tobacco companies from around the globe were quick to say they did not use pig haemoglobin in any of their products.

Regardless of whether the above brands contain porcine traces or not, the main aim of Dr Mackenzie and Professor Chapman's 2010 publication exercise was achieved: to highlight how little we know about what makes its way into cigarettes. We are all aware that tobacco smoking is unhealthy and may cause cancer and a number of other illnesses, but what are cigarettes actually made of? Most of us could probably name several ingredients, such as tobacco and tar, but it turns out that cigarettes have a lot of them; hundreds of additives are *approved* by the EU for the manufacture of cigarettes. Additives are used, for example, to make cigarettes more taste-friendly for children, or to make smoking as addictive as possible. The additives used include boric acid, cognac oil and rum ether (SANHA's leaflet was right on that count), and shellac, a type of resin secreted by lac insects such as *Kerria lacca*. So cigarettes are not only bad for you, but potentially *haram*, *treif* (non-*kosher*) and not vegan-friendly.

When Snoop <insert animal of choice here> decided he wanted to be a Rastafarian, but wanted to continue eating pork, he probably didn't realise that becoming a member of a religion isn't about picking and choosing what you like most about it, but rather about abiding by *all* its rules. It is only when all the members follow and respect all of the religion's guidelines that the group's identity and cohesion can be asserted. As discussed in this chapter, many groups throughout the world define their separate identities by avoiding, among other things, the consumption of pork. Their shared eating habits and other behaviours are what binds them together and sets them apart from others. Many explanations of an ecological, medical or other nature have been sought to understand the specific avoidance of pork by many groups, but no consensus has yet been reached.

Whatever the explanation for it, what is certain is that pigs and pork have, throughout history, been used to divide and unite people, with the Spanish Inquisition probably being the most extreme of the examples highlighted here. This pork targeting, however, is not just a thing of the past: as discussed in the following chapter, what people eat (or don't eat) today continues to be a source of conflict and group targeting and pigs are once again in the limelight.

ADAFINA (SPANISH CHOLENT) (SEPHARDIC SPAIN)

By The Peppermill, Brooklyn, New York

Serves 4

Given the Jewish origin of this dish, *adafina* obviously contains no pork. The pot was placed to cook on Friday evening to be later consumed on Saturday, the Shabbat. In order to make sure that non-*kosher* ingredients are not added to the pot, and to avoid anyone tampering with it during the period when it is forbidden to cook, a water-and-flour paste is used to seal the pot – if anyone were to take the lid off disturbance to the paste would show the tampering.

Ingredients

For the meat

1 large onion, diced
1kg 2¼lb (1kg) beef flank or ribs and beef bones
100g (3½oz) chickpeas
100g (3½oz) white beans
2 medium-sized potatoes, cubed
1 medium-sized sweet potato, cubed

Salt and pepper to taste
½ teaspoon turmeric
¼ teaspoon nutmeg
½ teaspoon cinnamon
¼ teaspoon paprika
Pinch of cayenne pepper

For the rice
180g (6½oz) rice
1 small sweet potato, diced
1 small onion, diced
½ teaspoon cinnamon
1 teaspoon cumin
½ teaspoon turmeric
Pinch of nutmeg
1 teaspoon of salt
Pinch of pepper
2 tablespoons canola oil
500ml (17fl oz) water
4 eggs, raw in their shells
cooking or roasting bags

Method

1. Dice and sauté the onion until it is golden.
2. Cut the beef into chunks and brown together with the onion.
3. After the beef has browned, add the chickpeas, beans, potatoes and sweet potatoes. Add the spices as directed or to taste. Place this mixture in a cooking bag in a slow cooker.
4. In a separate bowl, mix together the rice, sweet potato and diced onion. Add the spices and seasoning. Add oil and water.
5. Place the rice mixture in a separate cooking bag and put in the slow cooker. Cover the bags with water.

Add the eggs in their shells. Cook everything together on a low heat for 12 hours.

6. Serve the contents of the bags in separate bowls, each with an egg on top.

COCIDO MADRILEÑO (MADRID STEW) (SPAIN)

By Reyes Lucini Rodríguez, my husband's aunt

Serves 6

'*A cada cerdo le llega su San Martín*' is a popular expression in Spain. It roughly translates as 'each pig will have to face its Saint Martin', and its English equivalent is 'to meet one's Waterloo'. The expression is linked to Spain's now-dying *matanza* tradition, in which pigs were slaughtered in town squares on the Catholic festivity of Saint Martin on 11 November. The original purpose of this autumn pig slaughtering season was to take advantage of the late-autumn and early-winter cold to air-dry the black pudding, chorizo and other sausages and meats made from the slaughtered pig. These products would later be used to prepare winter stews such as this one.

Ingredients

300g (10oz) chickpeas
3 beef marrow bones
2 ham hock bones
700g (1½lb) shank of beef
250g (9oz) chicken meat
150g (5oz) bacon

1–2 chorizo sausages (of the uncooked variety for boiling)
1–2 blood sausages
500g (1lb) carrots
500g (1lb) small, whole, peeled potatoes
1kg (2¼lb) cabbage
150–200g (5–7oz) filini pasta
2 garlic cloves, thickly or thinly sliced, or even crushed
4 tablespoons olive oil
About 2–3 teaspoons salt, according to taste

Method

1. Leave the chickpeas to soak overnight.
2. Fill a big pot to about two-thirds with cold water. Place all the meats (except the sausages) and bones in the pot, then heat until the water starts to boil. Remove the foam that has formed on top.
3. Drain the chickpeas and place them in the pot, and bring to the boil again. Reduce heat and simmer for 3½ hours. After 2½ hours, add some salt and the carrots. Half an hour later (3 hours in), add the potatoes.
4. Boil the cabbage separately (12–15 minutes).
5. Once the cabbage has boiled, cook it for about 2–3 minutes in a pan with the garlic and some olive oil.
6. Boil the blood sausage for 15–20 minutes. Make sure it is at room temperature, and also introduce it into boiling water to prevent the skin from breaking.
7. Boil the chorizo sausage separately, in the same fashion as the blood sausage, but for only 15 minutes.
8. Once the main pot has done boiling and the chickpeas are cooked, remove the broth with a strainer to another pot.
9. Bring the broth to a boil and cook the pasta for 3–4 minutes.

Presentation

Put the pasta soup in a tureen. Place all the vegetables (cabbage, carrots and potatoes) on a serving platter, and all the meats on another serving platter.

Personal Notes

1. The chickpeas, carrots and potatoes can be boiled in a cooking mesh (each ingredient on its own) in order to make removing them from the water easier.
2. The potatoes and bacon can disintegrate, so they may need to be removed from the broth ahead of time.
3. The broth from the chorizo sausage can be used as an accompanying sauce.

CHAPTER EIGHT

Identities and pork politics

In the Apuan Alps in the Italian region of Tuscany stands Colonnata, a small village first settled around 40 BC and now home to about 300 people. The village is known for its marble, which is extracted from the various quarries surrounding it, and which has been exploited since Roman times. Michelangelo's sculpture of David was made using a block of marble extracted in the nearby city of Carrara. Colonnata is also well known for its *lardo*, which is not lard as English speakers understand it, but rather fat from the pig's back. Though it may not be to everyone's taste, *lardo* is in fact considered a delicacy by many, and the village's four-day, very well-attended *Lardo di Colonnata* festival in late August is testament to this, with hundreds of kilos of pork fat being avidly consumed by the festival goers. But the *Lardo di Colonnata* has come to be more than just a piece of fat, playing an important role in Italian politics and cultural identity. Surprisingly, it all has to do with the way this fatty delicacy is produced.

Every January raw fat from the backs of locally reared and slaughtered pigs is cut into marble-like slabs at least 3cm (1¼ in) thick and weighing 250g–5kg (½–11lb). These fat slabs are then placed inside rectangular marble basins known as *conche* that have been rubbed with garlic on the inside. Salt, pepper, garlic, rosemary and other herbs and spices are placed between the neatly stacked layers of *lardo.* Once all the layers have been arranged within the *conche*, a piece of bacon is placed on top of the pile in order for the pickling process to kick off. The *conche* are then placed in dark, cool cellars for a minimum of six months, during which time the salt draws moisture from the fat, creating a brine that, in turn, protects the slabs of pig fat from the air and from getting spoilt. After the curing process is complete, white with pinkish undertones, translucent, soft slabs of fat emerge ready to be thinly sliced and consumed with tomato and onion on a crusty piece of bread – in the same way that the marble quarry workers of Colonnata ate them back in the days when *lardo* was not a global delicacy phenomenon, but rather the high-energy food of the working classes.

Lardo production and consumption had been all fine and dandy in Tuscany for millennia, until in the mid-1990s the EU put forward a set of standardised food rules enforcing the use of non-porous materials in cheese and cured meat production. Though to the naked eye marble may not seem like the most porous of materials, it is in fact *slightly* porous, so the EU wasn't happy about the way *lardo* was aged. Why was the EU worried about the tiny pores in the marble? Well, you see, small holes are ideal spaces for mean and nasty bacteria to hide and proliferate in. The *conche*, as you can imagine, are a health inspector's worst nightmare, because not only do they have tiny holes potentially full of nasty diseases, but they're also stained from having been used for decades (or even centuries), and are kept on the potentially dirty floors of cellars; this is not quite the pristine stainless steel-tank environment food-health inspectors tend to have in mind.

Food-safety tests carried out on the meat, however, showed it to be perfectly safe for human consumption, and the millions of people who at some point in their lives have eaten *lardo*, and have not died or become sick, have attested to this. As a matter of fact, the food-safety tests actually showed the importance of the marble in *reducing* the risk of contamination. It was found that the cellars' humidity, together with the porosity of the *conche*, gave rise to the most optimal conditions for the production of brine within the marble containers, the presence of which makes bacterial proliferation and contamination of the meat almost impossible.

It seems, however, that we humans don't seem to learn from our mistakes. A similar case of food-safety legislation not taking microbiology into account was that of the so-called 'cheese nun', Mother Noella Marcellino, a Benedictine nun at the Abbey of Regina Laudis in Bethlehem, Connecticut, in the US. She learned how to make St Nectaire cheese using the traditional French recipe and methods, which include the use of a wooden vat to store the milk while it turns into curd. When the Food and Drug Administration (FDA) found out about Sister Noella's cheese-making technique, it was horrified and asked her to stop producing the St Nectaire cheese using the wooden barrel where, it claimed, bacteria could easily hide, and to use stainless steel vats instead where, they told her, there were no pockets for *Listeria* and other harmful bacteria to hide and multiply. Mother Noella complied with the law and started using the FDA-approved stainless steel vats. These new containers, however, not only did not reduce the amount of bacteria, but actually made things worse. *E. coli* measurements went through the roof, leaving the FDA inspectors wondering what had gone wrong. Luckily for them, Mother Noella has an avid interest in microbiology, and she decided to conduct a study – for which she would later earn a PhD – on why the evil bacteria flourished in the supposedly sterile stainless steel vat, but not in the wooden barrel. What she found was that the *lactobacilli* (the bacteria that produce lactic acid from the fermentation of carbohydrates) that live in the wooden barrel digest the lactose from the milk, turning it into lactic acid, which in turn kills the *E. coli* in the milk. The wooden bacteria-hiding pockets were therefore a good thing in terms of food safety. Needless to say, the FDA admitted its mistake and Mother Noella was once again allowed to make cheese in her wooden barrel. If only the EU inspectors had known about this...

The potentially new EU food-safety regulations on the way *lardo* would have to be produced (and St Nectaire, for that matter, as it is a French product) were viewed by many Italians as an attack on their national identity (food, after all, is at the centre of Italian life and culture), and the cured meat soon became one of the first so-called 'nationally endangered foods' for the 'Slow Food' organisation founded in Italy in 1989. This gastronomic institution was set up with the aim of, among other things, preventing the disappearance of local food cultures and traditions, and to show people where the food they eat comes from and how our food choices affect the world we live in. It believes that food, as we have seen throughout this book's examples, is tied to many aspects of life, including culture, agriculture and the environment, so that what and how we consume is of utmost importance. In the end, the EU backed off and allowed the *lardo* to be produced using the traditional technique, further strengthening the role of the Slow Food movement, which has grown extensively over the years and is now present in more than 160 countries, including the US and UK.

As a results of this movement a project by the name of Ark of Taste has been set up in the UK, which includes 95 small-scale quality products and animal breeds that the organisation deems under threat from disappearing from our edible heritage and, in a way, define who the people of the isle are. Of the 95 listed British endangered products, 11 are pork-based or actual pig breeds; that's quite the representation, especially considering the UK's love of bacon and ham. Among the pig breeds listed we find, for example, the Berkshire, of 'Pig War' fame (see the next chapter), thought to have been discovered by Oliver Cromwell in 1650 during another conflict, the English Civil War. Its decline is mostly due to changes in our food preferences and fashions, in part dictated by the factory farming sector, which prefers and therefore focuses mostly on raising lighter coloured and leaner breeds. Berkshire pigs have many black hairs, which are difficult to remove, as well as a blemished skin. As we have become accustomed to the more pinkish meat varieties found in supermarkets today, the meat of Berkshire pigs is no longer considered 'attractive' and is therefore difficult to sell; the breed is thus in decline as a result of the fall in demand for its pork. The Berkshire, however, isn't the only 'non-desirable' breed: there is also the Large Black pig, the only all-black pig in the British Isles; and the Oxford Sandy and Black pig, also known by the cutest of names: 'Plum Pudding'. This breed has been around in the UK for more than 200 years, but is now one of the rarest because, as ridiculous as this may sound, its flesh isn't pink enough to be sold at your local Tesco or Sainsbury's. The Tamworth, with its distinctive golden-red coat and pricked ears, is the oldest pure English breed,* yet it's slowly being forgotten for the very same reason as all of the above. Changing fashions really are strange human phenomena.

It's not all pig breeds on the Slow Food's Ark of Taste list, though. There are three pork dishes most of us in the UK have probably never heard of, but that were common, at least locally, not so long ago: Bath chaps, Huntingdon fidget pie and Lincolnshire stuffed chine. I don't know about you, but if it wasn't for the pie bit I'd probably have had trouble knowing these were food dishes just by their names. So what do they consist of, and how have they become 'endangered', potentially leading to a loss of a part of who we are?

Bath chaps doesn't refer to a group of men from Jane Austen's favourite city, but rather to the cheek and tongue of a pig, tied into shape and later boiled, skinned and breaded. Because offal is no longer such a popular food choice as it was half a century or so ago, dishes such as Bath chaps (which, by the way, used to be made from the Gloucestershire Old Spot breed,† also under threat) are quickly disappearing, and pig entrails and inner organs are instead being used to produce processed or pet food.

The Huntingdon fidget pie, on the other hand, doesn't contain offal, but is instead filled with bacon or ham as well as apples, and in some cases cider and onions, all cooked inside a pastry case with a small hole on the top to provide a sneak peek of its fragrant and heart-warming contents.

---

* In the eighteenth century a pig-breed improvement programme was implemented in many parts of the world. In the UK it entailed the crossing of native breeds with mostly Chinese ones to improve productivity. The Tamworth wasn't very popular at the time and no efforts were made to cross it with other foreign breeds, so it now is the proud owner of the oldest pure English breed 'achievement certificate'.

† White ('pink') breed with black dots.

This was the food of harvest workers, who would cook the dish when apples were abundant in Cambridgeshire during the early autumn. Pies used to be popular in this region back in the day when wheat was more popular than potatoes, but such has been the shift in the area's gastronomy towards a more commercial and standardised diet (and a greater use of potatoes), that most people in this English market town are probably unaware of the pie's existence, let alone its disappearance.

Last, but not least, there is the Lincolnshire stuffed chine, which, like the *Lardo di Colonnata,* had its livelihood threatened by politics back in 1996. That was the year when, again, changes to EU legislation were proposed that would require slaughtered pigs to be split only down the backbone. This new kind of butchering would have unfortunately meant the end of the traditional 'chine cut'. Why was that? Well, it all had to do with the pig breed from which the meat was derived: the Lincolnshire Curly Coat, now extinct. These pigs had the ability to grow seriously big and chunky. Due to their massive size it was extremely difficult to cut through their backbone, which was covered by a thick layer of fat. The carcasses of these hefty beasts were therefore processed by removing the sides of the animals and leaving the backbone ('chine' in Old English) and its top layer of fat intact, from which square blocks would be cut. The exposed fatty meat slabs would then be left to go mouldy. They were later cleaned and herbs such as nettles, marjoram and blackcurrant leaves inserted into deep cuts before the meat was boiled in a copper pot. The whole thing, the preparation of the meat, picking of the herbs, cooking and eating of the stuffed chine, was a community affair and one linked to a special celebration, such as a local festivity or the christening of a child. Somehow it's sad to think that many of these dishes, and their accompanying traditions and social interactions, are being lost and replaced by TV dinners and lonely sandwich lunches eaten in front of computer screens by people who are unaware of the existence of this Old English-named 'chine' cut and the many stories behind it.

There have been other instances in which even if legislation and cultural gastronomic traditions have not clashed, they have not been to everyone's liking and have caused controversies. Take, for example, the EU's views on the stunning of animals before slaughter: it requires animals to be stunned to minimise their pain, *but* understands that religions such as Judaism and Islam have a different view, and because of this makes an exception when it comes to the *kosher* and *halal* meat consumed by the more than thirty million Jews and Muslims currently living in countries in the EU; this exception, of course, doesn't apply to pigs as their consumption is forbidden to members of both religions. This 'special status' isn't to everyone's (Christian) liking, though, and concerns have been raised about what this all means in terms of the animals' well-being and how 'humane' this type of religiously guided slaughter actually is. There are countries like Denmark where a number of its politicians feel pretty strongly about this. So strongly, in fact, that in February 2014 this Scandinavian country's government decided to fully ban the religious slaughter of animals. Speaking to Denmark's TV2 at the time, Dan Jørgensen, the then Danish Minister for Agriculture and Food, argued that the new legislation had been approved because 'animal welfare takes precedence over religion', even if the EU choses to make an exception when it comes to *halal* and *kosher* meat. This legislative move was indirectly criticised by Rabbi Eli Ben Dahan, then Israel's Deputy Minister of Religious Services, who told the *Jewish Daily Forward* that 'European anti-Semitism is showing its true colour across Europe, and is even intensifying in the government institutions'. Based on the rabbi's words, history appeared to be to be once again repeating itself, just like it had during the Spanish Inquisition: food was being used as a form of religious 'persecution'.

Though Denmark's measure had little to do with pork – pigs, as noted earlier, are not *kosher* or *halal* – it was part of a number of events in which, once again, the consumption or rather avoidance of pork was allegedly being used as a political way to segregate and point fingers at people because of the religious beliefs they ascribe to. There had already been some religious tension in Denmark a year earlier, when the sensationalist newspaper *Ekstra Bladeta* revealed that the town of Ishøj, south-west of Copenhagen, had completely banned pork at all municipal day care centres. Similarly, in Vestegn all council-run day care centres were told not to serve one of Denmark's national dishes, *frikadeller*, flat meat balls, the main ingredient of which is pork mince. In the capital itself several childcare establishments did not only not serve *frikadeller* or pork, but they also only served the children halal meat because, they argued, they didn't want to discriminate on religious grounds. On finding out about this, the right-wing Danish People's Party claimed that not allowing children to eat *frikadeller* was actually an act of discrimination against Danish food culture.

The Danish government's religious slaughter ban wasn't only criticised by Israel's Deputy Minister of Religious Services, but also by many others, including environmentalists and journalists, who viewed this as a clear case of human hypocrisy that had little to do with animal welfare. Denmark, alongside Spain and Germany, is the top producer of pork in the EU. Its approximately 5,000 farms raise and slaughter around 28 million pigs each year, which works out at around 77,000 pigs *every single day*. Raising and slaughtering that many pigs every day obviously requires an intensive system for it to happen, and in an intensive system human gain – as opposed to animal welfare – tends to prevail. This, many argued, is what the Danish government should be focusing on and tackling, as opposed to unnecessarily worrying about the religious identities and food preferences of its multifaith citizens.

It is not only Danish politicians who use pork in their culture wars: throughout the past few years, using the flesh of pigs as part of political campaigning has become quite the thing among many European right-wing politicians. Take, for example, the case of France: in 2014 the leader of the French National Front, Marine Le Pen, said that regional state-run school canteens in towns governed by her party would no longer be allowed to serve pork-substitute dishes on the days on which this meat was on offer. The way she framed it was that in France the public sector and religion don't mix, and thus need to be kept apart. Others in her party put forward different 'excuses' for this subtle pork praising, including that the party was concerned about the amount of food that gets wasted when schoolchildren are given too many food choices in their canteens. Whereas in the case of the politicians it is on many occasions more talk and less action, some citizens have been taking this pork imposition on Muslims and Jews too literally. In Bristol, for example, two men were jailed in 2016 for tying bacon to the door handles of a mosque in this western English city, and shouting abuse at the worshippers visiting the temple. In another case, four pig heads were found dumped outside a community centre in Solihull in the West Midlands, England, which was thought to have been (illegally) used as a mosque. No culprits were found in this case, but this is in no way an isolated incident: similar incidents are known to have taken place in Australia, Austria, the US and other countries.

It was in January 2015 on the BBC's Radio 4 *Today* programme that its then-presenter Jim Naughtie revealed the contents of a letter sent by Oxford University Press (OUP) to one of its authors of English Language Teaching (ELT) textbooks. In it it said that her book had to have no mention of 'pigs plus sausages, or anything else which could be perceived as pork'. However, it soon emerged that this policy was not unique to OUP, but it was rather widespread in this kind of publishing, so much so that ELT publishers and authors have come up with a clever acronym to more easily remember all the thematic restrictions they need to abide by: PARSNIP. 'P' for politics, 'A' for alcohol, 'R' for religion', 'S' for sex, 'N' for narcotics, 'I' for isms (such as fascism) and 'P', of course, for pork. Naughtie's words were soon picked up by the national press, which published cleverly titled stories such as 'Pigs won't fly in textbooks: OUP tells authors not to mention pork',* and 'Oxford University Press bans sausages and pigs from children's books in effort "to avoid offence"'.†

These articles were then picked up by international media, and OUP had to publicly respond to all the criticisms by clarifying that they hadn't banned books on pigs, as some media sources were reporting, but rather that these guidelines were put together to remind authors of cultural sensitivities, especially as many of the English-language learning texts are aimed at people living in Muslim-majority countries; it is all, they said, about common sense. For example, an English-language reading exercise in which two male friends are chatting about their latest female conquests while eating pork chops and drinking beer is not realistic for someone living in, say, Morocco, and therefore not something they can relate to and learn better from.

It wasn't all about 'banning' pigs from just textbooks, though: in late 2016 the BBC reported that Islamic leaders in Australia were pushing for a Muslim alternative to *Peppa*

* *Guardian*, 14 January 2015.

† *Daily Mail*, 13 January 2015.

Pig, the hugely popular yet slightly irritating cartoon.* The headline caused quite a stir and soon the broadcasting corporation found itself having to issue a correction: the Australian National Imams Council (ANIC) had nothing against the pig character; it was just that it wanted to crowdfund a cartoon that more specifically supports Muslim values and shows children what it's like to be a practising Muslim, which obviously *Peppa Pig*, who isn't Muslim, does not. This new TV show would not be replacing *Peppa Pig*, but rather complementing it, providing children with Muslim viewing alternatives. As many have pointed out, the pig (the animal in itself) is not really *haram* (forbidden), but rather its consumption, so watching *Peppa Pig* is not a problem from an Islamic point of view. The same should apply to watching *Babe*, or reading the tale of the 'Three Little Pigs' or *Charlotte's Web*.

Pigs and pork – who would have thought that even today these two would be so influential in how we view ourselves, others and the differences between us? They do say that we are what we eat, and as the above examples have shown, many people feel very strongly about what goes into their their bodies and nourishes them, and how their gastronomic preferences/rules dictate who they are and, most importantly, who they are not. From rural Alpine Italians all the way to Australian toddlers obsessed with Peppa Pig and her family, suids most definitely are being used, among other things, as a prop in the fragmentation of our modern-day societies. Though up until now it's mostly been political discourse and a few pig heads outside mosques, things can quickly get out of hand – and as described in the following chapter, even the death of a single pig was capable of triggering an international war.

* If you're the parent of a *Peppa Pig*-obsessed child, like I am, I'm pretty sure you'll understand why I find her and her relatives irritating.

DIFFERENT WAYS TO USE *LARDO*

By Chichi Wang of *The Nasty Bits*

- Shaved thinly and served with nuts, *lardo* makes a simple yet memorable antipasto dish. You can drizzle the nuts and *lardo* with honey, or serve the platter of fat with olives.
- *Lardo* pizza. Grill or bake your pizza crust, then top with thin shavings of *lardo* and drizzle with olive oil.
- *Lardo* on bread, toast or crostini. Same concept as pizza, though I sometimes make mine sweeter, with honey.
- *Lardo* and steak. Thin slices of *lardo* set on top of a grilled or pan-fried steak.
- Potatoes browned in *lardo* – or really, any mild-tasting root vegetable that allows the flavour of the pork fat to come through.
- *Lardo*-wrapped dates or prunes. Grill or broil briefly, only until the edges of the fat begin to curl and brown.
- *Lardo* pastry. Cut cubes of lard into the flour until it has a slightly rougher than cornmeal consistency, and use it for either a savoury or sweet tart.
- Rendered and whipped *lardo*. Use in place of butter on toast and bread.

Note Many '*lardo* purists', including my godfather Franco who, by the way, introduced my husband and I to this Italian delicacy a few years ago at a Christmas Eve celebration at his house, would argue that *lardo* is best enjoyed on its own or over grilled bread; adding it to pizza, he says, is quite the gastronomic abomination! Each to their own, I guess.

FRIKADELLER (MEATBALLS) (DENMARK)

By Jane Hansen, the mother of my Danish neighbour Anita

Serves 4

This recipe has been passed down through four generations of a family living on the island of Lolland in Denmark. It was first put together by Jane's great-grandmother, Christiane Svendsen (1863–1943), who then passed it to her daughter Emilie Hansen, and she in turn passed it to her daughter Karen M. Christensen, Jane's mother. The way *frikadeller* are prepared is different in every region. For example, in some areas breadcrumbs or potato flour rather than wheat flour are used (or have been used), in other areas a mixture of the two is used, and in other areas still only pork is used. On the island of Lolland, where Jane grew up, they have primarily used flour and a mixture of veal and pork, and this recipe reflects this local version of *frikadeller*.

Ingredients

250g (9oz) minced lean veal
250g (9oz) minced lean pork
1 medium-sized onion, peeled
1 litre (2 pints) whole milk
2 medium-sized eggs or 1 large egg
2½–3 tablespoons white flour
2 teaspoons salt, or to taste
1 teaspoon freshly ground black pepper, or to taste
Freshly ground herbs to taste, for example parsley or a little thyme or basil (optional)
Minimum 2 tablespoons of butter for frying (amount varies depending on pan)

Method (the modern way)

1. Blend together all the non-meat ingredients to create an even mixture. The onion should be cut into 4 pieces.
2. Mix the blend thoroughly with the meat, using spoon or dough mixer for 5 minutes.
3. Let the mixture rest in the fridge or another cool place to 'pull together' for ½–1 hour.
4. Put the butter in a pan and heat to medium heat.
5. Form meatballs with the help of a tablespoon dipped into the melting butter (the meat does not stick and gives a nice crisp surface). Take a large spoonful of the mixed meat and form into a meatball in one palm of your hand until it has an oval shape.
6. When the butter has just melted (be careful not to let it turn brown) place the meatballs in the pan.
7. While the meatballs are frying on the first side, drizzle the melted butter over the raw surfaces, using a spoon.
8. Turn over the meatballs to fry them on the opposite side after 5–10 minutes, and let them fry for yet another 5–10 minutes, this time not drizzling butter over them.
9. Add more butter to the pan while frying, if needed.

Method (the old-fashioned way, without a blender)

1. Grate/shred the peeled onion.
2. Whisk the eggs.
3. Pour milk into the whisked eggs and whisk together.
4. Knead the flour and seasonings thoroughly into the meat with your hands.
5. Add the shredded onions, and knead them in thoroughly.

6. Add the egg and milk blend, and knead together for 5–10 minutes, until even, sticky and slightly 'heavy'. If the mixture is too liquid, add 1 more tablespoon of flour and knead again for 5 minutes; be careful not to add too much flour to avoid the meatballs tasting like 'flour balls'.
7. Follow directions 3–9 in the 'modern way' above.
8. Serve with boiled white potatoes, thickened brown sauce (made from the melted butter gravy left in the pan), and sweet pickled red beets or sweet pickled red cabbage. Alternatively, serve with boiled white potatoes and cooked white cabbage tossed in a white milk-based thick sauce.

CHAPTER NINE

Pig wars

Fidel Castro was one of the Marxist leaders of the Cuban Revolution that successfully overthrew the Fulgencio Batista right-wing US-friendly government in 1959. The revolution and Castro's close links with Nikita Khrushchev, leader of the Soviet Union, made the Eisenhower administration (1953–1961) extremely uncomfortable, and led the CIA to develop a plan to train Cuban exiles to invade the Caribbean island and eliminate Castro. In February 1961, just after John F. Kennedy came to power, preparations for an invasion were actually authorised. Despite an air strike by US jets on Cuban airfields the night before the invasion, and gossip and newspaper articles in the US and Cuba, Kennedy wanted to do everything he could to hide the US involvement in the invasion.

The landing of the troops at the Bay of Pigs was part of that plan: the bay is an isolated area on the southern coast of Cuba, where a night landing of the Cuban exile army would allow them to enter the country with little or no resistance from the locals, and would help conceal any US involvement. The invasion took place on the night of 16–17 April 1961 and, as is now generally agreed, was a total fiasco: more than 100 men died; around 1,200 'traitors' were forced to surrender and imprisoned; and the US eventually had to pay out $53 million's worth of baby food and medicines in exchange for their release. But the greatest costs to the Kennedy administration were the domestic political embarrassment for having launched such an ill-managed venture, and the strengthening of Castro in Cuba as a result. The failed tactics of the Bay of Pigs invasion, however, were not the only mishandled aspects of this story.

I have never been to Cuba, but the name Bay of Pigs conjures up images of invaders, faces blackened, wading ashore alongside pigs swimming in the sea, just as they do in the crystalline waters of the nearby Bahamas, and wandering along the island's beautiful coastline. Disappointingly, the truth is far from that. Although the bay is bordered by beautiful coral reefs on its western side and by large areas of swampland to the north and south, its name is a confusing misnomer; the area is entirely devoid of pigs. Pigs, as a matter of fact, have never really had much of a presence in the region and are not even indigenous to the American continent. Like many of the other things that went wrong in the planning and execution of this doomed attempt to liberate Cuba from communism, the communications completely broke down from the outset.

The Bay's name in Spanish is *Bahía de Cochinos*, which should be translated into English as Cochinos Bay, in the same way as is done for Guantánamo Bay, or the Bay of

Buena Vista (the Bay of Good Sight if literally translated). The correct translation, Cochinos Bay, was used in the documents distributed by American instructors to the Cubans training for the invasion in Nicaragua on 14 April 1961, two days before the invasion, but between then and 17 April, the bay's name somehow got lost in (literal) translation, and instead became the 'Bay of Pigs' now so familiar to English speakers. Indeed *cochinos* does mean 'pigs' in Spanish, but according to the *Diccionario de la Real Academia Española*, it can also mean *four* other things. The other meanings are: 1. a very dirty person; 2. a mean, stingy person; 3. a rude person; 4. a pig fattened up for slaughter; and 5. a definition specific to Cuba: a teleost fish of the Plectognathi order. The *Bahía de Cochinos* is thus not the Bay of *Pigs* of popular imagination, but rather more mundanely only the Bay of *Triggerfish*. Although Cubans also use the word *cochino* to refer to pigs, when the term is used in an aquatic context, as in the name of this bay, it refers solely to the queen triggerfish, old wife or turbot (*Balistes vetula*).

What are queen triggerfish? Well, they live in the eastern Atlantic Ocean, in the area stretching from Ascension Island to southern Angola. Populations are also found in the western Atlantic, from Canada all the way south to warmer Brazil. They are fond of tropical to warm-temperate waters, and quite like living on coral reefs like those in the Bay of Pigs. Most of the genus' forty species are benthic, meaning that they live close to or at the bottom of the sea. They feed on hard-shelled invertebrates such as crabs, from which they obtain meat by using their strong, incisor-like teeth to chisel their way through the hard carapaces of their prey. They also live on zooplankton (floating animal organisms), and get their five-a-day from algae. The queen triggerfish is a very colourful creature, with yellow, green and blue colouring to its skin, and light bluish lines running across its fins, snout and back. It is, despite its colourfulness, also rather flat in the physical sense, oval and reaches average lengths of 30cm (11¾in). In terms of its behaviour, it is generally shy, but can be extremely aggressive during the breeding season, so if you are lucky enough to ever encounter one during a swim, make sure you keep your distance. But the question remains: why are these fish known as *cochinos* in Cuba when they clearly have nothing to do with pigs? As some believe, perhaps it is because their bodies and heads are covered in rough, thick scales, making them tough-skinned creatures just like our friend the pig. But given the tenuous nature of this explanation, this could just be an old wives' tale.

What can be said for certain is that no pigs (or triggerfish, for that matter) were involved in the Bay of Pigs invasion (until proven otherwise by currently undisclosed CIA documents). There have, however, been instances when pigs have been the actual protagonists of historical battles. This happened in the case of the Pig War of the mid-1800s, the last border conflict between the US and Canada.

Between Vancouver Island and the US mainland lie the San Juan Islands, a group of around 400 islands, some of which are only visible during low tide, and of which only 172 are named. The three largest and most important are Orcas, Lopez and San Juan. This beautiful archipelago, home to killer whales, or orca (*Orca orcinus*, hence the name of one of the largest islands), harbour seals (*Phoca vitulina*), Steller sea lions (*Eumetopias jubatus*) and numerous other marine creatures, was also the setting of what could have ended up being a mini replay of the American War of Independence (1775–1783), and this time a pig would truly have been to blame for it all.

Archaeological evidence has shown that human hunters-gatherers were present on the San Juan Islands as early as 8,000 years ago. The first Europeans to arrive were the Spanish in 1791. The islands were not only attractive to the Spanish; the Brits and the newly independent Americans were also interested given the islands' numerous resources such as wood and beaver fur. The islands' positions were also used to justify claims of control over Oregon Country (the states of Washington, Oregon, Idaho, and parts of Wyoming and Montana, and the province of British Columbia), so in 1818 the US and Britain reached an agreement to jointly occupy the area (Spain had left by this point, ceding its land to the US). The Americans wanted to extend their border along the same parallel all the way to the Pacific Ocean, but the Brits were having none of that and insisted instead that the northern border should be placed west of the Columbia River, and should follow its course to the ocean. No agreement was reached in the end, and the two countries decided that it would be best to put the territorial dispute in abeyance and revisit it in ten years' time. When 1827 came along, the two nations were still at loggerheads, could do nothing but agree to disagree and postponed the matter indefinitely (it was, however, agreed that if the matter was to be discussed again a year's notice was required from either side – all very civilised).

The Webster-Ashburton Treaty of 1842 partly established the northeastern US-Canada border, but the Oregon Territory border was still to be fully established. Tension started to mount following the presidential election of Democrat James K. Polk in 1844, as during his campaign he had focused heavily on the westwards expansion of the US, and in particular the annexation of the whole of Oregon Country. Polk was a man true to his word, and fulfilled each and every one of his electoral promises during his four years in office. By now you're probably wondering what this all has to do with pigs, but please bear with me. Fed up with what seemed to be a never-ending dispute, Polk determined to settle the territorial question once and for all and, together with the British Minister to Washington (a chap named Richard Pakenham) and the Secretary of State, James Buchanan, finally reached a compromise. The boundary dividing the US and Canada (British North America) would lie 'along the forty-ninth parallel of north latitude to the middle of the channel which separates the continent from Vancouver island, and thence southerly through the middle of the said channel, and of the Strait of San Juan de Fuca, to the Pacific Ocean'.

After so many years of wrangling, you would think that all was now nice and dandy, and the Americans and Brits could get along together, and relax a little about where to draw the (border) line. If only things were that simple. Geographic knowledge and cartographic representation of the area were rather more primitive back then (there was no GPS or GIS in the 1800s), and the 'said channel' referred to in the treaty turned out to be something that could mean two different things: either the Rosario Strait on the east side (supported by the Brits) or the Haro Strait along the west part of the San Juan Islands, favoured in turn by the Americans. To resolve this ambiguity, a new Boundary Commission was set up in 1856 to determine where the international border should be placed. Meetings were held and letters were exchanged, but neither party could agree, and in December 1857 they were again forced to agree to disagree. Both nations continued to claim land rights over the San Juan Islands, with the Brits settling in the southern part of San Juan island and establishing the Belle Vue sheep farm, and a few dozen American settlers setting up small farms throughout.

One of the American settlers was Lyman Cutlar. Originally from Kentucky, he had not had much luck with his ventures in the Gold Rush and decided he might do better on San Juan. He made his way to the island and settled there, claiming that the Donation Land Claim Act of 1850 gave him the right to do so (the Act specified that any white male citizen over twenty-one years of age was entitled to 160 acres/65ha of land for free). What Cutlar did not seem to know was that the island was still not yet *technically* US territory, and that the Act did not apply to lands in dispute; his claim was therefore invalid. Even if he had known he would probably not have cared anyway; this man was no great fan of the British, so he set up his potato farm very close to British Belle Vue farm, then run by an Irishman named Charles Griffin. The animosity between the two was reciprocal. Griffin did not like American settlers one bit, claiming they made his farming and life in general quite difficult. To make matters worse, the Americans brought cattle with them to the island, and let them graze on the sheep pastures. However, angry though he was with the Americans, Griffin had no political authority, and all he could do was moan (then moan some more), while looking after the Hudson Bay Company's 4,500 sheep, 40 cattle, 10 oxen, 35 horses and… 40 pigs.

On 15 May 1859, a Griffin pig decided to have a culinary adventure and set off to 'explore' Cutlar's potato patch. This, it turns out, was not the pig's first such excursion, and there had been an earlier gastronomic visit to the American's 'land plot'. Understandably, Cutlar had not been happy at the result of the first visit and had told the Irishman that he would kill the pig if it were to happen again. On the morning of Sunday, 15 May 1859, Cutlar was woken by the sound of another of the island's inhabitants cracking up with laughter at the sight of the pig nuzzling through the precious patch and tucking into his potatoes with relish. Furious, he grabbed his rifle and shot the porcine beast. While revenge was sweet, Cutlar soon realised that what he had done was not going to go unnoticed, and so paid Griffin a visit to offer him compensation for the greedy pig. The Irishman said he would accept $100, but Cutlar baulked at such audacity and first offered $5, then $10, and that was tops. A heated argument ensued in which Cutlar threatened to kill all of Griffin's animals and him as well if any of them dared trespass on his farm again. As an American, he proudly proclaimed, he had the right to live on American territory, and San Juan was American territory because the American authorities had told him so (as you will have gathered by now, Cutlar still had no right to settle on San Juan). After Cutlar left, Griffin wrote to the Hudson Bay Company director telling him what had happened. As a result, several British authorities were dispatched, and landed on the island a few weeks later and threatened Cutlar with imprisonment. The American was unimpressed by this show of force and, together with other American settlers, asked his own government for military protection (their explanation being that they had heard how horrible British prisons were and did not want to have to spend any time in them).

So a conflict began. On 27 July 1859, 66 American soldiers arrived in San Juan with the mission to stop the British taking over more of the island. The British, now worried that more American 'squatters' would settle on the island and further disturb the running of Belle Vue Farm, sent three warships. The escalation continued and by mid-August nearly 500 American soldiers were ready to battle the more than 2,000 Brits stationed on the five warships anchored offshore from the island. Both sides, however, had been given the same strict instruction: *do not fire the first shot*. Thus the two sides ended up facing their opponents, shouting insults in the hope of provoking the other to open fire. Despite some highly creative slander concerning the mothers and sisters of their opponents, and a lot of well-honed national insults, both parties resolutely refused to fire the first shot. The bullet-free war of words continued for some time, a true forerunner of some Monty Python-style sketch.

When news of the Pig War standoff reached London and Washington, both governments were less than amused and hurriedly sent representatives to the island to try to negotiate an amicable solution. Both nations agreed once again to jointly occupy the San Juan Island until a final resolution of the dispute could be found, with the Americans setting up the 'American Camp' in the south and the Brits the 'British Camp' in the north. The dispute was finally settled by international arbitration in 1872: Kaiser Wilhelm I of Germany, together with two others, set the border to lie along the Haro rather than the Rosario Strait, so that in the end the island was ceded to the Americans. The Union Jack, however, still flies above the 'British Camp' in remembrance of the war that never really was, and it would be nice to believe perhaps also in memory of its sole victim: the potato-loving Berkshire pig.

Berkshire hogs are a breed supposedly first recognised by Oliver Cromwell in 1650 when he and his troops were stationed in Reading, Berkshire during the English Civil War. Word soon spread of the superb quality of this suid's bacon and ham, and for many years thereafter the Berkshire was the favourite of the British upper classes, including more latterly Queen Victoria. As Mrs Beeton, the nineteenth-century culinary writer, put it in her household management 'bible': 'The Berkshire pig is the best known and most esteemed of all our domestic breeds.' The Berkshire we know today (black-coloured, prick-eared, white socks and white tip) looks a little different from what Oliver and Victoria would have been familiar with, as a result of the mixing of the 'original' breed with Chinese and Siamese specimens. Before this, Berkshire hogs were brownish to black in colour, and sometimes had white spots and patches across their bodies. Berkshires are no longer as popular as they were during Victorian times because of the trend and increased demand since the 1960s for a leaner pig meat, such as that of the Large White (which looks rather more pink than white), probably the breed most of us are familiar with. As a matter of fact, such was the fall in demand for the sometimes slightly darker, flavourful meat of the Berkshire that it is now considered a rare breed in the UK as we saw in the previous chapter, and its pork is mostly sold in specialist markets. In Japan, however, it is still a highly prized meat, and is known as *Kurobuta* pork ('black pork') and has the same high ranking among gastronomes as the more widely known Kobe beef. The latter, the meat of *wagyū* cattle, a closed herd raised in Kobe since the seventeenth century, are fed beer and rubbed down with sake to improve their coat and skin, which the Japanese believe improves the quality of this highly marbled, exquisite and super expensive (£100+ for a single steak in Tokyo) juicy beef.

As noted earlier, pigs are not indigenous to America and were introduced there by Spanish explorer Hernando de Soto during one of his voyages, which first landed in sunny Florida in 1539. The Berkshire breed didn't arrive in the US until 1823, a mere thirty-six years before the Pig War. Just as in Britain, it was a favourite of the American elites until the middle of the twentieth century, when the Yorkshire breed, first imported from England in 1830, began to gain in popularity. Though initially not as popular – the Berkshire was still the 'king' breed – Yorkshire pigs gained favour with American farmers as soon as they realised that though the pigs grew at a slower rate, these large whites produce bigger litters and are physically longer in size, so more meat can be obtained from each individual. As a result, demand for Yorkshire imports increased, and American Yorkshire pigs are now the most common pig breed in the US and Canada.

Disputes of the late nineteenth and early twentieth centuries involving pigs were not always as 'amicably' resolved in other parts of the world as they were between the US and UK. Take the case of Serbia: after gaining independence from the Ottoman Empire in 1878, this mainly agricultural economy traded almost exclusively with the Austro-Hungarian Empire. Between 1901 and 1905, 53 per cent of all Serbia's imports were Austro-Hungarian in origin, and more than 83 per cent of Serbia's produce – mostly pigs – was exported to the empire. That's not surprising considering the geographical magnitude of Austro-Hungary and the position of Serbia relative to it: in order to access most of Europe's markets Serbian produce *had* to make its way through Franz Joseph I's vast lands. In an attempt to break free from the grip of the Austro-Hungarian Empire, Serbia initiated trading links with France. In January 1904, Serbia was able to secure a long-term deal with a French businessman who agreed to buy 150,000 Serbian pigs every year, and with this money the Serbs were able to place a large artillery order with the French munitions company Schneider. As can be imagined, the Habsburgs were not happy at this Serbian entrepreneurial initiative. Until that time most of Serbia's pork had fed the empire, and the Serbs had bought their munitions from the Austro-Hungarian Skoda plants in Bohemia. To add insult to injury, in 1906 Serbia proceeded to set up a customs union with Bulgaria, which placed taxes on Austrian goods, making them prohibitively expensive and impossible to sell in Serbia. This was the straw that broke the Austro-Hungarian camel's back, and later that year the Habsburgs hit back where it hurt Serbia the most: by imposing a ban on *all* Serbian pork; pigs, they declared, were welcome to the empire from everywhere except Serbia.

This did not seem to bother the Serbs too much: after all, they had secured a massive pork deal with the French and had even managed to obtain further funding from *La République* to construct industrial-scale meat-packing plants to further boost their international pork trade (up until this point pig farming and pork production had been locally run individual family affairs across Serbia). The Serbs further upset the tottering Habsburg Empire by deciding to build the plants using materials sourced from Germany, an arch commercial rival of the Austro-Hungarians. To make matters even worse, Serbia began to pressure the then Austro-Hungarian provinces of Bosnia and

Herzegovina for a trade route through their territory as a means of accessing the Adriatic Sea, and thereby gaining quicker access to France and other potential non-Habsburg trade partners. These attempts were all aided and abetted by the Russians, whose involvement nearly led them into a war with the Austro-Hungarian Empire – a German ultimatum in 1909 luckily put a stop to that, and the Russians backed down from further supporting Serbia's expansionist trading tactics. Eventually tempers cooled, and not long after Serbia and the Habsburgs signed a new commercial treaty, and once again Serbian pork was filling the bellies of the subjects of the empire. It would be nice to be able to finish this little historical account by saying à la Shakespeare 'all's well that ends well', but sadly this was not to be the end of the story. Despite the new treaty, Serbia continued to stir trouble in Bosnia and Herzegovina, and this ultimately became one of the many causes leading to the First World War.

Pigs have not only triggered human conflict, but also actively participated in it. Armies past and present have made use of pigs and other animals such as dogs, horses and even rats to help them win battles and conquer lands. For example, legend has it that Alexander the Great used squealing pigs to panic the war elephants of his enemies – a trick he had learned from an Indian warlord. According to Pliny the Elder, a Roman naturalist and author living in the first century AD, this was a tactic also used by his fellow Romans to repel the war elephants of the Greek general Pyrrhus – who, as Alexander's cousin, should have known better than to use elephants. Procopius, a Roman historian writing about the wars of Justinian in the sixth century AD, describes another example of how a squealing pig hung from the walls of the besieged town of Edessa in Mesopotamia was used to frighten the elephant of the Persian emperor camped outside. Yet another historian of antiquity, Polyaenus, an author from Macedonia, reported that the siege of Megara in Greece, which took place in the first century BC, was broken when pigs doused in pitch and set alight were driven towards the enemy's massed war elephants, which promptly stampeded, trampling many of Megara's attackers to death.

In more recent times 'military pigs' have been used, for example, on the Maginot Line – a set of fortifications and other military installations built by the French along their borders with Switzerland, Luxembourg and Germany following the First World War – where miniature breeds were used to find hidden mines. The Nazis employed pigs, alongside cows and camels, to check for minefields on the German army's movements across Egypt during their attempt at invasion in 1942. As recently as 2003 the idea of 'sniffer pigs' continued to be a popular one: Geva Zin, an Israeli de-mining specialist, after observing the olfactory excellence of wild boar rooting for food in Croatia, came to realise that specially trained pigs could be particularly good at finding all sorts of explosives using only their noses. He put his theory to the test by training a miniature year-old piggy called Dora, showing the world how a sniffer pig can be just as good as or even better than the sniffer dogs we are all so accustomed to.

The Israeli Army has yet to approve the use of pigs for mine detection, though it seems that this decision has nothing to do with the Jewish pig taboo; this would not be a problem as the pigs would be used for a good cause, saving human lives. As a matter of fact, according to an article published in March 2000 in Israel's oldest newspaper, *Haaretz*, the Israeli Defence Forces (IDF) regularly use pigs as well as rats and sheep in their warfare-related experiments, the purpose of which, they say, is to improve the conditions and care of those injured at war. According to the latest data, in 2015 more than 600 animals were exploded and subjected to all kinds of violent experiments by the IDF.

The extent of animal warfare experimentation carried out by the IDF is modest by comparison to what goes on inside Porton Down, the UK's Ministry of Defence's laboratory in Wiltshire. First opened in 1916 to investigate the gas attacks on British troops by the Germans during the First World War, the centre currently carries out more than 2,000 animal experiments each year. A large number involve exploding live pigs to assess whether humans would be able to survive this sort of extreme battlefield injury and, if they did, to figure out what would be the best blood-clotting solutions for this kind of trauma. As part of the centre's experimental programme, pigs are also shot repeatedly and later operated on by army doctors, or are made to inhale mustard gas to assess how this toxic gas affects human concentration levels and orientation. Though it is illegal to test on animals in the UK if there are other ways of obtaining results, Porton Down continues to experiment in the name of warfare science, and pigs appear to be one of its preferred models.

In the US in 1957, Operation Plumbbob, in which twenty-nine nuclear tests were carried out in Nevada by the US military, involved experimenting with 1,200 pigs to assess the effects of radiation on biological life. The experiments included putting the pigs in cages wearing suits made of different materials in order to assess which would provide humans with the best protection in the case of an atomic blast. Another test involved placing pigs in pens at different distances from glass panels to assess the extent of damage that would be produced by flying debris during an atomic blast. This wasn't the first time the US had used pigs in atomic bomb testing, though. In 1946, at Bikini Atoll in the Marshall Islands of the Pacific Ocean, 147 pigs, 3,030 rats, 109 mice, 57 guinea pigs and 176 goats were, as part of Operation Crossroads, placed in ships close to where the first atomic bomb was dropped to assess the extent to which the radiation would affect them. Many of the animals died then and there, and the rest only managed to survive a couple of weeks following the blast, except for one: Pig 311. Not only did she survive the blast, but she also managed to escape the sinking ship on which she had been placed, and was later found swimming towards the safety of one of the lagoon's shores. Following her rescue, she was sent to the Naval Medical Research Institute in Maryland, where she was studied for three years. Pig 311 spent her final year of life at the Smithsonian's Zoological Park, where she died in 1950. She left no offspring, and it was thought that this may have been due to the radiation, which probably rendered her sterile. What test or war will pigs be a part of next?

CUBAN-STYLE ROAST LEG OF '*PUERCO*' (CUBA)

A Cuban family recipe

Serves 8

Cuba is home to the Black Creole Cuban pig, which is now mostly raised in rural areas of the country. It is very well adapted to the Cuban environment, and is known to thrive on royal palms and the subproducts derived from agricultural activity. Its origins are not yet fully understood, but it's thought to be descended from the *Ibérico* breed, which the Spanish brought to the island more than 500 years ago. It may also be descended from pre-Hispanic Black Canarian pigs, as ships sailing from Spain to America used to stop on the Canary Islands in the Atlantic before making their way to the New World.

Ingredients

1 leg of pork, weighing 3kg (6.6lb)
1 head of garlic cloves, crushed
1 tablespoon oregano
2 teaspoons cumin
½ teaspoon pepper
2 tablespoons salt
8 bitter oranges, juiced
500g (1lb) onions, sliced

Method

1. Clean the leg of pork, place on an oven dish and prick the surface with a knife.
2. Mix together the crushed garlic, oregano, cumin, pepper, salt and orange juice. Spread the paste over the whole leg and cover with the sliced onions. Cover the dish with cling film and place in a fridge for a minimum of 10 hours.
3. Leave at room temperature for 30 minutes, and preheat the oven to 165 °C (325 °F).
4. Cover the leg with foil paper. Roast in the oven for 4 hours, or until it reaches an internal temperature of 85 °C (185 °F).
5. Serve with white rice, black beans and ripe plantain.

LESKOVACKA MUCKALICA (Лесковачка мућкалица), (PORK AND PEPPER STEW) (SERBIA)

By my Serbian friends Tonko and Vida Rajkovaca, adapted from *Jasna's Kitchen Creations*

Serves 4–6

Muckalica is a popular stew in Serbia and its name is derived from the Serbian word *muckati*, meaning to stir, mix or shake (so it's perhaps an apt recipe choice for a chapter on wars!). This recipe, the *Lesckovacka* variety, derives from the city of Leskovac in southern Serbia, where it is generally made using pork tenderloin as opposed to the more traditional pork shoulder cut. *Muckalica* is generally served with rice or bread and a dollop of sour cream, known as *kaymek* (*Кајмак*) in this Balkan nation.

Ingredients

1–1.5kg (2¼–3¼lb) of pork (pork shoulder is most commonly used)
200g (7oz) of smoked bacon, sliced
5 onions, diced
6 cloves of garlic
1kg (2¼lb) of red peppers
1 tin of tomatoes
2 tablespoons of vegetable oil, or lard to make it extra porky
Chilly powder or flakes, to taste
Salt and black pepper

Method

1. Season the meat and grill it (preferably on a wood-fired barbecue). For this, leave it in large pieces (which will be sliced later), or thread cubes onto skewers (adding a few bacon slices in between).
2. Grill the peppers or bake them in an oven until their skins turn slightly black and look blistered. To bake the peppers in the oven, cut into quarters and coat in about 1 tablespoon of oil per pepper. Add coarse salt to taste. Bake in the oven (preheated to 180 °C/360 °F) in a roasting pan for about an hour, stirring them every 20 minutes or so.

3. Set aside the peppers to cool. Peel off the skins from the peppers, then slice them.
4. Heat the oil in a pan and add the bacon and onions. Cook until the onions change colour slightly.
5. Once the onions turn slightly translucent, add the garlic, tomatoes, sliced peppers and grilled meat. Season to taste.
6. Cover and place in an oven preheated to 160–180 °C (320–360 °F) for a minimum of 45 minutes.

CONCLUSION

Carnism, or why I used to eat pork

It took me some time to pluck up the courage in the summer of 2016 to write to Jim and Anna, who I had been working with at my publisher, to tell them about a moral dilemma I had been having for quite some time: I was now reluctant to include the pork recipes in the book that were proposed when we first discussed the project. You see, when I put together the proposal for *Pig/Pork* back in the summer of 2013, things were a little different in my life. I was a postdoctoral researcher studying Palaeolithic hunting sites in southern Ukraine and very much the omnivore myself. I really didn't question my consumption of meat and other animal products back then. I guess, in part given my job, I had a bit of a palaeodiet frame of mind. Much of my focus was on what meat people from the past were hunting and eating, and I just didn't pay much attention to what we are all eating now, and what this consumption really entails. Thinking more about it, who am I kidding? I *was* probably aware, but just didn't want to know anything about it; I was happy furthering my knowledge of Palaeolithic food procurement while munching my way through supermarket packaged meat. It may seem like a very obvious contradiction to you (and me now), but back then it all sort of made sense, or at least in my head I pretended it did.

Things started to change following the birth of my son in the summer of 2014. I won't bore you with many of the soppy details, but it was all a bit overwhelming at first, and the experience of breastfeeding him was nothing like I had imagined it to be. Let me tell you it's nothing like it's shown in the films, or as predictable as some parenting books make it out to be. The whole nursing experience got me thinking about our own consumption of milk as a species, and the more I thought about it, the weirder it became in my head. Why do we as adults continue to drink milk? Why do we drink the milk of other species? Most intriguingly, why, out of all the mammal species out there, do we only milk cows, goats and a few other animals?* During the many hours, days and months spent nursing my child I read numerous articles on the importance of breastfeeding, its immunological benefits, how my body produces a milk tailor-made to the needs of my child and so on. From a species-survival point of view all this research I was reading about made a lot of sense, but it also made me realise how such a well-established

* Pigs are extremely difficult to milk and that's probably the reason why they're not used as dairy animals, but this is not true for other mammalian species.

product, dairy, is in fact not really an ideal source of nourishment for humans. This is when my first moral dilemma arose: here I was, physically and emotionally drained from my son's non-stop nursing, yet I was adding cow's milk to my coffee and eating yogurt.

It was at this point that something clicked: a cow somewhere out there was having the same physical and emotional demands placed on her just so I could have my coffee white – and she didn't even have her child's life as a source of comfort. It just didn't feel right to ask that from another species, especially if this was to consume a food product that my body, I now realised, didn't even need in the first place. This realisation triggered a whole rethinking of my food choices and the kinds of relationships I/we have with animals. By this point I had already written parts of the chapters on modern-day pig farming and medical experimentation, and typed out and tested a number of the recipes in the book. Yet, on rereading them I realised how little attention I had been paying to the wider picture of these and other pig-related topics.

Were many of the farming practices I had read and written about really necessary? Factory farming is, after all, a system after maximum productivity and profitability; animal welfare, from what I found, was generally not a top priority. Examples like that of the *Ibérico* breed, however, provided me (and my meat-eating habits) with some reassurance. Their acorn feasts on the *dehesas* and the care with which this precious breed is treated were clear examples of how pig welfare and food production can, in a way, go hand in hand… right? I couldn't ignore the fact, however, that in order for pork to make its way to my plate a pig must first be slaughtered. Obviously I had known about this aspect of food most of my life – long gone were those sweet innocent childhood years – but the whole breastfeeding and cow-welfare reasoning had touched a nerve. I again found myself thinking about my food choices and wondering: why do we eat some species and not others?

That's when I came across the concept of 'carnism', a term coined by psychologist Dr Melanie Joy, author of *Why We Love Dogs, Eat Pigs and Wear Cows*. The way she explains carnism goes something like this: when we think of food activism at the table, most of us tend to associate this with vegetarians and vegans. Not much attention is paid to the meat eaters as they are considered the 'normal' ones. Yet, as Joy explored as part of her PhD at Saybrook University in Oakland, California, eating meat isn't something we do because it's inherent in our nature, but rather because we've been conditioned to do it by an invisible belief system that 'encourages' us to eat animals. This belief system, carnism, is shared by all meat-eating cultures: of the various million possibilities, only a few animals are classed as edible; the rest, the belief systems states, are disgusting and shouldn't be eaten. This is why, say, someone in the US may find it emotionally impossible to roast and eat a dog, whereas another person in rural China might salivate at just the thought of a crispy puppy. This belief system would also explain, for example, why the French eat horse, whereas the British find this culinary practice an abomination. Proof of this rejection of horses as food was best exemplified in the UK's 2013 horsemeat scandal, in which it was found that mince labelled as beef in many cases contained horsemeat. Had it been chicken, people may perhaps have felt cheated, but they wouldn't have felt as repulsed as they did at the thought of having unknowingly eaten horse mince.

As discussed in Chapter 7, pigs (or rather pork) play an important role within this 'carnism' system: praised by many, their meat is taboo to many others. Numerous explanations have been sought to understand the pig taboo, including its replacement by the more compact and easier to raise chicken or the trichinellosis-pork connection, but these are, as we know, not applicable to all groups of people.

That is the thing with carnism: each group dictates which species are edible and which are not. This really was quite a revelation to me. I ate pork because my family ate pork, because the society in which I grew up in reveres pork, because pork was here, there and everywhere. Did I really have a choice? Thinking about it, I probably didn't have much leeway, but then, chorizo and ham are tasty so there was no reason for me to complain. Knowing what I now know, however, I have to realise that today I do have a choice, and mine is not to eat pork. As a matter of fact, I have chosen not to consume any kind of meat or any type of animal-derived product. It is only now that I can truly say I love pigs, but not pork. All those chorizo days are now far behind me. I would find it difficult to justify both to myself and to others that I admire and respect pigs, yet that their suffering and death is worth a few minutes of my gastronomic satisfaction. Call it carnism or what you like; it just doesn't make sense in my head any more. My sudden shift to veganism has surprised many of those closest to me – and I do not blame them. This has been quite a drastic transition, but one I feel very proud of – I hope many others will consider it, too.*

Despite shifting to veganism, on balance I do feel that having recipes in the book is important from a historical, gastronomic, identity, you-name-it point of view. As this book has hopefully shown, pigs and pork are such an important part of who we are and our (pre)history, that not including the many shapes and forms in which they have made it to our plates, battles, health, disease and many other areas would be missing a key part of the human-pig connection. You don't have to make the recipes – as a matter of fact, I urge you not to, especially the raw varieties – but they are interesting in themselves and how

* Curious? You can sign up to the Vegan Society's 30-day vegan pledge at any time on their website.

they connect to each chapter's themes, and I'm grateful to all those who shared them with me.

While I am sitting here editing these final lines, news has broken in the UK that the new £5 note contains traces of tallow, a rendered form of beef fat. Numerous vegetarians, vegans and Hindus have spoken out to let the Bank of England know how problematic the presence of this animal fat is to many of them. For some it's a matter of purity and respect for a creature they consider sacred, whereas for others it's a matter of principle, a matter of belief that all forms of animal exploitation and cruelty should be excluded as far as is practicable and possible, as defined by the Vegan Society. Many people wonder whether it was really necessary to add animal fat to such a product. Even if the amount is extremely small, why couldn't a non-animal alternative be sought? Why had the presence of the tallow not been openly disclosed from the start?

This case, as the many others throughout this book have highlighted, is not an isolated one: there is so much we as consumers don't really know about. I remember when I first came across an article on 'vegan wines', when I thought that surely wine is vegan because it's made of grapes. I felt slightly cheated when I found out about how wines are improved and filtered – as though I hadn't been given the full information about what I was drinking and, to a certain degree, this made me feel vulnerable as a consumer. Further research revealed more interesting/shocking discoveries about the extent to which pigs/pork can be found in all sorts of foods and everyday products, ranging from brushes all the way to cigarettes. Though it was good to know that at least pig by-products are being made use of by all types of industry, the not-fully disclosed ingredients list of many products was a little troubling. Veganism, I soon realised, was not just about not eating pork.

Researching *Pig/Pork* has made realise how little I knew about the world I live in, the products I consume and many aspects of the history that has shaped us into what we are today. Wild boar, pigs and pork, as we've seen, have played a tremendous role in our development and survival as a species, but at what cost to them? The price they've paid for 'innocently' approaching our settlements in Turkey and China many millennia ago has tied them into a permanent partnership, which though it appeared mutualistic at first, has seen them progressively more and more enslaved so that they, through their bodies and reproduction, can fulfil our food, medical and a variety of other needs. Just like with the £5 note, I ask: is this really necessary? Is it really necessary to our survival to treat another species in such a way?

Such reflections make me think about, for example, my husband, who in his early twenties was diagnosed with melanoma. If it wasn't for the kind of dermatological research that has been carried out on pigs and other animals, he might not have made it. For that, of course, I'm grateful to the pigs and every one else who makes it possible for our medical knowledge to advance each and every day. While researching Chapter 4, however, I stumbled on a practical guide which, with the aid of photographs, showed researchers how to handle and position specifically bred pigs when carrying out different skin experiments on them. There was nothing particularly gory about the photographs, but they really struck another nerve in me: again, is this really necessary? What if instead of showing pigs, the photos showed humans handling other humans to be experimented on? There would be a massive outcry, yet here we are, treating animals not as the independent, self-sufficient living organisms that they (just like us) are, but as mere objects for us to use and easily discard.

I never used to give these kinds of things this much thought, and just assumed them to be necessary and therefore right in my then-omnivorous world of existence.

I have learned, however, that this much suffering of pigs and other animals for our own medical benefit is, on many occasions, simply not necessary. If pain and suffering can be avoided, why make that choice? I recently learned about the Dr Hawden Trust (DHT), the UK's leading non-animal medical research charity, and knowing of its existence has given me hope and a further charity to support. As I've learned and as DHT points out, many human diseases do not exist in animals, and when they do the way an animal deals with them can be very different from how the human body experiences it. DHT is right: as we saw in Chapter 4, medical research on pigs has provided us with much knowledge on our own diseases, but there have also been many limitations. I think the fact that, for example, the medical community has had to breed a specific pig that develops melanoma in a similar way to us, but not quite, demonstrates why maybe animal experimentation is not the only way forwards.

The purpose of DHT is to fund research that proves medical studies can, and should, take place without using animals. I agree. As DHT notes on its website, animal use is so historically embedded in the design of experimental protocols that very few people question these approaches, even if, on many occasions, the trials just produce negative or unhelpful results. It's a bit like my chorizo-eating habits: they are so embedded in the environment I grew up with that neither I nor anyone else questioned them. I guess if my mother had been giving me sliced fancy rat meat sandwiches, most people would have been disgusted by her choice of snack, but what's the difference?

Going back to animal experimentation: information is power, and the more aware we become that it's time and it's possible to invest in innovative animal-free and human-relevant research, the sooner, I believe, both we and the millions of animals that are experimented on each year will benefit from this alternative approach. Some may disagree with me or think this may be completely impossible, and I can see why, but wouldn't it be better if the treatment of human suffering didn't have to come from the suffering of another species like the highly intelligent and sensitive pig? This change in the biomedical community will not happen overnight and will be a slow process, but I think it is something we can achieve – we invented the wheel, and this is nothing by comparison! Arthur Schopenhauer, the German philosopher, wrote in his *The Basis of Morality* (1841): 'The assumption that animals are without rights and the illusion that our treatment of them has no moral significance is a positively outrageous example of Western crudity and barbarity. Universal compassion is the only guarantee of morality.' I think he had a point. I hope the 'squealing pig' experiment days will soon be over and there will be no more pig wars; love pigs, not pork.

Given the above, it makes sense for me to end this book – and this journey of porcine discovery – not with a recipe featuring pork, but rather a vegan recipe like the ones I get to enjoy nowadays. I hope you'll try it. *Bon appétit!*

LENTEJAS SIN CHORIZO (LENTILS *WITHOUT* CHORIZO) (SPAIN)

By yours truly

Serves 4

This dish is perfect for a chilly winter's evening. The original version, made with chorizo, is a specialty from Ávila, a city to the north-west of Madrid (where I grew up). The fact that I no longer cook it using chorizo results in it being slightly lighter than a version containing meat, so it can easily be consumed late in the day. The original hearty version is probably best eaten for lunch followed by a restorative siesta! Though I no longer eat chorizo, I do miss the flavour it gives to these kinds of dishes, so it is replaced by paprika, garlic, white wine and, of course, salt. These are some of the non-meaty ingredients found in chorizo, and they help give this lentil dish a chorizo kind of flavour. Serve it with crusty bread.

Ingredients

400g (14oz) dried green lentils, presoaked in cold water for 12 hours
1 large onion, finely chopped
1 clove of garlic, finely chopped
2 teaspoons paprika
4 carrots, peeled and cut into small chunks
2 large potatoes, peeled and cut into small chunks
White wine
Water
1 vegetable stock cube
1 laurel leaf
Olive oil
Salt

Method

1. Heat some olive oil and add the onion and garlic. Cook on a low to medium heat to avoid burning the garlic (this would make the dish taste bitter). Add the paprika so that the onion and garlic are slightly coated by it; stir slightly to avoid any burning.
2. A minute or so later add the small chunks of carrot and potato, and a glug of white wine, and mix.
3. After another minute or so add the drained lentils. Add water to cover all of the vegetables and lentils,

then add the stock cube. Stir to dissolve the stock cube as much as possible.

4. Add the laurel leaf and bring to the boil. Leave to simmer for 20–25 minutes.
5. Add salt to taste.

APPENDIX

A note on pig breeds

When asked to imagine a pig, the average person probably thinks of a fat pink creature with a curly tail, probably going 'oink oink'. There is, however, more to *Sus scrofa domesticus* than this particular breed, which, by the way, is known as the Large White or English Large White, even if it's more pink than white (or at least, that's how I see it). Just as in the case of cats, dogs and other domesticated animals, humans have, through selective breeding, produced different kinds of pig breed to suit their individual needs. According to *The Pig Site*, the go-to website for all those interested in the global pig industry, there are currently 73 registered pig breeds. The breeds most commonly used in the farming industry include the Large White, British Landrace and American Yorkshire, all white/pink varieties. There are other breeds that many of us rarely or never get to hear about, let alone come across or see, so here is a shortlist of some of the most peculiar breeds out there that highlights the diversity of domesticated pigs present throughout the globe today.

Arapawa Island Arapawa or Arapaoa Island, found in the Marlborough Sounds of New Zealand, is home to the Arapawa Island feral pig breed. These fairly hairy pigs are generally tan in colour with black patches throughout, though fully black individuals have also been spotted. These rather peculiar pigs are believed to have been introduced to the island by whalers in the first half of the nineteenth century. However, legend has it that the pigs living on the island today are descended from others released there by James Cook, the British explorer and

Royal Navy captain, in the 1770s during his third and final voyage. The breed nearly became extinct in the 1990s, but a breeding programme set up in 1998 following the capture of four individuals has led to population numbers increasing as a result of these rescue efforts.

Belarus Black Pied Also known as the White-Russian Black Pied or Spotted (among other names), this breed is today found in the area around Minsk, the capital city of the Republic of Belarus in eastern Europe. The breed was created in the mid-1800s by crossing local pigs with Large Whites, Middle Whites, Berkshires and Large Blacks imported from England, where these breeds originate. The Belarus Black Pied is light brown in colour and has very characteristic black spots all over the face and back. It is quite a fatty and meaty breed, and was very popular until the mid-twentieth century, when lard and full-fat meats were still in vogue.

Hampshire Despite its English county name, the Hampshire is in fact a US-developed breed. The British connection, however, lies in the original stock from which the Hampshire derived, one from Wessex, a region in England encompassing the counties of Hampshire, Devon, Dorset, Somerset, the Isle of Wight and Wiltshire, from where it was imported to the US in 1832. Between 1832 and 1890, this US breed was known as the 'Thin Rind' because of the leanness of its meat, a quality it still possesses, which makes it a favourite among pig farmers when cross-breeding to improve performance.

Mangalitza The Mangalitza breed is probably one of the most peculiar out there due to its woolly hair. Such is the distinctiveness of its coat that it is also known as the 'Woolly Pig'. It is currently found in Germany, Austria, Switzerland, Romania and Hungary, and is particularly popular in the latter. The pigs are quite fatty and used to be revered for the large amount of fat they produced, but they are now more commonly used in the making of salami sausages and hams, which the Hungarians are particularly fond of. Compared with the fat of other breeds, the fat of the Mangalitza comprises a higher percentage of monounsaturated fat, which helps keep rancidity at bay for longer and is perfect for making cured products such as sausages.

Mukota This black-coloured breed, also know as the 'Rhodesian Indigenous' or 'Zimbabwe Indigenous', is thought to have first been introduced to this southern African nation by traders from Europe and China back in the seventeenth and eighteenth centuries. There are currently more than 70,000 of these pigs living in Zimbabwe, and the neighbouring Mozambique and Zambia. The difficult tropical environment in which they live, in which there can sometimes be little food and water, and the high temperatures have made this breed extremely resilient and nutritionally efficient.

Ossabaw Island This island is found on the Atlantic Ocean opposite the US state of Georgia. The spotted black-and-white pigs living here are descended from those brought to the island by the Spanish in the sixteenth century. When sailing to America from Spain, Spanish ships would first stop in the Spanish-owned Canary Islands off the coast of Morocco, and it is from these islands' local breeds that the Ossabaw Island pigs are thought to be descended – and not from the mainland Ibérico breed, which is a fully black creature. In general, these are small pigs, weighing 90–136kg (200–300lb). Their small size is a direct result of their isolation, an ecological phenomenon described earlier.

Oxford Sandy and Black This two-hundred-year-old rare breed, also known by the names of 'Plum Pudding' or

'Oxford Forest Pig', is one of Britain's oldest and its origins are thought to lie somewhere in the Thames Valley in Oxford. When this ginger and black-spotted animal was first bred, it was mostly kept as a family pig in rural areas; it was fed with scraps, and sacrificed in the autumn to provide the families with a meat source throughout the winter months.

Select Bibliography

Pig/Pork would have not been possible without the research carried out and the publications written by all those listed below and on my website. I am greatly indebted to all of them for studying and writing about the many fascinating aspects of the pig world, and I hope I have done their findings justice in this book. For a full bibliography please visit: piaspry.com/pigpork.html

A note on pig evolution

Frantz, L., Meijaard, E., Gongora, J., Haile, J., Groenen, M.A.M. & Larson, G. 2016. The evolution of Suidae. *Annual Review of Animal Biosciences* 4: 61–85.

Naish, D. 2010. Babirusas can get impaled by their own teeth: that most sought-after of objects does exist! (babirusas, part VIII). *Science Blogs: Tetrapod Zoology*. Available at: scienceblogs.com/tetrapodzoology/2010/03/08/babirusa-impales-own-head/

Watson, L. 2004. *The Whole Hog: Exploring the Extraordinary Potential of Pigs*. London: Profile Books Ltd.

Chapter 1: Once upon a boar

Aubert, M., Brumm, A., Ramli, M., Sutikna, T., Saptomo, E.W., Hakim, B., Morwood, M.J., van den Bergh, G.D., Kinsley, L. & Dosseto, A. 2014. Pleistocene cave art from Sulawesi, Indonesia. *Nature* 514: 223–227.

Borgia, V., Boschin, F. & Ronchitelli, A. 2016. Bone and antler working at Grotta Paglicci (Rignano Garganico, Foggia, southern Italy). *Quaternary International* 403: 23–39.

Evin, A., Girdland Flink, L., Krause-Kyora, B., Makarewicz, C., Hartz, S., Schreiber, S., von Wurmb-Schwark, N., Nebel, A., von Carnap-Bornheim, C., Larson, G. & Dobney, K. 2014. Exploring the complexity of domestication: A response to Rowley-Conwy and Zeder. *World Archaeology* 46(5): 825–834.

Freeman, L.G. 1987. *Altamira Revisited*. Chicago: Institute for Prehistoric Investigation.

Krause-Kyora, B., Makarewicz, C., Evin, A., Flink, L.G., Dobney, K., Larson, G., Hartz, S., Schreiber, S., von Carnap-Bornheim, C., von Wurmb-Schwark, N. & Nebel, A. 2013. Use of domesticated pigs by Mesolithic hunter-gatherers in northwestern Europe. *Nature Communications* 4: 1–7.

Harvati, K., Darlas, A., Bailey, S.E., Rein, T.R., El Zaatari, S., Fiorenza, L., Kullmer, O. & Psathi, E. 2013. New Neanderthal remains from Mani peninsula, southern Greece: The Kalamakia Middle Paleolithic cave site. *Journal of Human Evolution* 64(6): 486–499.

Leduc, C., Bridault, A. & Cupillard, C. 2015. Wild boar (*Sus scrofa scrofa*) hunting and exploitation strategies during the Mesolithic at Les Cabônes (Ranchot Jura, France), layer 3. *Journal of Archaeological Science: Reports* 2: 473–484.

Rice, P.C. 1992. The boars from Altamira: Solving an identity crisis. *Papers from the Institute of Archaeology* 3: 23–29.

Rowley-Conwy, P. & Zeder, M. 2014. Mesolithic domestic pigs at Rosenhof–or wild boar? A critical re-appraisal of ancient DNA and geometric morphometrics. *World Archaeology* 46(5): 813–824.

Sato, H. 2012. Late Pleistocene trap-pit hunting in the Japanese Archipelago. *Quaternary International* 248: 43–55.

Soffer, O. 1985. *The Upper Paleolithic of the Central Russian Plain*. London: Academic Press.

Speth, J.D., Meignen, L., Bar-Yosef, O. & Goldberg, P. 2012. Spatial organization of Middle Paleolithic occupation X in Kebara Cave (Israel): Concentrations of animal bones. *Quaternary International* 247: 85–102.

Stepanchuk, V.N. & Moigne, A.-M. 2016. MIS 11-locality of Medzhibozh, Ukraine: Archaeological and paleozoological evidence. *Quaternary International*: 241–254.

Chapter 2: Old MacDonald had a farm

Albarella, U., Dobney, K. & Ervynck, A. (eds). 2008. *Pigs and Humans: 10,000 Years of Interaction*. Oxford: Oxford University Press.

Albarella, U., Dobney, K. & Rowley-Conwy, P. 2006. The domestication of the pig (*Sus scrofa*): New challenges and approaches, in Zeder, M., Bradley, D.G., Emshwiller, E. and Smith, B.D. (eds), *Documenting Domestication: New Genetic and Archaeological Paradigms.* Berkeley: University of California Press, 209–227.

Claudio, O. et al. 2012. Pig domestication and human-mediated dispersal in Western Eurasia revealed through ancient DNA and Geometric Morphometrics. *Molecular Biology and Evolution* 30(4): 824–832.

Cucchi T., Dai, L., Balasse, M., Zhao, C., Gao, J., Hu, Y., Yuan, J. & Vigne, J.-D. 2016. Social complexification and pig (*Sus scrofa*) husbandry in ancient China: A combined geometric morphometric and isotopic approach. *PLoS ONE* 11(7): e0158523.

Cucchi, T., Hulme-Beaman, A., Yuan, J. & Dobney, K. 2011. Early Neolithic pig domestication at Jiahu, Henan Province, China: Clues from molar shape analyses using geometric morphometric approaches. *Journal of Archaeological Science* 38(1): 11–22.

Ervynck, A., Dobney, K., Hongo, H. & Meadow, R. 2001. Born free? New evidence for the status of '*Sus scrofa*' at Neolithic Çayönü Tepesi (Southeastern Anatolia, Turkey). *Paléorient* 27(2): 47–73.

Evin, A., Cucchi, T., Cardini, A., Strand Vidarsdottir, U., Larson, G. & Dobney, K. 2013. The long and winding road: Identifying pig domestication through molar size and shape. *Journal of Archaeological Science* 40(1): 735–743.

Frantz, L.A.F., Schraiber, J.G., Madsen, O., Megens, H.-J., Cagan, A., Bosse, M., Paudel, Y., Crooijmans, R.P.M.A., Larson, G. and Groenen, M.A.M. 2015. Evidence of long-term gene flow and selection during domestication from analyses of Eurasian wild and domestic pig genomes. *Nature Genetics* 47(10): 1141–1149.

Jing, Y. and Flad, R.K. 2002. Pig domestication in ancient China. *Antiquity* 76(293): 724–732.

Larson, G., Dobney, K., Albarella, U., Fang, M., Matisoo-Smith, E., Robins, J., Lowden, S., Finlayson, H., Brand, T., Willerslev, E. & Rowley-Conwy, P. 2005. Worldwide phylogeography of wild boar reveals multiple centers of pig domestication. *Science* 307(5715): 1618–1621.

Larson, G. et al. 2007. Ancient DNA, pig domestication, and the spread of the Neolithic into Europe. *PNAS* 104(39): 15276–15281.

Peasnall, B.L., Redding, R.W., Nesbitt, R.M. & Rosenberg, M. 1998. Hallan Çemi, pig husbandry, and post- Pleistocene adaptations along the Taurus-Zagros Arc (Turkey). *Paléorient* 24(1): 25–41.

Pennisi, E. 2015. The taming of the pig took some wild turns. *Science Magazine* [online]. Available at: www.sciencemag.org/news/2015/08/taming-pig-took-some-wild-turns

Vigne, J.-D., Zazzo, A., Saliege, J-F., Poplin, F., Guilaine, J. & Simmons, A. 2009. Pre-Neolithic wild boar management and introduction to Cyprus more than 11,400 years ago. *PNAS* 106 (38): 16135–16138.

Yale University. 2016. *Pig Out Panel 1: Porcine Pre-History: Domestication* [video online] Available at: www.youtube.com/watch?v=6i90ZUKOHa4

Zeder, M.A. 2012. Pathways to animal domestication, in Gepts, P. *et al.* (eds), *Biodiversity in Agriculture: Domestication, Evolution, and Sustainability.* Cambridge: Cambridge University Press, 227–259.

Chapter 3: Food waste and modern farming

Díaz Yubero, I. 2013. *Gastronomía del Cerdo Ibérico: El Mito, la Cocina… y Hasta sus Andares.* Madrid: Yeguada Marqués S.L.

Duke Energy. 2016. Pork power gets new meaning with Duke Energy deal in N.C., *Duke Energy News Center* [online]. Available at: news.duke-energy.com/releases/pork-power-gets-new-meaning-with-duke-energy-deal-in-n-c

Golovan, S.P. *et al.* 2001. Pigs expressing salivary phytase produce low-phosphorus manure. *Nature Biotechnology* 19(8): 741–745.

Harpster, H.W. 2000. Case studies in utilizing food-processing by-products as cattle and hog feed, in Westendorf, M.L. (ed.) *Food Waste to Animal Feed.* Ames, Iowa: Iowa State University Press, pp. 145–162. Johnson, D.M. 2016. Hog lagoons in North Carolina, after Hurricane Matthew, *The New York Times Opinion Pages* [online]. Available at: www.nytimes.com/2016/11/05/opinion/hog-lagoons-in-north-carolina-after-hurricane-matthew.html?_r=1

Jones, R. 2001. Farrowing and lactation in the sow and gilt, *The Pig Site* [online]. Available at: www.thepigsite.com/articles/1101/farrowing-and-lactation-in-the-sow-and-gilt/

Mizelle, B. 2011. *Pig.* London: Reaktion Books.

Myer, R.O., Brendemuhl, J.H. & Johnson, D.D. 2000. Dehydrated restaurant food waste as swine feed, in Westendorf, M.L. (ed.) *Food Waste to Animal Feed.* Ames, Iowa: Iowa State University Press, pp. 113–143.

National Pig Association. 2013. *NPA position on feeding 'waste food' to pigs.* Warwickshire: National Pig Association.

Stuart, T. 2009. *Waste: Uncovering the Global Food Scandal.* London: Penguin.

Wasley, A., Hansen, K. & Harvey, F. 2016. Revealed: MRSA variant found in British pork at Asda and Sainsbury's, *The Guardian* [online] 3 October. Available at: www.theguardian.com/environment/2016/oct/03/revealed-mrsa-variant-found-in-british-pork-at-asda-and-sainsburys [Accessed 3 October 2016].

zu Ermgassen, E.K.H.J., Phalan, B., Green, R., & Balmford, A. 2016. Reducing the land use of EU pork production: where there's a swill, there's a way. *Food Policy* 58: 35–48.

Chapter 4: Fluorescent green pigs

Brubert, J. 2016. *Dance Your PhD 2016 WINNER: A polymeric prosthetic heart valve* [video online] Available at: www.youtube.comwatchv=3pqHVersEik&feature=youtu.be

Crovara Pescia, A., Astolfi, P., Puglia, C., Bonina, F., Perrotta, R., Herzog, B. & Damiani, E. 2012. On the assessment of photostability of sunscreens exposed to UVA irradiation: From glass plates to pig/human skin, which is best? *International Journal of Pharmaceutics* 427(2): 217–223.

Curnutte, M. 2014. The problem with mini-pigs. *National Geographic* [online] 1 October. Available at: news.nationalgeographic.com/news/2014/09/140930-animals-culture-science-miniature-pigs-breeders-sanctuaries/

Glover, T. *Mating Males: An Evolutionary Perspective on Mammalian Reproduction.* Cambridge: Cambridge University Press.Gross, C.G. 1998. Galen and the squealing pig. *The Neuroscientist* 4: 216–221.

Herzog, H. 2011. The impact of pets on human health and psychological well-being: Fact, fiction, or hypothesis? *Current Directions in Psychological Science* 20: 236–239.Kauffman, G.B. & Adloff, J-P. 2009. The 2008 Nobel Prize in Chemistry - Osamu Shimomura, Martin Chalfie, & Roger Y. Tsien: The Green Fluorescent Protein. *The Chemical Educator* 14: 70–78.

Miller, J.S. 1997. *Fetal Pig Dissection Guide, Including Sheep Heart, Brain and Eye.* 3rd Edition. Goshen: Goshen College.

Reardon, S. 2015. New life for pig-to-human transplants. *Nature* 527: 152–154.

Reiland, S. 1978. Growth and skeletal development of the pig. *Acta Radiologica Supplementum* 358: 15–22.

Vehling, J.D. (ed.) 1977. *Apicius: Cookery and Dining in Imperial Rome.* Toronto: General Publishing Company, Ltd.Vincent-Naulleau, S. et al. 2004. Clinical and histopathological characterization of cutaneous melanomas in the melanoblastoma-bearing Libechov Minipig model. *Pigment Cell Research* 17: 24–35.

Chapter 5: What doesn't kill you…

Arends, J.P. & Zanen, H.C. 1988. Meningitis caused by *Streptococcus suis* in humans. *Review of Infectious Diseases* 10:131–137.

Bianchin, M.M., Dal Pizzol, A., Cabral, L. S., Martin, K. C., de Mello Rieder, C. R., de Andrade, D. C., Rodrigues, C. L., Castro, L. H. M., Machado, L. R. & Caramelli, P. 2010. Cognitive impairment and dementia in neurocysticercosis: A cross-sectional controlled study. *Neurology* 75(11):1288–1295.

Del Brutto, O.H. & Del Brutto, V.J. 2012. Calcified neurocysticercosis among patients with primary headache. *Cephalalgia* 32(3): 250–254.

Greger, M. 2012. Ractopamine and yersinia in US pork, Nutrition Facts [online] 29 November. Available at: nutritionfacts.org/2012/11/29/ractopamine-and-yersinia-drugs-and-bugs-in-pork/

Huong, V. T. L., Hoa, N.T., Horby, P., Bryant, J.E., Kinh, N.V., Toan, T.K. & Wertheim, H.F.L. 2014. Raw pig blood consumption and potential risk for *Streptococcus suis* infection, Vietnam. *Emerging Infectious Diseases* 20(11): 1895–1898.

Pacelle, W. 2015. This drug, banned in Europe, Russia and China, may be in your lunch, *Reuters Blogs* [online] 31 March. Available at: blogs.reuters.com/great-debate/2015/03/30/if-you-eat-meat-in-the-united-states-buyer-beware/

Poletto, R., Cheng, H.W., Meisel, R.L., Garner, J.P., Richert, B.T. & Marchant-Forde, J.N. 2010. Aggressiveness and brain amine concentration in dominant and subordinate finishing pigs fed the b-adrenoreceptor agonist ractopamine. *Journal of Animal Science* 88(9): 3107–3120.

Ramírez-Bermúdez, J., Higuera, J., Sosa, A. L., López-Meza, E., López-Gómez, M., & Corona, T. 2005. Is dementia reversible in patients with neurocysticercosis? *Journal of Neurology, Neurosurgery, and Psychiatry* 76(8):1164–1166.

Ruetsch, C. et al. 2016. Inadequate labelling of pork sausages prepared in Corsica causing a trichinellosis outbreak in France. *Parasite* 23: 27.

Stephens, P. 2014. One in 10 sausages 'carries risk of hepatitis E virus', *BBC* [online] 20 November. Available at: www.bbc.co.uk/news/health-30006977

Chapter 6: Cooking pork science

Boles, J.A. and Pegg, R. N.D. *Meat color* [pdf]. Montana State University and Saskatchewan Food Product Innovation Program University of Saskatchewan. Available at: www.cfs.purdue.edu/fn/fn453/meat%20color.pdf>

Claus, J.R. 2007. Color changes in cooked beef [pdf]. Beef Research: Beef Facts, Product Enhancement. Available at: www.beefresearch.org/CMDocs/BeefResearch/PE_Fact_Sheets/Color_Changes_in_Cooked_Beef.pdf

Exploratorium. N.d. What is meat? | What gives meat its color? | What gives meat its flavor? | What makes meat juicy and tender? *The Accidental Scientist: Science of Cooking* [online]. All four available at: https://www.exploratorium.edu/cooking/meat

FAO. N.d. Raw-fermented sausages, *FAO Corporate Document Repository* [online]. Available at: //www.fao.org/docrep/010/ai407e/ai407e11.htm

Ferry, G. 2008. *Max Perutz and the Secret of Life*. London: Pimlico.

López-Alt, J.K. 2012. The food lab: The truth about brining turkey, *Serious Eats* [online] November. Available at: www.seriouseats.com/2012/11/the-food-lab-the-truth-about-brining-turkey-thanksgiving.html

National Cancer Institute. N.d. Chemicals in meat cooked at high temperatures and cancer risk, *National Cancer Institute, About Cancer: Causes and Prevention* [online]. Available at: www.cancer.gov/about-cancer/causes-prevention/risk/diet/cooked-meats-fact-sheet

Nathan. 2013. The Maillard Reaction, *Modernist Cuisine* [online]. Available at: modernistcuisine.com/2013/03/the-maillard-reaction/

Toldrá, F. (ed.). 2010. *Handbook of Meat Processing*. Iowa: Wiley-Blackwell.

Viegas, O., Yebra-Pimentel, I., Martínez-Carballo, E., Simal-Gandara, J. and Ferreira, I.M. 2014. Effect of beer marinades on formation of polycyclic aromatic hydrocarbons in charcoal-grilled pork. *Journal of Agricultural and Food Chemistry* 62(12): 2638–2643.

Viegas, O., Moreira, P.S. and Ferreira, I.M. 2015. Influence of beer marinades on the reduction of carcinogenic heterocyclic aromatic amines in charcoal-grilled pork meat. *Food Additives & Contaminants: Part A* 32(3):315–323.

Chapter 7: The swine; he is unclean to you

Anderson, J.M. 2002. *Daily Life during the Spanish Inquisition*. Santa Barbara: Greenwood Publishing Group, Inc.

Domingo, C., Touitou, I., Bayou, A., Ozen, S., Notarnicola, C. *et al.* 2000. Familial Mediterranean fever in the 'Chuetas' of Mallorca: A question of Jewish origin or genetic heterogeneity. *European Journal of Human Genetics* 8: 242–246.

Douglas, M. 2002. *Purity and Danger: An Analysis of Concept of Pollution and Taboo*. London: Routledge.

Liebman Jacobs, J. 1996. Women, ritual, and secrecy: The creation of Crypto-Jewish culture. *Journal for the Scientific Study of Religion* 35(2): 97–108.

MacKenzie, R. and Chapman S. 2011. Pig's blood in cigarette filters: How a single news release highlighted tobacco industry concealment of cigarette ingredients. *Tobacco Control* 20(2):169–172.

Meindertsma, C. 2007. *Pig 05049*. New York: Flocks.

Redding, R.W. 2015. The pig and the chicken in the Middle East: Modeling human subsistence behavior in the archaeological record using historical and animal husbandry data. *Journal of Archaeological Research* 23(4): 325–368.

Roth, C. 1992. *A History of the Marranos 5th Edition*. New York: Sepher-Hermon Press.

United States Department of Agriculture. N.d. Trichinellosis (trichinosis), *National Agricultural Library, Special Collections: Exhibits* [online]. Available at: www.nal.usda.gov/exhibits/speccoll/exhibits/show/parasitic-diseases-with-econom/parasitic-diseases-with-econom/trichinosis

Valavanidis, A., Vlachogianni, T. and Fiotakis, K. 2009. Tobacco smoke: Involvement of reactive oxygen species and stable free radicals in mechanisms of oxidative damage, carcinogenesis and synergistic effects with other respirable particles. *International Journal of Environmental Research and Public Health* 6(2): 445–462.

Weiner, J. 2013. The lion smokes tonight. *Rolling Stone Middle East,* [online]. Available at: www.rollingstoneme.com/print/the-lion-smokes-tonight

Chapter 8: Identities and pork politics

BBC. 2016. Religious leader backs drive for cartoons for Muslim children, *BBC News* [online] 9 December. Available at: www.bbc.co.uk/news/world-australia-38218118

Dolamore, A. 2003. Jack Spratt's horror: Lardo rediscovered, in Walker, H. (ed.), *The Fat of the Land: Proceedings of the Oxford Symposium on Food and Cooking 2002*. Bristol: Footwork, pp. 76–81.

Leitch, A. 2013. Slow food and the politics of pork fat: Italian food and European identity. *Ethnos* 68 (4): 437–462.

Leitch, A. 2013. Slow food and the politics of 'virtuous globalization', in Counihan, C. and van Esterik, P. (eds), *Food and Culture: A Reader*. 3rd Edition. Abingdon: Routledge, pp. 409–425.

Slow Food in the UK. N.d. *Bath Chaps | Huntingdon Fidget Pie | Lincolnshire Stuffed Chine* [online]. All available at: www.slowfood.org.uk/ff-products/

Chapter 9: Pig wars

Atomic Heritage Foundation. N.d. *Operation Plumbbob – 1957* [online]. Available at: www.atomicheritage.org/history/operation-plumbbob-1957

Coleman, E.C. 2009. *The Pig War: The Most Perfect War in History*. Stroud: The History Press.

Hall, R. 2003. Serbia, in Hamilton, R.F. and Herwig, H.H. (eds), *The Origins of World War I*. Cambridge: Cambridge University Press, pp. 92–111.

National Museum of Natural History Unearthed. 2011. *PIG 311 – the Smithsonian and Operation Crossroads* [online] 10 May. Available at: nmnh.typepad.com/100years/2011/05/pig-311-the-smithsonian-and-operation-crossroads.html

Neering, R. 2011. *Pig War: The Last Canada-US Border Conflict*. Victoria: Heritage House Publishing.

Vouri, M. 2013. *The Pig War: Standoff at Griffin Bay*. Seattle: Northwest Interpretive Association.

Conclusion: Carnism, or why I used to eat pork

Joy, M. 2011. *Why We Love Dogs, Eat Pigs, and Wear Cows: An Introduction to Carnism*. Newburyport: Red Wheel/Weiser.

Zeltner, A. 2013. *Handling, Dosing and Training of the Göttingen Minipig* [pdf]. Ellegaard educational package. Available at: minipigs.dk/fileadmin/filer/Education_package_New/Handling__Dosing___Training.pdf

Appendix: A note on pig breeds

The Pig Site. N.d. *The different breeds of pig* [online]. Available at: www.thepigsite.com/info/swinebreeds.php

Acknowledgements

Firstly, massive thanks go to my father, Eddie Spry, who, just like he did for my equally long doctoral thesis, read, edited and commented on the many thousands of words that make *Pig/Pork*. I also owe massive thanks to Joe Owen, pig GM expert and a dear friend of mine since our fun days at York – he read many of the chapters, and provided useful pointers and corrections to my work. Siniša Radović helped me with the polishing of the chapters on archaeology, on which he is an expert. *Hvala!* Others who also kindly agreed to read and comment on various drafts of several chapters are Erasmus zu Ermgassen, Haskel Greenfield, Chloe Nahum-Claudel, José Manuel Maíllo Fernández, Vida Rajkovaca and Nuria Avilés Thurlow. Your feedback was invaluable and I thank you for taking the time to read some of my work. This book wouldn't have been possible without all those who kindly gave me permission to reproduce their recipes here – massive thanks therefore go to (in order of appearance): Anna Colquhoun, Amelia Ijiri, Douglas Santry, George and Vicki Psarias, Yuying Qiu and Ningning Dong, Marisol Jiménez, Mar Izvaz, Carly Morgan, Cándido López, the Peppermill Inc. in Brooklyn, New York, Reyes Lucini Rodríguez, Franco Savoia, Jane Hansen and Anita Friis Sommer, Mabel Valcárcel, Tonko and Vida Rajkovaca. Massive thanks also go to Anna MacDiarmid and Jim Martin at Bloomsbury for providing me with the opportunity to write this book, to Krystyna Mayer for her thorough copyediting, and Samantha Goodlet for her wonderful illustrations. I am also grateful to Fitzwilliam College, Cambridge, for supporting me during the final stages of this project. The most special thanks go to my husband, Alejandro Lucini, without whom this book would have most definitely not been possible. At all. *Gracias* for keeping Daniel entertained when I was writing, and *muchas gracias* for putting up with my craziness and worries. Thank you also to Daniel for teaching me so much from day one and making me realise that there was something within me that I didn't even knew I had. I am bound to have forgotten lots of people here – I am sorry for that. I appreciate you all and I hope you know that! You all rock.

Index